The Great Sayings of Jesus

THE CLASSIC BIBLE BOOKS SERIES

The Song of Solomon: Love Poetry of the Spirit
Introduced and Edited by Lawrence Boadt;
Foreword by John Updike

The Hebrew Prophets: Visionaries of the Ancient World
Introduced and Edited by Lawrence Boadt;
Foreword by Desmond Tutu

The Great Sayings of Jesus: Proverbs, Parables and Prayers
Introduced and Edited by John Drane;
Foreword by Richard Holloway

The Gospel of St John: The Story of the Son of God
Introduced and Edited by John Drane;
Foreword by Piers Paul Read

Forthcoming

The Book of Job: Why Do the Innocent Suffer?
Introduced and Edited by Lawrence Boadt;
Foreword by Alice Thomas Ellis

Genesis: The Book of Beginnings
Introduced and Edited by Lawrence Boadt;
Foreword by Sara Maitland

The Psalms: Ancient Poetry of the Spirit
Introduced and Edited by Lawrence Boadt and F. F. Bruce;
Foreword by R. S. Thomas

Sayings of the Wise: The Legacy of King Solomon
Introduced and Edited by Lawrence Boadt;
Foreword by Libby Purves

Stories from the Old Testament: Volume I
Introduced and Edited by Lawrence Boadt;
Foreword by Monica Furlong

Stories from the Old Testament: Volume II
Introduced and Edited by Lawrence Boadt;
Foreword by Morris West

The New Testament Epistles: Early Christian Wisdom
Introduced and Edited by John Drane;
Foreword by Roger McGough

Revelation: The Apocalypse of St John
Introduced and Edited by John Drane;
Foreword by Richard Harries

THE GREAT SAYINGS OF JESUS
Proverbs, Parables and Prayers

INTRODUCED AND EDITED BY JOHN DRANE
FOREWORD BY RICHARD HOLLOWAY

St. Martin's Griffin
New York

ISBN 0-312-22211-4 cloth
ISBN 0-312-22078-2 paperback

Library of Congress Cataloging-in-Publication Data
is available from the Library of Congress.

First published in Great Britain by Lion Publishing plc, 1997.
First St. Martin's Griffin edition: June 1999
10 9 8 7 6 5 4 3 2 1

Contents

ACKNOWLEDGMENTS

The text of 'The Great Sayings of Jesus in Literature' has been selected from *A Dictionary of Biblical Tradition in English Literature*, edited by David Lyle Jeffrey, copyright © 1992 by permission of Wm B. Eerdmans Publishing Co.

The text of 'The Great Sayings of Jesus' has been taken from the Authorized Version of the Bible (The King James Bible), the rights in which are vested in the Crown, by permission of the Crown's Patentee, Cambridge University Press.

Margaret Avison, 'For the Murderous: the Beginning of Time', has been reproduced from *sunblue* (1978). Published by Lancelot Press: page 194.

T.S. Eliot, extracts from 'The Love Song of J. Alfred Prufrock', 'East Coker' and 'Journey of the Magi', published by Faber and Faber Ltd: pages 183, 193 and 204.

Foreword

One of the most fascinating things about human nature is the way we all see the same things differently. Ask eyewitnesses at a road accident or crime scene for an account of the same event and they are likely to come up with as many descriptions as there were onlookers. This does not mean that any of them is lying, though some of them may have a better eye for certain kinds of detail; it does mean that, since we all see things from different perspectives, we unavoidably bring something to the events we observe, as well as taking something from them. We are even told that scientific experiments are not exempt from this law. The observer influences the event that is looked at. All of this has particular importance when we come to the history of the lives and sayings of great figures. What we get is the truth of history filtered through the hearts and imaginations of observers, not to mention the way the material has been edited and altered by succeeding generations. This does not cause us to despair of ever knowing the truth about anything; but it does serve to remind us that truth is a complex, dynamic reality, and that the attitude we bring to it is as important as the news it brings to us.

It used to be thought that the first three gospels, Matthew, Mark and Luke, were straight reporting, while John was the result of theological reflection on the raw events of the life of Jesus. We know now that the first three gospels, though different in perspective from the fourth gospel, differ in subtle ways between themselves, and that each of them has its own voice or, to use a metaphor from the cinema, a particular 'take' on the life of Jesus. In other words, none of the gospels is the result of a simple verbatim piece of reporting. They are all theological documents in the sense that they bring to their account of the life and sayings of Jesus the perspective of faith and a conviction about the significance of this life for all other lives. That is why the narratives about him are called gospels, not biographies. They are testimonies to the effect this life had on those who encountered it; they are the recorded memories or traditions of those who gave up everything else to serve and bear witness to this life. That is what gives the gospel narrative its intensity; it is also why it continues to confront people today and change their lives. Through these written words, we encounter the living word God spoke in the life of Jesus.

But these written words have their own history. We are fairly certain that the first three gospels were not written down the way a writer of a novel would work today, creating the narrative from his or her own imagination. The process is more like the kind of thing that goes on when a musical historian goes round the highlands and islands of Scotland to record folk tales, poetry and songs that are in the memories of people, but have never been written down. Most of the great literary traditions had a long life as stories by the fire side before they were committed to ink on paper. The gospel writers would have been engaged in a similar exercise. They would listen to and meditate upon stories about Jesus, the memories that were handed down, maybe even some of the sermons or meditations that were the result of long thinking on the meaning of that story. In time, these would be woven into a whole garment, but only whole in the sense that a patchwork quilt is whole, stitched together out of many pieces.

The beauty of this volume of the great sayings of Jesus is that it helps us to get the feel of what the pre-written tradition might have felt like. Because of the way the parts of this book have been edited, we get a strong sense of a living tradition that is spoken, rather than written, passed on round the fire side, rather than lifted off a bookshelf. And the fact that the translation is in the classic form also serves to emphasize the original oral power of the tradition. These extracts are meant to be listened to. Even if we read them to ourselves we can hear them in our own heads. I hope that readers will not just go through them from cover to cover, but will read and ponder, putting the book down on their knees from time to time, and looking into the distance as these great and ancient words echo in their minds.

There has been no false attempt to harmonize these extracts from the first three gospels into a single narrative. Instead, we are given five great themes from the story of Jesus, bracketed between a prologue that includes the the birth narratives and an epilogue that points to the possibility of a living encounter with the meaning and message of Jesus in our own time. The sayings of Jesus as presented to us in this book have a tremendous sense of energy and movement.

We can almost hear the words spoken by Jesus as he strides from town to town, or from a disciple as he slowly tries to express what he remembers of those days and what it has come to mean to him. As well as enormous compassion and a sense of the unconquerable love God has for us all, we get from these stories a sense of passionate anger against all human systems, religious or political, that come between God and God's children. In the sermon on the mount, in particular, we get from Jesus something of God's dream for a transformed creation. But the epilogue reminds us that the dream is costly, that dreamers are cruelly disposed of by the world as we know it. Yet the dream lives on, nothing can kill it for long; and Jesus goes on breaking out of the tombs into which we have consigned him. Whether we like it or not, the last word in this book is a promise or a threat, take it how we will, that Jesus will be with us to the end of the world.

Richard Holloway

INTRODUCTION

Understanding the Gospels

What is a gospel?

The modern reader approaching one of the gospels for the first time may think it looks very much like a biography of Jesus. But a quick glance through any one of them will show that it is hardly that. A good biography usually begins with an account of the subject's childhood years, and progresses consecutively through adolescence and adulthood to show how the mature person has developed in response to the various influences of early life and environment. By contrast, the main emphasis in the gospels is not on the course of Jesus' life, but on the events of the last week or so. This is prefaced by reports of Jesus' teaching and accounts of a few incidents from the three years immediately preceding his death, with virtually no mention at all of his childhood and adolescence. If this is a biography, then it is certainly no ordinary biography.

We can most easily find out what it is by turning to the gospels themselves. Rather than trying to classify them as a modern librarian would, we should ask what their authors thought they were doing as they wrote. Take Mark, for instance, the gospel commonly thought to be the earliest of the four. The author describes his work in the opening sentence as 'The beginning of the gospel of Jesus Christ'. This statement stands as a kind of title or heading to what follows, and two words are important here for an understanding of the purpose of the gospel: the words 'beginning' and 'gospel'. 'Gospel' is simply the English equivalent of Mark's Greek word *euangelion*, and it was originally chosen because the two words had the same meaning: 'good news'. Mark, then, was writing about 'the beginning of the good news'.

What does this mean? Mark and the other gospel writers had

11

heard the 'good news' about Jesus. They had accepted its authority and recognized Jesus as Lord of their lives. Mark himself had subsequently become deeply involved in the work of the church, and an important part of this work was preaching and teaching the message that had changed his own life.

So when Mark describes his gospel as 'the beginning of the good news', he is saying that his purpose is to describe the first stage in the development of the message to which he and others had responded. The story he tells was an integral and important part of their own story and experience as Christians. Luke had a similar intention: he writes so that his readers may know the full implications of the Christian message which they had heard so often. Indeed, Luke felt it necessary to emphasize the continuity of the life of the church with the life of Jesus by writing a second volume (the Acts of the Apostles) to bring the story more fully up to date.

When we call the writers of the gospels 'evangelists' we are therefore accurately describing their intention. For they were primarily concerned to deliver the message about Jesus to their own contemporaries, and only secondarily, if at all, with the normal interests of a biographer. This fact has at least three important consequences for our understanding of the gospels they wrote.

(1) We must regard the gospels as a *selective* account of the life and teachings of Jesus. In their preaching of the message the apostles and others no doubt spoke of incidents from Jesus' life in much the same way as a modern preacher may use appropriate illustrations to explain his theological points. Mark and the other evangelists had no doubt heard these incidents used to illustrate many a sermon, and they incorporated them into their gospels for broadly similar purposes. Indeed Papias, one of the Fathers of the early church, claimed that Mark's Gospel consists of material extracted from the preaching of none other than Peter himself.

The fact that the information contained in the gospels was first used to illustrate the message of the church also explains some of the difficulties we often feel about the apparent incompleteness of the gospel accounts. All four of them put together would hardly contain enough information to document three years of anyone's life, let alone someone as active as Jesus. But when we realize that the information we have has been preserved because of its relevance to the life of the earliest churches, we can readily understand why so much that we would like to know has been left out.

This probably explains why we find no mention in the New Testament of the early childhood of Jesus, nor for that matter any descriptions of what he looked like, or the kind of person he was. Had the evangelists been writing merely to satisfy people's curiosity about Jesus, they would have included that sort of information. But that was not their intention. They were primarily concerned to win other people to faith in their Lord and Master, and for this purpose such details were quite irrelevant.

(2) If the gospels are illustrations of the apostolic preaching, this means that we cannot regard their contents as simple stories about Jesus. They must be closely related to the theology of the evangelists. At one time it was fashionable to suppose that it was possible to recover from the gospels a picture of a simple Galilean teacher which had later been altered by Paul and the others into a theological message about the Son of God. But it is now widely recognized that the gospels are themselves among the most important theological documents of the early church, and we can never in fact discover a picture of Jesus as a simple Galilean teacher. As far back as we can go, the Jesus whom we find in the pages of the New Testament is always a person who makes great claims for himself and utters definitive pronouncements on the relationship of men and women to God. All his teaching and every incident recorded in the gospels has something specifically theological to tell us.

(3) If, as we have suggested, the authors selected their materials to serve their own purposes in writing, it follows that we can probably discover something about them and their readers by comparing their relative selection and use of information about Jesus. In the case of the first three gospels we can do this quite easily, for they tell roughly the same story in the same order, and each of them repeats large sections of the material that is found in the others. By comparing the different ways that Matthew, Mark and Luke have used the deeds and teaching

13

of Jesus in their narratives, we can readily learn something about them and the situation in which they lived and worked.

So to understand the gospels fully is a rather complex business. We need to know why the evangelists wrote as and when they did. Then we need to try to understand the way they assembled their material, and why they used it in one particular way rather than in another. And always we need to bear in mind that their gospels were intended to serve the preaching ministry of the church: they were not written as biography, history or even theology in the usual sense.

Preaching and writing

An obvious question to ask about the gospels is: Where did the evangelists get their information, and what did they do with it? This may seem at first to be a rather irrelevant question, a kind of theologian's 'Everest', demanding to be conquered just because it happens to be there. But it is a helpful question for a satisfactory understanding of the nature of the gospels. Tracing sources and investigating an author's method of using them can be an important part of understanding what he or she is saying. If we know what the author is doing, then we can understand more clearly what he or she may be getting at. And if we misunderstand the method, it is quite likely that we will also fail to grasp the author's essential message.

Since the gospels almost certainly developed in the context of the preaching of the early church, we may expect to find some clues to their origin by examining the church's message. This essentially contains three major themes. First, the Christian gospel was connected with the promises of the Old Testament. Then came a series of statements about Jesus and his significance. Finally there was a challenge to men and women to repent and accept the message.

Old Testament texts

The message began with the statement that the promises of the Old Testament had been fulfilled in the life of Jesus. In the New Testament summaries of the preaching, this statement is often made in a rather generalized way. But of course in real-life situations it must have been a more specific declaration. For anyone familiar with the Old Testament would not be content until they had found out just which prophecies Jesus was supposed to have fulfilled. We know from other evidence that one of the favourite occupations of the Jews was the compilation of lists of Old Testament passages which the Messiah would fulfil when he came. The people at Qumran, for example, kept such lists, and so did other Jewish groups. These lists are generally referred to by scholars as *testimonia*.

There are a number of indications in the New Testament that these text-lists were probably in regular use among Christians from the earliest times. In both Matthew and John a great number of texts from the Old Testament are cited, with an indication that they were fulfilled in some particular incident in the life of Jesus. Yet it is striking that they hardly ever used the same passages. This may well have been because they were using different collections of *testimonia*.

In some of Paul's letters, too, we find Old Testament texts strung together in continuous passages in what often seems to be a rather arbitrary fashion. Again, it is reasonable to think that Paul originally found these grouped together under the same heading in his collection of Old Testament texts. It may well be that the collection of these texts from the Old Testament was the very earliest form of literary activity in the Christian church. They would be assembled for the convenience of Christian preachers, so that they could cite specific examples to support their claim that Jesus had fulfilled the Old Testament promises concerning the Messiah.

Word of Jesus

But the central element in the message was the series of statements about Jesus himself. No doubt in the very earliest days of the church's existence it would be possible to proclaim the message with no more than a passing reference to Jesus' life and teachings. For most Christians were Jews and the church was still a local Palestinian sect, and many people in Palestine must have known something about Jesus, however little. But it was not very long before Christian missionaries were spreading out to far beyond Palestine and carrying their teaching to parts of the Roman empire where Jesus was quite unknown. It must have been essential at this stage for the preachers of the good news to include in their message some kind of factual information about Jesus himself, if only the account of the events of his death and resurrection.

Once people had become Christians they would require further instruction in their new faith. This instruction would include information about Christian beliefs, as well as the kind of advice about Christian behaviour often found in the New Testament letters. One obvious and important source of such teaching must have been the remembered statements of Jesus himself. This would not necessarily be given as information about Jesus, as we can see from Paul's advice in Romans 12–14. Much of what he says there is so close to Jesus' teaching in the Sermon on the Mount that it is hard to believe that the two do not derive from the same source. Yet Paul never identifies his advice with the teaching of Jesus himself. Other parts of Paul's writings also show that the traditions of Jesus' teaching were familiar to the early Gentile churches.

It is therefore quite likely that long before the gospels were written in their present form the sayings of Jesus would be collected together as a kind of manual for the guidance of teachers in the early church. No doubt there would be a number of such collections of Jesus' teaching, made for different purposes and occasions in the church's life. Scholars often call these collections of sayings by the name *logia*.

In addition to the general considerations already mentioned, there are several more substantial reasons for believing that this was one of the earliest types of Christian writing about Jesus.

(1) We know that there were later collections of this kind, even long after the writing of the New Testament gospels. A number of papyrus fragments dating from the 3rd century AD, found at Oxyrhynchus in Egypt, contain sayings of Jesus, some of them different from those found in the gospels. A whole book of such sayings written in Coptic has also been found in Egypt. This is known as the Gospel of Thomas. It contains sayings of Jesus not found in the New Testament, some of which could be authentic. Whether or not they are genuine, however,

these documents do show quite clearly that it was the custom of the early church to make such collections of the sayings of Jesus.

(2) About AD130–40 Papias, the bishop of Hieropolis, wrote a five-volume *Exposition of the Oracles of the Lord*. Though most of this work is now lost, we do possess a few fragments of it in the form of quotations given in the writings of other people. Writing of Matthew, Papias says that he 'compiled the *logia* in the Hebrew language, and each one interpreted it as he could'. The precise implication of this statement is uncertain, but most scholars believe that the *logia* to which Papias refers is a collection of the sayings of Jesus rather than the book we know as the Gospel of Matthew.

(3) The organization of the material in the gospels often seems to suggest that Jesus' sayings had been grouped together before they were placed in their present context. There are many groups of sayings which are only loosely linked together and do not form any kind of consecutive argument. For example, the sayings about salt in Mark really seem to be quite different from each other, and may well have been put together in a collection simply because they all mention salt.

Then there is the whole of the Sermon on the Mount. Anyone who has ever tried to discover the argument of the sermon will realize the impossibility of the task, for there is no consecutive argument. What we have is the body of Jesus' teachings collected together because they all deal with ethical issues. But they hardly follow on in the same way as a modern sermon is expected to do. According to Professor Jeremias, the reason for this is that the sermon originally formed a collection of sayings of Jesus strung together to make them easily accessible to new converts to the Christian faith.

(4) A strong reason for assuming the existence of collections of Jesus' sayings early in the church's history is the fact that Matthew and Luke have a large amount of material that is common to both their gospels, but which is altogether absent from Mark's Gospel. This material consists almost entirely of Jesus' teachings, but it also includes the story of one miracle, the healing of the centurion's servant. The generally accepted explanation of this common material is that

Matthew and Luke both used the same collection for Jesus' sayings and incorporated it into their respective gospels.

Scholars call this supposed sayings collection Q. It may have been a written document, or perhaps a body of oral tradition. Its existence in some form is certainly credible, especially since its alleged contents are closely parallel to the collections of prophetic oracles that we find in the Old Testament. In addition to the prophet's words gathered together and edited by his disciples, the prophetic books also often contain an account of the prophet's call and one or two incidents in his life. This is precisely what we get in the tradition called Q: an account of the baptism and temptation of Jesus (which can reasonably be equated with his call), and an illustration of the most typical of his activities: a healing miracle. But the main emphasis is on his teaching.

From the evidence assembled so far, we may conclude that from the very earliest times the church's main interest was in two kinds of literature: the *testimonia*, and the *logia* of Jesus. They may also have had a commonly agreed outline of the course of Jesus' life and teaching. But before too long it began to be necessary to gather all this material together in a more permanent form. This process did not, of course, take place overnight. Indeed it may not really be a separate process at all, but just the natural extension and completion of the work already begun in making collections of *testimonia* and *logia*. But the end product was to be the four documents we now know as the gospels of Matthew, Mark, Luke and John.

Putting the gospels together

The first three gospels are called the synoptics because they are so much alike; and the precise way in which their writers transformed *logia* into gospel is at the centre of the 'synoptic problem'.

These gospels are in effect three different editions of what is more or less the same basic material. Much of their resemblance can of course be explained by the assumption that these evangelists may have been using the same collections of sayings that had been circulating among different groups of Christians. But the resemblances are more complex than that, for there are so many instances where the three gospels use precisely the same language, vocabulary and grammatical constructions that most scholars believe they must have shared written sources.

As early as the 4th century AD, Augustine believed that Matthew must have been written first, and Mark later made a summary of it. Then Luke came along and wrote his gospel on the basis of both Matthew and Mark. Until almost the beginning of the 20th century, this was the most widely held view. There were, of course, variations on it. One of them – the 'Griesbach hypothesis' (put forward by the German J.J. Griesbach, 1745–1812) – has recently been the subject of much interest by contemporary scholars. Griesbach agreed with Augustine that Matthew was the first gospel to be written, but he believed that Luke came next, and that Mark later used both Matthew and Luke as a basis for his work.

There are a number of difficulties with this view:

(1) Why would anyone have wanted to condense Matthew and Luke in order to make a gospel like Mark? Compared with the two longer gospels, Mark's short narrative can hardly be regarded as comprehensive. It has no mention at all of Jesus' birth or childhood, comparatively little about some of his most distinctive teaching, and only a very abbreviated account of the resurrection. We have already seen that the gospel writers selected their materials according to the interests and concerns of their readers. So, in principle, there would be no reason why an abbreviated version of Matthew and Luke should not have been produced. But given the absolute centrality of precisely those elements which are either missed out or underplayed in Mark, it is virtually impossible to envisage a Christian group that would have been satisfied with Mark's account of Jesus if they had already had access to Matthew and Luke. Indeed, it was not long before Christians almost universally preferred Matthew and Luke for this very reason. If Mark was written last, in full knowledge of the other two synoptic gospels, it is very difficult to explain why it was written at all.

(2) Much of Mark's language seems to point to the same conclusion. If Mark used the polished accounts of Matthew and Luke, why did he

so often write Greek that is virtually unintelligible? The parable of the mustard seed is a good example here. Both Matthew and Luke use eloquent expressions, which are quite similar to each other. Mark, by contrast, has a complicated Greek sentence without any verb in it that really makes imperfect sense. If he was copying Matthew's or Luke's account, then it looks as if he went out of his way to avoid using their words – and it is very difficult to think of a good reason for doing that!

(3) It is almost as difficult to believe that Luke read and used Matthew's Gospel. If he did, then here again he must have adopted some rather strange literary procedures. Matthew contains one of the greatest masterpieces in any of the gospels, the Sermon on the Mount. If Luke had that before him as he wrote, why did he break it all up, using some of it in his own Sermon on the Plain, but scattering the rest of it in small sections all over his own gospel?

There are many other examples of the same problems at other points in these three gospels. This is why most modern scholars have preferred a rather different explanation of their relationship with each other.

The more generally accepted explanation of the resemblances between the synoptic gospels is that Matthew and Luke both used two source documents in writing their own accounts of Jesus' life and teaching. These were the sources we now know as Mark's Gospel and the hypothetical document Q. It is, of course, certain that Luke, at least, used a variety of sources in composing his gospel, for he explicitly says that he had sifted through the work of other people, selecting those parts of their record that were suitable for his own purpose in writing. In view of the close literary connections with Mark and Luke, it seems certain that the author of Matthew used the same method in his work.

New light on old problems

Much of the emphasis in New Testament scholarship is now moving away from a 'mechanical' analysis of the gospels. Though the two-source theory of gospel origins is still widely accepted, a number of new questions are being asked, some of which may have a decisive influence on our understanding of the way the New Testament came to be written.

(1) Questions continue to be asked about the two-source hypothesis itself. Was Mark really the first gospel to be written? Did Q ever exist independently as yet another 'gospel'? If so, why was it originally written, and what was its distinctive message? And is it really necessary to suppose that Q represents a fixed collection of *logia* rather than just a looser collection of traditions known by both Matthew and Luke? Debates that seemed to have been settled fifty years ago are now being reopened, and much of the evidence for the two-source theory is being looked at again. We can now see that the way a question is posed can have important effects on the answers that are produced. For instance, the order of events in the gospel narrative has generally been held to prove conclusively that Mark was written first and that Q had a more or less fixed form. If we accept the suggestion that Q had a form similar to that of the Old Testament prophetic literature, then its form may well have been a written form too.

(2) The older idea of a linear development from *testimonia, logia* and *kerygma* (the message) to a finished gospel is now being questioned. What we know of the earliest churches suggests they were for the most part independent of one another. Churches in different parts of the Roman empire would therefore develop at their own rate, and it is quite likely that Christians in different geographical locations would not be at the same stage of development at the same time. This means that it is unrealistic to suppose that in the collection of traditions about Jesus there was a period when all the interest was in collecting *logia*, and this was then followed by a period of intense literary activity during which the gospels came to be written. It may well be that the type of information about Jesus current in any given church varied according to the needs of the particular congregation.

This has an important bearing on the question of dating the gospels. If it is necessary to suppose a long history of development from *logia* to gospel, then we need to allow time for this in our dating of the gospels. But if *logia* and gospel were both being formed at the same time, to meet the requirements of different churches, then there is no reason why we cannot date the gospels somewhat earlier than is usually done.

(3) A similar point has been made with regard to the 'theological development' some suggest can be traced within the gospels. In his book *Redating the New Testament*, Dr John Robinson has pointed out that a sophisticated theology does not necessarily indicate a later date than a primitive theology. For example, Mark's Gospel is undoubtedly less sophisticated than John's Gospel – and this has been one reason (though not the only one) why Mark has generally been dated first, and John last. But of course this assumes a direct evolutionary progression working through all the gospels. If, however, the different gospels were written to serve the needs of independent churches in different places, it is not difficult to believe that churches with a primitive theology could have existed at the same time as churches with a more sophisticated belief – and so 'theological development' is not necessarily a very useful concept in studying the gospels we now have.

So there are a number of new questions being asked about the gospels today, and they are of a rather different kind from those asked by earlier generations. It is now widely recognized that, wherever the information actually comes from, each evangelist has written what is essentially an original work, distinctive in important respects from the work of any of the others. Much of our interest is now focused on *what* the evangelists were doing, rather than on finding out *how* they were doing it. And that is a question that calls for a theological answer to supplement the earlier findings of the literary critics.

What Do the Gospels Tell Us about Jesus?

In all we have said so far, we have taken it for granted that we can actually learn something about Jesus from the gospels of the New Testament. We have recognized that the gospels are not so much biographies of Jesus, as selective accounts of his words and actions compiled because of their usefulness in the preaching ministry of the earliest churches. But we have not taken that fact as a reason to doubt the general reliability of their account of Jesus' life and teaching. At most points we have felt justified in treating these records as a picture of Jesus as he really was, rather than regarding them as psychological case studies of the Christians who first wrote about him.

It must be frankly admitted, however, that this assumption has been called into question from a number of different directions. We do not need to take seriously those writers who occasionally claim that Jesus never existed at all, for we have clear evidence to the contrary from a number of Jewish, Latin and Islamic sources. But when people who have studied the New Testament for a lifetime claim that the gospels reveal nothing of importance about Jesus, then we need to take serious account of their arguments.

Perhaps the most radical expression of this viewpoint in our generation has been associated with the name of Rudolf Bultmann. In a book first published in 1934, he made the remarkable statement: 'I do indeed think that we can now know almost nothing concerning the life and personality of Jesus.' The precise implication of what Bultmann meant by that must be decided in the light of some of his other writings, where he makes it clear that he does believe certain elements of Jesus' teaching as found in the gospels to be original to Jesus himself. But to his dying day Bultmann remained sceptical about both the possibility and the value of knowledge about 'the historical Jesus'.

Not all Bultmann's followers have been quite as sceptical as he was. We can see this clearly enough from Gunther Bornkamm's book, *Jesus of Nazareth*, which shows that even from a radical form-critical standpoint there is still a good deal that can confidently be known about Jesus. But for all that, those scholars who have been most influenced by Bultmann and his form-critical approach to the gospels have generally taken it for granted that the gospels are primarily a record of the beliefs of the early church about Jesus, rather than any sort of account of Jesus as he actually was.

Clearly, our knowledge of Jesus is not the same as our knowledge of, say, Winston Churchill, or Martin Luther, or even of Paul. For we can know these people through their writings and recorded utterances. Indeed, in the case of Luther and Paul, the main source of the information about them is the books that they themselves wrote. But Jesus did not write a book. He spent his brief life as a wandering teacher, working in a more or less remote corner of the Roman empire, among people who were probably not very interested in literary matters.

It is quite unlikely that Jesus' words and actions had ever been written down, either by himself or by any of his contemporaries. Furthermore we know that Jesus lived in a society whose main language was Aramaic, and yet our knowledge of his teaching comes from documents written in Greek. It is possible that Greek may have been familiar to someone brought up in Galilee. But it is certain that most of Jesus' teachings were not originally given in this language, and that the gospels are therefore a translation of the words of Jesus into the major language of the Roman empire.

Moreover, one of the consequences of handing on Jesus' sayings in Greek is that we now have variant accounts in our gospels of what is obviously the same basic tradition. If we take the Lord's Prayer, for example, we find that Matthew and Luke preserve different versions. The similarities are so close that there can be no doubt we are dealing with the same basic tradition. But the differences are too striking to be explained merely as variant translations. The same observations could be made at many other points in the gospels, and they are the basic facts with which source, form and redaction critics are concerned.

We must not exaggerate the problems. Many generations of gospel readers ignorant of the findings of modern scholars have found little difficulty in dealing with such matters. For all the distinctiveness of the various stories about Jesus and the reports of his teaching, there is clearly an inner coherence in the gospels as a whole. It is not difficult to gather together an account of what the gospels effectively present to us as 'the teaching of Jesus' – and the basic elements of that teaching are the same in all four gospels.

A positive approach to the gospels

Many scholars find the scepticism of Bultmann and his followers quite unacceptable. They argue instead that there are a number of good reasons for starting from the assumption that the gospels are reliable, rather than unreliable, as records of Jesus as he actually was. A number of important arguments point in this direction.

(1) To begin at the most general level, we must not forget that ancient writers were not, on the whole, either fools or frauds. Many modern theologians (though not as many historians) speak so disparagingly of the historians of the Roman world that we are often given the impression that the concept of accurate history writing was quite unknown to them. It is of course true that the ancient historian did not have at his disposal all the modern aids we have today. But that is not to say he simply invented his stories. Both Latin and Greek historians had high standards, and though they did not always keep to them, it was certainly not for lack of trying. The principles outlined by people like Lucian and Thucydides make it quite clear that they operated within guidelines that would not be out of place even today.

Whatever else may be said about the people who wrote the gospels, it is clear that they thought they were working within this kind of historical tradition. Luke explicitly says that he sifted all his sources of information and carefully compiled his story on that basis. Since the other synoptic writers used a more or less similar technique in dealing with their sources, it is natural to suppose that they also worked on the same lines. Certainly they all thought they were giving actual information about a person who had really lived in the way they described. They were not conscious of reporting sayings made up by their contemporaries and attributed to Jesus. They believed that their risen Lord was actually a Galilean rabbi, and that as a wandering teacher he lived and spoke as they depicted him.

(2) This argument is of course not very strong by itself, for the evangelists could have been mistaken and deluded. But it gains considerable added force when we discover that the details of their accounts do actually give an authentic picture of life in Palestine at the time of which they purport to write. When we recall that they all wrote in Greek for a more or less non-Jewish readership, and that at least two of them were not living in Palestine when they wrote, this is all the more remarkable. At point after point we find that the

background of the gospels is authentic. Moreover, at places where their record was once believed to be mistaken (as in the case of John's Gospel), subsequent discoveries of new information have often shown that the gospels preserve reliable accounts of a number of important geographical and social details.

(3) The gospels have also been firmly rooted in a Jewish context by the work of two Scandinavian scholars, Harald Riesenfeld and his pupil Birger Gerhardsson. Gerhardsson has put forward the view that the teaching of Jesus was very similar in form to that of the Jewish rabbis, and in an extended analysis of their teaching methods he has shown how the rabbis took great pains to ensure that their sayings were accurately remembered and passed on by word of mouth to their followers. Gerhardsson suggests that Jesus adopted the same methods, and that he formulated his teaching with a view to his disciples learning it by heart so that they could pass it on to their own followers in the same easily memorized form. It is suggested that the teaching of Jesus was handed on in this way as 'holy word' in the early church, and that the gospels represent the writing down of accurately transmitted traditions going right back to Jesus himself.

We have no evidence that the early Christians regarded themselves as the transmitters of tradition, however. They were preachers of the good news, explaining how the life and message of Jesus was relevant to the needs of their own generation. We also have the unanimous testimony of the gospels that Jesus was quite different from the Jewish rabbis. He taught 'with authority' and did not simply hand on memorized sayings from one group of disciples to another.

Yet, though the case of Riesenfeld and Gerhardsson may be exaggerated, they have reminded us that Jesus' teaching was given in a Jewish context, and that in the context of the teaching of an authoritative leader was treated with great respect. Even if the earliest disciples did not learn Jesus' sayings by heart, they would certainly have a high regard for them.

There is also ample evidence for the reliable oral preservation of stories in the wider Hellenistic world. Take the *Life of Apollonius of Tyana*. This man Apollonius was a contemporary of Jesus, though he lived on into old age and died towards the end of the 1st century. The account of his life, however, was not written down until the beginning of the 3rd century. Though the author collected the stories of his life from a number of different sources, and though he was not an impartial biographer, very few ancient historians would have serious doubts about the reliability of the main outline of his account. In the case of the gospels we are dealing with documents that were written down very shortly after the events of which they speak. To most ordinary people it would seem absurd to assume that such accounts are useless for the purpose of knowing something of Jesus himself.

(4) According to the German scholar Joachim Jeremias, the gospels do indeed bring us into close contact with Jesus as he actually was. Jeremias has scrutinized the linguistic and grammatical features of the gospels, and argues that in them we can discover the authentic voice of Jesus.

Occasionally we come across actual Aramaic words, even in the Greek text of the gospels. In many other cases there are passages where an idiomatic Aramaic construction has been used in the writing of the gospels in Greek. Jeremias also outlines a number of ways of speaking which he says were characteristically used by Jesus. Much of his teaching is given in the form of Aramaic poetry, recognizable even in an English translation. At other points, as we have already said, it has been shown that when sayings attributed to Jesus are translated back into Aramaic, they often assume a typically Semitic form, and even display alliteration and assonance that could have had meaning only in Aramaic. Then there are the parables, which are quite different from the teaching of the rabbis; and Jesus' special use of the words *Amen* and *Abba*.

Features such as these do not themselves prove that the gospel traditions go back to Jesus. Strictly speaking, the most they can show is that they go back to a form in which they were preserved by Aramaic-speaking Palestinian Christians. But when we get back into that context we are also back to a time shortly after the events of Jesus' life, death and resurrection. At this time many eye-witnesses must still have been alive to challenge any accounts which were pure fiction.

These facts therefore favour the authenticity of the gospel accounts of Jesus' teaching. Jeremias for one has no doubt that they place the burden of proof squarely on those who would dispute their accuracy: 'In the synoptic tradition it is the inauthenticity and not the authenticity of the sayings of Jesus that must be demonstrated.'

(5) Another consideration that gives us confidence in accepting the gospels as generally authentic records of Jesus' life and teaching is the fact that they are so different from what we know of the life and concerns of the early non-Jewish churches. It is wrong to assume that, because the gospels were written to serve the needs of the churches, they are little more than a mirror reflecting the early life of the church. The rest of the New Testament shows that the church had many needs that are not even remotely met in the gospels.

There is, for example, no real teaching on the church itself in the gospels. This is so obvious a gap as to render it necessary to ask whether Jesus was interested in founding a church at all. It has been suggested that the emergence of the church was by no means incompatible with Jesus' teaching, but we still need to admit that there is virtually no specific guidance on the subject in the gospels. Even baptism, which very soon became the rite of initiation into the Christian fellowship, is never mentioned by Jesus, apart from one isolated instance. Jesus himself did not baptize, nor did he make baptism a central part of his teaching. Yet this was a matter of great importance to the early church. If they did indeed make a regular practice of manufacturing 'sayings of Jesus' to meet their needs, they certainly missed an important opportunity here.

We find the same lack of specific guidance on other crucial topics. The question of Jews and non-Jews, for example, is not really dealt with in the gospels, though we know from the rest of the New Testament that it soon became one of the most important matters of all.

In other places the gospels make quite a different emphasis from the rest of the New Testament. The term 'Son of man', for instance, is the most widely used name for Jesus in the gospels, but it hardly appears anywhere else. Likewise, 'the kingdom of God', which was the heart of Jesus' teaching, is hardly mentioned in the rest of the New Testament.

The fact is that if we were to try to reconstruct the church's life-situation from the gospels, we would never arrive at the kind of picture we know to be true from the New Testament letters. For there are so many features of the gospel stories about Jesus that are quite different from the life and concerns of the early church.

In the light of facts such as these, it seems reasonable to conclude that there are good reasons for supposing the gospels preserve authentic reminiscences of Jesus as he actually was. The whole character of their picture of Jesus is such that we would need very strong and coherent arguments to show that they are fundamentally mistaken.

This assumption does not of course mean that we can adopt a naïve and uncritical attitude. The evangelists were not mere recorders of tradition. They were interpreters of the facts handed on to them, and we need to scrutinize their work carefully in order to understand the precise nature of what they were doing. But it does give us confidence in thinking that the tradition they interpreted for their first readers was itself authentic, and that in general terms they have preserved a realistic account of the life and teaching of Jesus.

John Drane

THE GREAT SAYINGS OF JESUS IN LITERATURE

Quotations and Images

Characters and Events

The following characters are to be found in the volume *The Gospel of St John*: John the Beloved Disciple, Judas Iscariot, Mary Magdalene, Mary, Mother of Jesus, Peter and Pontius Pilate. The Resurrection is to be found in *The New Testament Epistles*.

Quotations and Images

Abraham's Bosom

This expression denotes, in the parable of the rich man (Dives) and
Lazarus, the place of repose to which Lazarus went after his death
(Luke 16:22ff.). The Jewish character of the image arises from the
custom in which an honoured guest at a feast might recline against
the chest of his neighbour, as John reclined on the breast of Jesus at
the Last Supper (John 21:20). Though rabbinic thanatology divided
Sheol into realms of the righteous and the wicked, the words of Jesus
do not precisely correspond – here 'Abraham's bosom' is not
identified with Sheol but distinguished from it. The image suggests to
subsequent commentators a 'paradise' where Abraham receives the
covenant faithful to the intimacy of an eternal feast. Christian
commentators relate Abraham's bosom to the 'perfect health' of
eternal felicity (e.g., St Augustine, *Sermo,* 97.3; 101.3–4).

King Richard, the errant rich man of Shakespeare's *Richard III,*
rationalizes to himself following his murder of the young princes in
the Tower that 'the sons of Edward sleep in Abraham's bosom'
(4.3.38); the allusion is parodied in *Henry V* when the Hostess
remarks on Falstaff's death, 'Nay, sure, he's not in hell; he's in
Arthur's bosom, if ever man went to Arthur's bosom' (2.3.9–11). A
similarly parodic reference occurs in Alexander Pope's *Dunciad,* where
'Shadwells' bosom' is a place of ignorant bliss.

In Matthew Henry's *Commentary on the Whole Bible* (1728) the
parable is made the basis for an argument for immortality of the soul:
the soul of the beggar 'did not *die,* or *fall asleep,* with the body… but
lived, and acted, and knew what it did, and what was done to it.'
Further, 'his soul was *removed* to another world, to the world of spirits;
it returned to God who gave it to its native country.' The carrying was
by ministering angels who, as Henry puts it, were no more offended
by the leprous sores on his body than was Abraham, 'the *father of the
faithful*', in whose bosom he lay:

> and whither should the souls of the faithful be gathered
> but to him, who, as a tender father, lays them *in his bosom,*

> especially at their first coming, to bid them welcome, and
> to refresh them when newly come from the sorrows and
> fatigues of this world? (5.759)

In Wordsworth's sonnet, 'It is a Beauteous Evening, Calm and Free', the poet addresses his illegitimate daughter Caroline in terms which do not mask, however gently phrased, his sense of the vast gulf which separates them: 'If thou appear untouched by solemn thought, / Thy nature is not therefore less divine. / Thou liest in Abraham's bosom all the year.' This sonnet is apparently a mediate influence upon Hardy's allusion in *Desperate Remedies*, where Cytherea discusses Springrove, whom she loves, with her rival. To her question, 'Are you fond of him?' the 'miserable Cytherea' obtains an ambiguous reply: '"Yes, of course I am", her companion replied, but in the tone of one who "lived in Abraham's bosom all the year", and was therefore untouched by solemn thought at the fact' (chapter 8). A more direct allusion (with a transference from Abraham to Jesus) comes in the guilty agony of the Chaplain of Shaw's *St Joan*, after Joan has been condemned to be burned. He cries, 'O Christ, deliver me from this fire that is consuming me! She cried to thee in the midst of it: Jesus! Jesus! Jesus! She is in thy bosom; and I am in hell for evermore.'

David L. Jeffrey
University of Ottawa

Beatitudes

A beatitude (Latin *beatitudo,* from Vulgate Romans 4:6–9) is a statement proclaiming the happiness, good fortune, or blessedness of certain types of people in the Old Testament and New Testament; beatitudes are also called makarisms because the most important series, in the Sermon on the Mount (Matthew 5:3–11) and in the Sermon on the Plain (Luke 6:20–22), begin with Greek *makarioi.* The many scattered Old Testament beatitudes (e.g., in Psalms 2:12; 32:1; Proverbs 8:34; Isaiah 32:20; 56:1–2) and other New Testament beatitudes (e.g., Matthew 11:6; 13:16; Romans 4:7; Revelation 1:3) will not be considered here.

Both the Matthean and Lucan series upend worldly values,

redefining conditions such as poverty and suffering. The beatitudes of both series state the blessing in the first clause and the reason for the blessing in the second clause: 'Blessed are... for...'. Otherwise the two series differ considerably. Luke's four blessings are followed by four exactly corresponding woes, all of which are in the second person. Focusing on external conditions such as poverty, the Lucan series stresses the vast social reversal which will occur through the coming of God's kingdom. Whereas Luke offers eschatological consolation, Matthew offers eschatological challenge, for in the Sermon on the Mount the blessed are those who live by certain spiritual values. Luke's poor are here the poor in spirit, and the hungry are those who hunger and thirst for righteousness. Matthew's eight beatitudes are addressed generally, in the third person, and are ethically conditional: only those who live by the specified spiritual values will be saved (*International Standard Bible Encyclopaedia*, 1.443–44). Of the two series, Matthew's has been more central to Christian doctrine because it begins the Sermon on the Mount; therefore, hereafter 'Beatitudes' will refer to the Matthew passage unless otherwise noted.

In Roman Catholic exegesis, which follows St Augustine (*De sermone Domini in Monte*, *Patrologia Latina*, 34.1229–1308) and St Thomas Aquinas (*Summa Theologica*, 1a2ae.69, 24.43–63), the Beatitudes are sequential stages in temporal spiritual growth ending with the person's becoming perfected in the divine image; they are also adjunct to the gifts of the Holy Spirit and to the vices and virtues. As such, the Beatitudes often appear in septenary schemes (e.g., *The World of Piers Plowman*, eds. J. Krochalis and E. Peters, 1975, 170–79). Thus, Dante's ascesis through Purgatory is marked by the Beatitudes, and in St Thomas More's *Dialogue of Comfort against Tribulation*, 1.10 and 1.19, the Beatitudes are key reminders of radical Christian detachment from the world.

Modern Protestant theology tends to see the Beatitudes as 'illustrative of a new set of mind and of the will, a disposition grounded on the consciousness that God is our all in all and that love, unlimited in its volition and free from all external constraints, is life's only good' (Windisch, 1951, 45). The 19th-century theologian Johannes Weiss saw the Beatitudes as an 'Interim-Ethik', binding only for the short period before the imminently expected Second Coming. Earlier theologians such as Luther and Calvin were much closer in spirit to the Augustinian view of the Beatitudes as an ethic for all Christians to attempt to live by (Luther, *The Sermon on the Mount*, in *Luther's Works*, ed. J. Pelikan, 1956, 21.3–4; Calvin, *Commentary on a Harmony of the Evangelists*, trans. W. Pringle, Calvin Translation Society, 1845, 1.260). The same holds true for Anglican theologians (e.g., Lightfoot, *Harmony, Chronicle, and Order of the New Testament*, 1655, 26; Poole, *Synopsis Criticorum Aliorumque Sacrae Scripturae Interpretum*, 1674, 4.114–15). In both Catholic and Anglican liturgies, Matthew 5:1–12 is the gospel for the Feast of All Saints (Novum 1).

Although the Beatitudes hold a central position in biblical commentary and in Christian theology, their occurrence in English literature is limited mainly to statements beginning 'Blessed be...' which seldom contain the rhetorical and ethical qualities of the originals, and which seldom have much significance for the works in which they occur. Nevertheless, some authors have used the Beatitudes or the beatitude form with great learning and wit, and sometimes with great thematic import.

Matthew 5:3 is one of the central ideas of Pacience's speech to Haukyn in *Piers Plowman* (B.14.214) and one of the main ethical messages of the poem's *Dowel* section (see R.W. Frank, Jr, *Piers Plowman and the Scheme of Salvation*, Yale Studies in English 136, 1957, 72–77). The homiletic, alliterative poems *Cleanness* and *Patience* both take Beatitudes as their themes (Matthew 5:8 and Matthew 5:3, 10 respectively). *Cleanness* discusses purity by contrasting it with profanation in the stories of the Flood, Sodom and Gomorrah, and the fall of Belshazzar; *Patience* focuses on the story of Jonah in such a way as to link patience with vocational obedience. Chaucer uses the beatitude form ironically in *The Miller's Tale,* where the carpenter's 'Ye, blessed be alwey a lewed man / That noght but oonly his bileve kan!' (*Canterbury Tales*, 1.3455–56) proclaims his ignorance and gullibility before the student Nicholas, who dupes the carpenter precisely by preying on his *bileve*. The avaricious friar in *The Summoner's Tale* uses Matthew 5:3 to wheedle a donation from the flatulent Thomas (3.1923). In *Melibee*, Matthew 5:9 is one of

Prudence's main themes in her efforts to get Melibeus to make peace with his enemies (7.1680), and thus one of the tale's central themes. *The Parson's Tale* concludes with a pastiche of Matthew 5:3, 5, 6.

In Spenser's *The Faerie Queene* (4.10.8.8–9) the inscription 'Blessed the man that well can use his blis: / Whose ever be the shield, faire Amoret be his' sends Scudamor on his quest. Throughout his works, Shakespeare adopts the beatitude form to express a blessing, although he alludes directly to only two of the Beatitudes per se. Matthew 5:9 is alluded to three times in the plays, but always ironically, since for various reasons the peacemakers are ineffectual and peace is impossible (*2 Henry VI*, 2.1.35; *Richard III*, 2.1.50–53; *Coriolanus*, 5.3.138–40). The Lucan beatitude form combined with a Lucan 'woe to...' reveals Falstaff's vindictive selfishness as well as his vain hope for preferment in *2 Henry IV*, 5.3.133–34: 'Blessed are they that have been my friends and woe to my Lord Chief Justice!' In *Eastward Ho,* by Chapman, Jonson, and Marston, Matthew 5:6 is applied by several characters in a humorously literal, appetitive sense: for example, to express Gertrude's desire for sex with Sir Petronel (2.2.431–32; cf. 2.2.164 and 3.2.246–47).

After the Renaissance the Beatitudes are usually pressed into the service of secular values. Pope's 'Ode on Solitude' makes a heaven of earth through two extended beatitudes celebrating rustic contentment and anonymity. Blake's letter to John Flaxman (19 October 1801) saw peace with Napoleon as the inauguration of an artistic eschaton: 'Blessed are those who are found studious of Literature and Humane and polite accomplishments. Such have their lamps burning and shall shine as the stars.' Wordsworth's Wanderer (*Excursion*, 2.591–92) exclaims at the sight of a rustic funeral procession: 'Oh! blest are they who live and die like these, / Loved with such love, and with such sorrow mourned!' although his optimism is soon challenged by the despairing Solitary. Thoreau pronounces the sixth Beatitude, in Transcendentalist fashion, on those who remain pure by avoiding knowledge of current events: 'Blessed were the days before you read a president's message. Blessed are the young, for they do not read the president's message. Blessed are they who have never read a newspaper, for they shall see Nature, and through her, God' (Thoreau to Parker Pillsbury, 10 April 1861).

The Beatitudes are central in Melville's *The Confidence-Man* and *Billy Budd*. In *The Confidence-Man* (chapters 3–7), the first three appearances of the confidence-man are 'types from the Beatitudes: the Negro Black Guinea, who solicits alms, the poor in spirit; John Ringman, the man with the weed, those who mourn; the man with the grey coat, those who hunger and thirst after righteousness' (Wright, 1949, 102). The Beatitudes are thus a vehicle for the confidence-man's manipulation of Christian virtues, which Elizabeth Foster saw as a 'criticism of religion itself and [an] attack on optimistic philosophy' (ed. pref., *Confidence-Man*, 1954, xlvii). In *Billy Budd*, Billy's being called a peacemaker ('Well, blessed are the peacemakers, especially the fighting peacemakers,' chapter 1) is ironically prophetic: by removing the evil Claggart, Billy is, in a way, a peacemaker, and by dying an innocent he remains a child of God. In Tennyson's 'Aylmer's Field', 753–56, Averill's sermon on the suicides of Edith and Leolin laments Aylmer's destructive avarice by reinterpreting 'poor in spirit' as vile.

M.W. Twomey
Ithaca College

Beelzebub

The Greek name *Beelzebul* or *Beelzeboul* means 'master of the heavenly dwelling', although in its Latin and Syriac version, *Beelzebub,* it can mean 'lord of the flies' (Matthew 12:24, 27; Mark 3:22; Luke 11:15, 18). A relatively obscure name for Satan or the prince of demons, Beelzebub was claimed by some enemies of Jesus to be the 'unclean spirit' (Mark 3:30) through which he performed miracles. The root of the etymology is both Aramaic and Hebrew: *be'el* ('master, lord') is Aramaic, and *zebul* ('height, abode, dwelling') the only Hebrew word ascribed to Jesus in the New Testament. The compound appears to have been a pejorative nickname for Jesus coined by the scribes (cf. Matthew 10:25). In origin the name may have referred to a Canaanite god, represented as Baal-zebub (2 Kings 1:2ff.). Postbiblical Hebrew, like Syriac, used *zbl* to mean 'dung, excrement', suggesting a further association to later writers. The accusation against Jesus is meant to imply demon possession, a charge which was laid also against John

39

the Baptist (Matthew 11:18; Luke 7:33) and which suggests sorcery; it is paralleled by explicit charges that Jesus had a demon (John 7:20; 8:48–52; 10:20). The claim, based on these associations, that Jesus was merely a magician is found in pagan sources (see Origen, *Contra Celsum*, 1.6, 38, 49, 53, 68; Justin, *Apology* 1.30; *Dialogue with Trypho* 69.7), in Jewish writings (e.g., Sanhedrin 43a), and in the Koran (5.113). Origen elsewhere observes that all 'those who invoke Beelzebub are magicians' (*In Numeros homilia*, 13.5).

Patristic commentary on the subject was slow to develop, but St Ambrose (*De poenitentia*, 2.4.21–26) connects Matthew 10:25 to the narrative of Simon Magus (Acts 8:21ff.). St Jerome regards the charge against Jesus to be the ultimate blasphemy (*Epistle* 42.1–2), an injury to the Lord so severe that comparable injury to his followers must seem by comparison much more bearable (*Epistle* 38.5). The *Glossa Ordinaria* etymologized the name as 'fly [or pest] of Baal' (*Patrologia Latina*, 114.119), hence 'Beelzebub is to say, the lord of the flies,' on account of the way in which the flies are attracted to the bloody filth associated with sacrifices to him (*Patrologia Latina*, 114.289). Calvin follows these sources in his commentary on Matthew 10:25, but opines from his northern perspective that the Philistines probably invoked their god Beel-zebub rather 'to save them from the flies which infested the district' (*Harmony of the Gospels*).

Belsabub, as he is called in the York cycle, is a vigorous captain of the underworld, reporting only to Satan himself (37.109–19). Both here and in the Towneley cycle, as Christ knocks at the gates he endeavours in vain to marshal the forces of hell against Christ's deliverance of the elect (the harrowing of hell): 'Harro! our yates begin to crak, / In sonder, I trow, they go' (Towneley, 25.194–95). Alluding to the Harrowing of Hell plays as much as to the Bible, Shakespeare has the porter in *Macbeth* respond to the imperious knocking at the gate with 'Knock, knock, knock! Who's there, i' the name of Beelzebub?' (2.3.3–4; cf. 17–19). Marlowe's *Tragicall Historie of Doctor Faustus* (1604) bears striking resemblance to the talmudic legends of Solomon's demise. After the appearance of Mephistopheles, when Faustus is told that 'the shortest cut for coniuring / Is stoutly to abiure the Trinitie, / And pray deuoutly to the prince of hell', the wise-man-turned-magician replies: 'So Faustus hath already done, & holds this principle / There is no chiefe but onely Belsibub' (1604, ed. Greg, 1.3.297–302). Later he admonishes himself to 'Despaire in God, and trust in Belsabub' (442), concluding:

> The good thou servest is thine owne appetite,
> Wherein is fixt the loue of Balsabub,
> To him Ile build an altar and a church,
> And offer luke warm blood of new borne babes. (448–51)

In Milton's *Paradise Lost* Beelzebub is still Satan's chief adviser, and Bunyan makes him captain of the strong castle near the Wicket-gate in *Pilgrim's Progress*. Melville's Ishmael refers to castaway whalers so queer that Beelzebub would pass unnoticed in their company, and later refers to the way he intends to deal with a potential mutineer: 'I'll just take the nape of his neck and say – "Look here, Beelzebub, you don't do it," and if he makes any fuss, by the Lord, I'll make a grab into his pocket for his tail' (*Moby Dick*, chapter 73). In Shaw's *St Joan* Bishop Cauchon appears to defend Joan, observing that 'the names on that white banner were not the names of Satan and Beelzebub, but the blessed names of our Lord and His Holy Mother' (4.44). William Golding's title *Lord of the Flies* unambiguously invokes the malignancy associated with the oldest references to Beelzebub in a modern parable of a fall from false innocence to neo-pagan horrors.

David L. Jeffrey
University of Ottawa

Blind Lead the Blind

When the disciples intimated to Jesus that he was apparently 'scandalizing' rather than persuading the Pharisees, he replied, 'Let them alone: they be blind leaders of the blind. And if the blind lead the blind, both shall fall into the ditch' (Matthew 15:14; Luke 6:39). This statement has become proverbial; Bunyan's pilgrim is one of many literary travellers who have looked into 'that ditch... into which the blind have led the blind in all ages.' Carlyle uses the phrase with reference to 'the Clergy of the Neighbourhood' who advise Carlyle's pilgrim to 'drink beer and dance with the girls' (*Sartor Resartus*, 3.1); elsewhere Professor Teufelsdröckh applies the figure knowingly to the typical progress of a university education. Both Wilkie Collins (*Moonstone*, 1.10) and G.K. Chesterton (*The Poet and the Lunatics*, 4) seem to have Carlyle as well as Matthew in mind in their citations. Anthony Hecht ironically characterizes 'Sloth' in his poem 'The Seven Deadly Sins' as blind discipleship (*The Hard Hours*, 52).

David L. Jeffrey
University of Ottawa

By Bread Alone

When Jesus had fasted forty days and forty nights in the wilderness, he was tempted by the devil. The first of three temptations was directed to his physical need: 'If thou be the Son of God, command that these stones be made bread' (Matthew 4:3). Jesus answered, quoting Deuteronomy 8:3, 'It is written, Man shall not live by bread alone, but by every word that proceedeth out of the mouth of God' (Matthew 4:4; cf. Luke 4:4). While the passage is occasionally adduced by patristic writers in support of the virtues of fasting as a preparation for spiritual struggle (e.g., St Ambrose, *Epistle*, 63.15), the *Glossa Ordinaria* summarizes what will become the conventional application when it says: 'No other power but the authority of scripture suffices for such combat' (*Patrologia Latina*, 114.84), then goes on to identify the Word of God as essential sustenance for the human spirit, adding that all the words (plural) which proceed from scripture constitute 'one word, that is the wisdom of God' (114.85). Later exegetes largely concur.

Milton's *Paradise Regained* provides a poetic elaboration of the passage (1.342–51). In later literature the traditional reading is loosely adapted, even trivialized. Ruskin makes the necessary bread natural beauty, 'the wild flower by the wayside' (*Unto this Last*, chapter 4). Trollope uses the passage to describe excessively functional architecture of a rectory (*The Warden*, chapter 8). Stevenson observes drily that 'Man is a creature who lives not upon bread alone, but principally by catch words' (*Virginibus Puerisque*, chapter 2), and Aldous Huxley, in his 'Guatemala City' essay in *Beyond the Mexique Bay*, conflates two orders of proverb to offer cynical wisdom: 'Men cannot live by bread alone. But neither can they live only by circuses.

To some extent, however, a shortage of bread can be made up for by a surfeit of circuses.'

David L. Jeffrey
University of Ottawa

By Their Fruits Ye Shall Know Them

In the Sermon on the Mount Jesus warned his hearers about false prophets who come 'in sheep's clothing, but inwardly are ravening wolves' (Matthew 7:15). A discerning eye will identify them, he indicated: 'Ye shall know them by their fruits. Do men gather grapes of thorns, or figs of thistles? Even so, every good tree bringeth forth good fruit; but a corrupt tree bringeth forth evil fruit... Wherefore by their fruits ye shall know them' (Matthew 7:16–20; cf. Luke 6:43–45). A variant of the figure was employed by Jesus on a later occasion when he said that 'the tree is known by his fruit' (Matthew 12:33).

In exegetical tradition from the writings of the early Church through medieval glosses (e.g., *Glossa Ordinaria*, *Patrologia Latina*, 114.110–11) to Reformation commentary (e.g., Calvin, in his *Harmony of the Gospels*) the false prophets identified by Jesus can be construed as heretics, but are most often seen as self-promoters or hypocrites.

This latter sense, linked closely to Jesus' denunciation of the Pharisees for their hypocrisy and religious pride, determines the typical force of literary allusion. William Cowper thus offers a scathing 18th-century portrait of a self-aggrandizing religious ascetic in his poem 'Truth': 'Such are the fruits of sanctimonious pride, / Of malice fed while flesh is mortified' (165–66). Although typically confounding Pharisaism with Puritanism and hypocrisy with prudery, D.H. Lawrence's *Lady Chatterley's Lover* invites a similar judgment: 'there's something wrong with the mental life, radically. It's rooted in spite and envy, envy and spite. Ye shall know the tree by its fruits' (chapter 3). Aldous Huxley is still thinking of pharisaical self-arrogation when he writes in *The Olive Tree*:

It is difficult for people whose main preoccupation is sensual enjoyment to do harm on a very large scale. But where the cravings to be justified are cravings for power, glory and the like, the case is different. The tree is known by its fruits. Judged by this standard, sympneumatism, for example, is a joke; nationalism, which is a theory intrinsically almost as preposterous as poor Oliphant's, is a tragedy and a menace. ('Justifications')

T.S. Eliot instances a further tendency in 20th-century humanism to associate science and technology with sanctimoniousness and fraudulent claims to moral authority, especially the scientists' habit of proclaiming successive hypothetical accounts of natural process as fact: 'Until science can teach us to reproduce such phenomena at will,' he notes, 'science cannot claim to have explained them; and they can be judged only by their fruits' (Introduction to *Pensée*).

In the Victorian period and in 20th-century usage, the phrase has been degraded to cliché, yet even ironic and jesting invocation tends to depend for its effect upon some recognition of the original association with hypocrisy and sanctimony. 'By the cigars they smoke,' writes John Galsworthy, 'and the composers they love, ye shall know the texture of men's souls' (*Indian Summer of a Forsyte*, chapter 1).

David L. Jeffrey
University of Ottawa

Camel through the Eye of a Needle

The story of the encounter between Jesus and the rich man seeking 'eternal life' appears in Matthew 19:16–30; Mark 10:17–31; Luke 18:18–30 and the noncanonical gospel of the Nazarenes, cited by Origen. In Mark and Luke, Jesus rejects the title 'Good Teacher'. Similarly in Matthew, he refuses to point to the 'good deed' which will win salvation (19:16). In all three gospels, the rich man is instead referred to God as the source of goodness (Matthew 19:17; Mark 10:18; Luke 18:19) and to the commandments as the traditional guides to right conduct (Matthew 19:18–19; Mark 10:19; Luke 18:20).

The rich man asserts his faithful observance of 'all these' commandments. In response, Jesus adds a new list of radical demands which exceed traditional piety. The rich man is told to sell his possessions, donate the proceeds to the poor, and undertake a life as Jesus' disciple. With sadness, the man declines to comply and leaves. His great wealth is cited as the reason for his refusal and consequent inability to gain 'treasure in heaven' (Matthew 19:22; Mark 10:22; Luke 18:23).

A dialogue continues between Jesus and his disciples. Jesus stresses the barrier wealth represents for those who seek to enter the kingdom of God with an oft-repeated maxim: 'It is easier for a camel to enter the eye of a needle than for a rich man to enter heaven.' To the amazement of those who doubt that anyone can then be saved, Jesus responds that although the situation is impossible by human effort alone, it is 'possible with God'.

The apostle Peter then asks what reward the disciples will receive, having 'left everything' and 'followed him' in sharp contrast to the reluctant rich man. Jesus not only promises the eternal life the rich man sought in vain but also rulership in Israel, judging the twelve tribes (Matthew 19:28). Furthermore, the sacrifices of disciples will be repaid abundantly, a 'hundredfold' in Matthew (19:29) and 'manifold' times in Luke (18:30). Mark adds more soberly that discipleship will also bring 'persecutions' (10:30). To stress that the disciples' reward is a matter of God's grace and not earned by human merit, the episode concludes with the admonition that many of those who are seemingly 'last' will be 'first' in the kingdom of God (Matthew 19:30; Mark 10:31; Luke 18:30).

In medieval exegesis the young man's riches were usually allegorized as works and honours obtained on his own merit, and Christ's call to radical divestment as an invitation to imitate him in his passion. In the light of the version in Mark 10:23–27, Jesus was not seen as prohibiting the rich but speaking of the difficulties for those who place their confidence in riches (e.g., *Glossa Ordinaria, Patrologia Latina*, 114.151; St Jerome, *Epistle,* 145; *Adversus Pelagianos,* 1.10); in one of his best-known letters, Jerome is at pains to emphasize the metaphorical character of Jesus' utterance. Calvin nonetheless observes that Satan holds the very affluent 'bound in chains', in that 'they bury and constrict themselves and enslave themselves completely to this world,' but adds that 'the simile of the camel' refers rather to 'a ship's rope than the animal' (*Harmony of the Gospels*, Matthew 19:23–26).

In Shakespeare's *Richard II*, the imprisoned king struggles with his soul's lack of elected peace: 'I have been studying how I may compare / This prison where I live unto the world' (5.5.1–2); he finds that those in religious doubt

> do set the word itself
> Against the word; as thus, 'Come little ones,'
> And then again,
> 'It is as hard to come as for a camel
> To thread the postern of a small needle's eye.' (5.5.13–17)

Anthony Trollope reflects the conventional interpretation: 'How hard it is for a rich man not to lean upon his riches! harder, indeed, than for a camel to go through the eye of a needle' (*Framley Parsonage*, chapter 8), while Charles Dickens incorporates the allusion as a satire on riches as poverty in *Little Dorrit*: its Antichrist figure, Mr Merdle, is an imperial tycoon of unknown and unquestioned sources of vast income, for 'it was the last new polite reading of the camel and the needle's eye to accept without enquiry' his riches (1.33; cf. *Martin Chuzzlewit*, chapter 25). Aldous Huxley takes up the Dickensian application in *After Many a Summer*, where he observes that 'Poverty and suffering ennoble only when they are voluntary. By involuntary poverty and suffering men are made worse. It is easier for a camel to pass through the eye of the needle than for an involuntarily poor man to enter the kingdom of heaven' (1.8), while in his essay 'On Grace' he adds that it is 'almost as difficult for the spiritually rich to enter the kingdom of heaven as it is for the materially rich' (*Music at Night*).

American literature often engages the phrase less soberly. Twain's antinomian humour leads to typical parody: 'It is easier for a cannibal to enter the Kingdom of Heaven through the eye of a rich man's needle than it is for any other foreigner to read the terrible German script' (*Notebook*, chapter 31). Rhett Butler executes an ante-bellum slur on Southern decorum in Mitchell's *Gone with the Wind*, turning the original point about riches inside out. Responding to Scarlett's assurances concerning his prospects ('If you've got money, people always like you') he retorts, 'Not Southerners. It's harder for speculators' money to get into the best parlours than for the camel to go through the needle's eye' (chapter 48).

Lenore Gussin
New York, New York
David L. Jeffrey
University of Ottawa

Dives and Lazarus

Jesus' parable of Dives and Lazarus (Luke 16:19–31) has two parts. In the first, the beggar Lazarus lies at the gate of a rich man (Latin *dives*, whence the traditional name), hungry and suffering from sores, while the rich man fares 'sumptuously every day' (v. 19). In the second, both have died, and the situation is completely reversed. Lazarus now rests in 'Abraham's bosom', whereas the rich man is tormented in the flames of the underworld. The rich man tries to persuade Abraham to send Lazarus with a drop of water. When Abraham refuses, because 'between us and you there is a great gulf fixed' (v. 26), the rich man asks for Lazarus to call his five brothers to repentance, 'lest they also come into this place of torment' (v. 28). Abraham refuses again, because they 'have Moses and the prophets' (v. 29).

The context of the parable suggests a comment on the divergence of earthly appearance and spiritual reality (cf. v. 15), but many interpreters either have used it as a source of information about life after death, or have emphasized its practical illumination of earthly life. Both interpretations were introduced by the Fathers. That the climactic statement has to do with one who 'rose from the dead', an evident allusion to the resurrection of Jesus, suggests that the story is also a polemic directed against those who refuse the gospel, failing to heed 'Moses and the prophets'.

Because of the rich man's fate, St John Chrysostom (in his *Homily on Ephesians,* 24) and others denied the possibility of repentance after death. St Augustine drew upon the text to prove the immateriality of the soul (e.g., *De anima et ejus origine*, 2.8 and 4.29) and concluded from the parable that part of the happiness of the blessed consists in contemplating the torments of the damned – a thought which later was taken up by St Thomas Aquinas (*Summa Theologica*, Supplement question 94.1).

Augustine also asks his listeners to rely on the heart and not on the eyes when judging human beings and concludes, 'Have respect unto the poor, do good works' (*Sermons on New Testament Lessons*, 52); cf. Chrysostom (*Homily on Thessalonians*, 9), who draws a parallel to Luke 14:12–14. Luther considers the parable 'a picture that is terribly and seriously against avarice, which makes people merciless; avarice is full of injustice and hinders every fruit of the gospel' (Sermon of 6 June 1535), and sees it as restricting the notion of personal property: 'But God's word suppresses this natural and civil right... Yes, a Christian owes help to everybody' (Sermon of 7 June 1523).

Lazarus is a Greek derivation of the common Jewish name *Eleazar* ('God helps') – the only proper name to occur in any of the parables. It entered the English language as *lazar*, meaning 'a poor and diseased person, usually with a loathsome disease; especially a leper' (*Oxford English Dictionary*).

The parable of Dives and Lazarus was paraphrased in various Middle English poems (*The Pricke of Conscience*, 84.3062–66; *Handlyng Synne*, 214.6635–6720), but truly literary treatment began with John Gower, who exploited its practical consequences. In his *Confessio Amantis* (6.975–1150), he retells the parable as an example of one of the seven deadly sins – gluttony. The parable shows that 'bodili delicacie / Of him which yeveth non almesse / Schal after falle in gret destresse.' The other exegetical strand is also found in Middle English literature. In Langland's *Piers Plowman* (B.16.252–71; A.11.38–57; C.11.279–90), William meets Abraham and sees the leper in his lap, 'amonges patriarkes and profetes pleyande togyderes'. Since the devil has claimed both Abraham and Lazarus, they wait for Christ to deliver them. This emphasis developed from the belief of the early Church in Christ's descent into hell (cf. 1 Peter 3:19; 4:6), reflected in apocryphal books such as the gospel of Nicodemus; the belief in a *limbus patrum* was given doctrinal status by Aquinas (*Summa Theologica*, Supplement question 69, 4, 5). The begging friar in Chaucer's *Summoner's Tale* hypocritically alludes to the parable when advising man to 'fatte his soule and make his body lene'.

Shakespeare's allusions to the parable are either ornaments or parodies. In *1 Henry IV* (3.3) Falstaff is reminded of 'hell-fire, and Dives that lived in purple' when looking at Bardolph's face. His charge of soldiers consists of 'slaves as ragged as Lazarus in the painted cloth, where the Glutton's dogs licked his sores' (4.2). In *2 Henry IV* (1.2) Falstaff refers to the rich man – 'Let him be damn'd, like the Glutton; pray God his tongue be hotter!'

Sir Thomas Browne denied the proximity of heaven and hell on the sole grounds of the 'discourse' [sic] between Dives and Lazarus, because that would mean an underestimation of the faculties of the glorified (*Religio Medici*, 1.49). A further reference to Lazarus accompanies a broad definition of charity: 'It is no greater Charity to cloath his body, than apparell the nakednesse of his Soule' (2.3).

Milton, in his *De Doctrina Christiana,* uses the parable to argue that miracles cannot produce belief (1.29). He distinguishes the luxury of the rich from Aristotelian 'elegance', a 'discriminating enjoyment of food, clothing and all the civilized refinements of life, purchased with our honest earnings' (2.9 – 'of the first kind of special virtues, connected with a Man's Duty Toward Himself'). In *Paradise Lost,* Milton uses the parable to depict the torments of Satan (1.56) and to refer to the 'gulf' which separates hell from heaven (e.g., 2.1027; 3.69–70; 10.253–54). Other contemporary references to Dives and Lazarus are found in poems by Richard Crashaw ('Upon Lazarus his Teares') and Thomas Traherne ('The World'). John Bunyan's Interpreter in *The Pilgrim's Progress* quotes verse 25 in characterizing the figures of 'Passion, of the men of this world; and Patience, of the men of that which is to come'.

The question raised by the parable concerning the state of the soul after death is dealt with in one of Boswell's conversations with Samuel Johnson. The latter supposes the parable either to be metaphorical or to support the Purgatorians, but does not want to make it an article of faith 'that departed souls do not all at once arrive at the utmost perfection of which they are capable' (*Life of Samuel Johnson,* Saturday, 28 March 1772). Laurence Sterne, in a 'Charity Sermon' (no. 23 of *The Sermons of Mr Yorick*), calls the parable 'one of the most remarkable in the gospel' and uses it to elaborate the wrong use of riches.

Tennyson alludes to the parable in 'To Mary Boyle', and it is one of the more frequent New Testament references in Lord Byron's poems (e.g., *Don Juan*, 2.683–88). There is a short reference to Lazarus as the patron saint of the lepers in Thomas Hardy's *The Return of the Native* (4.3), and a specific use of the parable in Charlotte Brontë's *Jane Eyre*: St John Rivers, the stern and exacting missionary, in one of his last attempts at persuading her to marry him, exhorts Jane to remember the fate of Dives, citing Luke 10:42 (chapter 9).

The parable's social implication made it a welcome source of illustrations for writers depicting social conflicts of the mid-19th century. A prominent example is Elizabeth Gaskell's *Mary Barton: A Tale of Manchester Life* (1848), in which Chartist and union man John Barton uses the parable as an illustration of the slavelike condition of the poor (chapter 1), and as a threat for the rich (chapter 9). John Ruskin makes a passionate appeal to the 'Judasian Dives' of his time to learn what alms mean, 'while Lazarus yet lies among the dogs' (*Fors Clavigera*, 7.82.24–25; cf. also 'The Crown of Wild Olive', 1).

The 19th century also provides whimsical treatments such as Charles Lamb's definition of a poor relative ('Poor Relations') as 'a Lazarus at your door'. Hilaire Belloc's poem 'To Dives' is a playful comparison of the lot of the poet and of the rich man, soon moving away from scripture towards Greek mythology: Charon will transport the light burdens of poets, 'the vain imaginaries', but not Dives' 'weighty things'.

American literature reflects similar adaptations. Poe briefly alludes to the crumbs which fell from the rich man's table ('Hop-Frog'), but Melville refers to the parable repeatedly. His Wellingborough Redburn, witnessing the death of a mother and two children, cries, 'Tell me, oh Bible, that story of Lazarus again, that I may find comfort in my heart for the poor and forlorn' (*Redburn*, chapter 37). Ishmael, the narrator of *Moby Dick*, ironically weaves the elements of the parable into his whimsical description of the Spouter Inn (chapter 2). The result is a curious combination of social criticism and attack against a divine world order which permits and even creates vast social differences. Melville's famous reference to the parable in Sketch First of *The Encantadas* is also more than a narrative adornment in that it introduces the metaphysical pessimism which pervades the sketches: 'Have mercy upon me,' the wailing spirit of the

Encantadas seems to cry, 'and send Lazarus that he may dip the tip of his finger in water and cool my tongue, for I am tormented in this flame.'

The sceptical modern attitude towards God's providence and love which Melville introduced can also be felt in Canadian poet W.W. Campbell's poem 'Lazarus'. It shows a humanistic pauper unable to rest in Abraham's bosom; he follows Dives' call for help, and then, 'Christ-urged, love-driven,' floats towards hell. Another modernist response emerges in T.S. Eliot's 'Love Song of J. Alfred Prufrock'. Whether its allusion is to Luke 16 or John 11 is not clear; it is connected with the Dantean motto ('but because no one ever returned alive from this depth') and warns against asking 'overwhelming questions'.

In Walker Percy's *Love in the Ruins,* Monsignor Schleifkopf, preaching a sermon on 'Property Rights Sunday', deliberately changes Lazarus from a poor man to one who 'lived comfortably in a home that he owned'.

Manfred Siebald
Johannes Gutenberg Universität, Mainz, Germany

Fishers of Men

Perhaps the most famous call to discipleship in the New Testament occurred when Jesus, walking by the Sea of Galilee, saw Simon Peter and his brother Andrew casting a net into the water. He spoke to them, saying, 'Follow me, and I will make you fishers of men' (Matthew 4:18–19; cf. Mark 1:16–17). The association of this episode with the future 'rock' upon which the new Church was to be built, and with the evangelistic Andrew, led to the phrase acquiring wide early association with the activity of soul-winning. Jesus subsequently called two other fishermen from their task, the sons of Zebedee, James and John (Luke 5:1–11), Peter's fishing partners, who, with him, obtained a miraculous draught of fish. In response to their astonishment Jesus said, 'Fear not; from henceforth thou shalt catch men' (v. 10).

Since the analogy in these passages suggested the fish as a symbol for the soul, it is not surprising that the fish became an important element in early Christian iconography. Souls, according to St Augustine, are fished away by the apostles and their successors from waters in which they are unwittingly captive to God's enemy (*De civitate Dei,* 20.30). Because of the widespread use of the symbol and the special association of the New Testament trope with St Peter and his apostolic vocation, it became natural to think of Peter's successors as occupying the chair of 'the great fisherman', so that 'the fisherman' became in time a nickname for the Pope. In later Protestant commentaries, such as that of Matthew Henry, the emphasis falls upon the apostolic activity of all Christians in evangelism as a response to Christ's 'Follow me', drawing people into 'the gospel net' (*Commentary on the Whole Bible,* 5.632; cf. 5.42–44).

The renegade Friar in Chaucer's *Summoner's Tale,* who regards himself as superior in prelatical efficacy to the parish priest, protests his apostolic vocation in terms which draw upon the traditional exegesis:

> I walke, and fisshe Cristen mennes soules
> To yelden Jhesu Crist his propre rente;
> To sprede his word is set al myn entente.
> (*Canterbury Tales,* 3.1820–22)

The pirate Lambro, in Byron's *Don Juan* (2.1001–03), is yet more obviously a parody:

> A fisher, therefore, was he – though of men,
> Like Peter the Apostle, – and he fished
> For wandering merchant-vessels, now and then.

Later in the poem Byron pictures the devil as a fisherman, baiting his hook with 'lies / Which Satan angles with for souls, like flies' (8.687–88). This infernal reading is echoed in Tennyson's *Harold,* in which the shipwrecked crew accuse their rescuer of having lured them with lights to their destruction. The fisherman replies, 'Nay then, we be liker the blessed apostles; / they were fishers of men, Father Jean says.' When a Provincetown clerk in Thoreau's *Cape Cod* lists a town representative as 'Master Mariner' rather than 'Fisherman', Thoreau reports himself as 'reminding' the clerk that 'Fisherman had been a title of honour with a large party ever since the Christian era at least.'

When the Jesuit rector in James Joyce's *A Portrait of the Artist as a Young Man* is endeavouring to lure Stephen Dedalus into a career in the Church he appeals to the shining example of St Francis Xavier:

> He had the faith in him that moves mountains [cf. 1 Corinthians 13:2]. Ten thousand souls won for God in a single month! That is a true conqueror, true to the motto of our order: *ad majorem Dei gloriam!*... A great saint, saint Francis Xavier! A great fisher of souls! (chapter 3)

More modestly, G.K. Chesterton's Father Brown gently distinguishes the spiritual servanthood involved in following the call of Christ into prelatical life, when the priest says to his sometimes mercenary associates: 'You are The Twelve True Fishers, and these are all your silver fish. But He has made me a fisher of men' ('The Queer Feet', in *The Innocence of Father Brown*). Morris West's *The Shoes of the Fisherman* is a novel based upon the life of Pope John XXIII.

David L. Jeffrey
University of Ottawa

Flesh is Weak

When Jesus in Gethsemane returned to find his disciples not praying but asleep he chided Peter, 'What, could ye not watch with me one hour? Watch and pray, that ye enter not into temptation: the spirit indeed is willing, but the flesh is weak' (Matthew 26:41; cf. Luke 22:45–46). The flesh is often said to be in conflict with the spirit in this way in the New Testament (e.g., Romans 8:13; Galatians 4:23, 29; 5:17; 1 Peter 2:11) – not that the physical nature *per se* is sinful but that it is frail and subject to temptation and sin.

The Fathers, reacting against preoccupation with the flesh and its appetites in decadent Roman culture, tended to make the weakness of the flesh equivalent to sin *sui generis*. Hence, for St Jerome, Christians are those who 'by abstinence subjugate our refractory flesh, [which is] eager to follow the allurements of lust. The eating of flesh, the drinking of wine, and fullness of stomach, is the seed-plot of lust. And so the comic poet [Terence, in *Eunuch*, 4.5–6] says, "Venus shivers unless Ceres and Bacchus be with her"' (*Adversus*

Jovinianum, 2.7). So great is Jerome's concern about the propensity of fleshly appetites to undermine spiritual health that he gathers a host of classical authors to support an argument (despite 'the liberty of the gospel') for vegetarianism as a preventative against carnal arousal (2.14). Similar sentiments abound in the writings of St Augustine, for whom, as he writes in his *Confessiones,* weakness of the flesh in sexual matters especially had been a major impediment to spiritual development. For the author of the 12th-century *De Fructibus Carnis et Spiritus* (ascribed to Hugh of St Victor, *Patrologia Latina,* 176.997–98), the fruits of the flesh, from the 'forbidden' fruit tasted in Eden on, are by nature corruptible, while the fruits of the spirit, love, joy, peace, etc., are not. In later theological writers and in Reformation theologians (e.g., Calvin, *Commentary* sup. Matthew 26:41), the weakness ascribed to the flesh is broadened to include general human limitations and frailty.

Both biblical and patristic notions of the frailty of the flesh became proverbial in medieval literature; one has only to reflect on Chaucer's Wife of Bath, for whom both the biblical text and Jerome's *Adversus Jovinianum* are authorities to be challenged, and whose motto is 'Freletee clepe I'. Much the same philosophy is claimed by another vivid personification of the weakness of the flesh, Shakespeare's Falstaff in *1 Henry IV.* When Prince Hal chides him for his behaviour with Mistress Quickly, Falstaff rejoins: 'Dost thou hear, Hal? Thou knowest in the state of innocency Adam fell, and what should poor Jack Falstaff do in the days of villainy? Thou see'st I have more flesh than another man, and therefore more frailty' (3.3.172–76; cf. *Richard II,* 1.3.195). Byron's *Don Juan,* which offers a considerable catalogue of the temptations to which flesh is vulnerable, includes the observation that in warm Mediterranean climes,

> howsoever people fast and pray,
> The flesh is frail, and so the soul undone;
> What men call gallantry, the gods adultery,
> Is much more common where the climate's sultry.
> (1.501–04)

Later in the same poem he inverts the relation in parody (5.878–80). Hardy's *Jude the Obscure* is a kind of fictive treatise on the frailty of the flesh. In *The Mayor of Casterbridge* Hardy applies the phrase to an incident of deception, as a rationale (chapter 13). In one of his *Letters* D.H. Lawrence uses the text to mask his lack of resolve to visit a sometime friend (385). Aldous Huxley offers a modernist rewriting of the biblical text which nevertheless constitutes a plausible psychological insight into the original remark of Jesus: 'It wasn't a case, he reflected ruefully, of the spirit being willing and the flesh weak. That was altogether the wrong antithesis. The spirit is always willing; but the person, who is a mind as well as a body, is always unwilling – and the person, incidentally, is not weak but extremely strong' (*After Many a Summer*, 1.8).

David L. Jeffrey
University of Ottawa

Generation of Vipers

The phrase 'generation of vipers' appears in Matthew 3:7 and Luke 3:7, on the lips of John the Baptist, and in Matthew 12:34 and 23:33, spoken by Jesus. Although Luke 3:7 has John addressing the crowds this way, in all the Matthean references the Pharisees (with the Sadducees in 3:7) are in view. The phrase seems to refer to the venomous hostility of those addressed. In the apocryphal 3 Corinthians (3:38), the term describes those who turn from the teaching of the gospel. The term's imagery may derive from such passages as Psalms 58:4; 140:3; and Deuteronomy 32:33, where the wicked are likened to poisonous serpents (cf. Romans 3:13). All this suggests strongly that the image is one of cruelty, and danger, especially for the innocent and righteous.

The *Glossa Ordinaria* relates the image in these contexts to the 'vipers that had slain their fathers', that is, the plague of serpents visited upon the children of Israel in the wilderness (Numbers 21), and allegorizes the phrase in Matthew 12:34 as 'the fruit of the tree of evil, issuing forth in blasphemy' (*Patrologia Latina*, 114.80, 127). The phrase 'generation of vipers' is used widely in polemical contexts, as, for example, in Wycliffite pamphlets attacking clerical abuse, and in religious controversy generally through to the 19th century wherever a charge of 'Pharisaism' could be levelled.

Shakespeare is concerned with a different kind of Pharisaism in *Troilus and Cressida*, where he has Paris jibe at Pandarus for his preoccupation in wartime with 'doves' and the 'hot deeds' of sexual encounter. Pandarus, the go-between, replies, 'Is this the generation of love – hot blood, hot thoughts and hot deeds? Why they are vipers. Is love a generation of vipers?' (3.1.139–47). In Trollope's *Barchester Towers* 'this generation of unregenerated vipers... still perverse, stiffnecked, and hardened in their iniquity' is the judgment, ironically, of a woman who is herself a *pharisienne* (chapter 43). François Mauriac's novel *Le noeud de viperes* (1933) deals similarly with a 'pharisaical' judgmentalism more damnable than the hypocrisy it believes it sees in the next generation, although in this case the story ends in regeneration for the old 'Pharisee'. Somerset Maugham uses the phrase against self-appointed guardians of religion who arrest a girl they take to be a witch in *Catalina* (chapter 19). It may be Aldous Huxley, however, who most succinctly grasps the force of the criticism of both Jesus and John the Baptist when he writes: 'Who are the Scribes and Pharisees? Simply the best citizens; the pillars of society; all right-thinking men. In spite of which, or rather because of which, Jesus calls them a generation of vipers' (*After Many a Summer*, 2.7).

Larry W. Hurtado
University of Manitoba

Get Thee Behind Me

When the devil tempted Jesus in the wilderness (Matthew 4:10; Luke 4:1–8), the condition of his promise of wealth and power was that Jesus should worship him. But 'Jesus answered and said unto him, Get thee behind me, Satan: for it is written, Thou shalt worship the Lord thy God, and him only shalt thou serve.' The same expression was used by Jesus in rebuking Peter when he resisted Jesus' resignation to his own imminent suffering, death, and resurrection: 'Get thee behind me, Satan... for thou savourest not the things that be of God, but those that be of men' (Matthew 16:21–23; cf. Mark 8:31–33).

The second instance, coming as it does immediately after the apostolic commission, 'Thou art Peter, and upon this rock I will build my church; and the gates of hell shall not prevail against it' (Matthew 16:18), is arresting, and has attracted considerable commentary. St Augustine takes the matter up directly:

> The very same Peter a little while before blessed, afterwards Satan, in a moment, within a few words! You may wonder at the discrepancy in these names; consider the divergent reasons for them... Mark the reason why he is blessed: 'Because flesh and blood hath not revealed it unto thee, but my Father which is in heaven'; therefore blessed... For if flesh and blood revealed this to you, it be your own insight... Now you have heard why he is 'blessed'... But why was he also the very thing we shudder to think of, or even to repeat – why else but because [his protest] was self-generated: 'For thou savourest not the things which be of God, but those that be of men'. (*Sermo,* 76.3)

Augustine goes on to apply the lesson of Peter to members of the Church, urging self-examination to 'distinguish what is of God and what of ourselves'. How much, he asks, is Peter like the whole Church, composed of both strength and terrible weakness: 'Yet see this Peter, who was then our figure; now he trusts, and now he totters; now he confesses the Undying, and now he fears lest he should die.' In another application to the life of the Church, Augustine connects this passage to Matthew 18:8–9, making the case that if loved ones or friends entice us to evil, however precious, the Christian must cut them off or 'put them behind' in order that, as in the case of Bunyan's Christian in *The Pilgrim's Progress,* those following Christ will not be impeded (*Sermo,* 81.4).

Calvin sees Peter's outburst as 'thoughtless enthusiasm', and the passage as teaching 'how much what are thought to be good intentions avail before God'. Accordingly, 'in the person of one man [Jesus] wanted everyone to restrain themselves and not give way to their enthusiasm' (*Commentary,* on Matthew 16:20–28). Theodore Beza says the intensity of Jesus' rebuke is attributable to the fact that Peter's sin is really the archetypal pride of Satan, a desire to have God do things his way, which makes Peter for the moment nothing less than the threat of Antichrist (*Commentary on the New Testament,* 58).

The temptation incident is repeated in Milton's *Paradise Regained* and is recollected by Carlyle in *Sartor Resartus:* 'Was "that high moment in the *Rue de l'Enfer*", then, properly the turning-point of the battle; when the Fiend said, Worship me, or be torn in shreds, and was answered valiantly with an *Apage Satana?*' (2.9; cf. Vulgate Matthew 4:9–10). In Sir Walter Scott's *Ivanhoe* Garth urges Wamba to restraint of passion, saying, 'It may all be as thou doest guess; but were the horned devil to rise and proffer me his assistance to set at liberty Cedric and the Lady Rowena, I fear I should hardly have religion enough to refuse the foul fiend's offer, and bid him get behind me' (chapter 20). In Thackeray's *The Newcomes* the temptation to sell tableware to pay debts is called 'the suggestion of *Satanas;* but I say to him *Vade retro*' (chapter 28; cf. Vulgate Matthew 16:23). One of Joyce's characters in *Dubliners,* recalling also the baptismal liturgy, says, '"We'll all renounce the devil... together, not forgetting his works and pomps." "Get behind me, Satan!", said Mr Fogarty, laughing' ('Grace'). G.B. Shaw, in his preface to *Back to Methuselah*, opines that 'A body of schoolmasters inciting their pupils to infinitesimal peccadilloes with the object of provoking them to exclaim, "Get thee behind me, Satan," or telling them white lies about history... would certainly do less harm than our present educational allopaths do.'

David L. Jeffrey
University of Ottawa

Golden Rule

The term *golden rule* is not biblical but has been applied to the injunction of Jesus: 'Whatsoever ye would that men should do to you, do ye even so to them' (Matthew 7:12; cf. Luke 6:31). 'This is the law and the prophets,' Jesus adds; in effect, his 'rule' is a broad summary of the Sermon on the Mount with respect to conduct, loosely paralleling the Great Commandment or summary of the Law (Matthew 22:37–40). It may be compared with the words of R. Hillel: 'That which displeases you do not do to another. This is the whole law; the rest is commentary' (Shabbat 31a). In the *Book of Common Prayer* 'Catechism', the phrase becomes part of one's answer to the question 'What is thy duty towards thy Neighbour?' According to Isaac Watts'

Improvement of the Mind the verse speaks of 'that golden principle of morality which our blessed Lord has given us' (1.14). In the 17th century the 'rule' is occasionally referred to as the 'Golden Law'.

The phrase from Matthew, along with slight variants from the Gospel of Luke, the *Prayer Book*, and elsewhere (i.e., 'Do unto others as you would have them do unto you'), is ubiquitous in English literature. Illustrating something of the range of adaptation (and frequent trivialization) during the Enlightenment are Pope and Blake. In Pope's 'Essay on Dedications' he observes, 'These, when they flatter most, do but as they would be done unto.' In Blake's *Miscellaneous Epigrams* he scorns Cromek: 'He has observed the Golden Rule / Till he's become the Golden Fool.' Thoreau reflects that 'The law to do as you would be done by fell with less persuasiveness on the ears of those, who, for their part, did not care how they were done by' (*Walden*, 'Economy'), a point Melville modifies in *Moby Dick:* '"I will not go," said the stranger, "till you say *aye* to me. Do to me as you would have me do to you in the like case. For you too have a boy, Captain Ahab"' (chapter 128). A commercial twist is on Dickens' mind in his *American Notes,* where he observes that 'the merits of a broken speculation, or bankruptcy, or of a successful scoundrel, are not gauged by his or its observance of the golden rule, "Do unto others as you would be done by," but are considered with reference to their smartness' (chapter 18).

A weakened form of the rule as modern creed is expressed in Somerset Maugham's *Of Human Bondage:* '"But what do you suppose you are in the world for?"... "Oh, I don't know: I suppose to do one's duty, and make the best use of one's faculties, and avoid hurting other people." "In short, to do unto others as you would they should do unto you?" "I suppose so"' (chapter 45). G.B. Shaw takes a calculatedly negative view of such a 'creed', saying in the Afterword to *Man and Superman:* 'Do not do unto others as you would they should do unto you. Their tastes may not be the same.' Later he adds cryptically, 'The golden rule is that there are no golden rules' (*Maxims for Revolutionists*, 227, 228).

David L. Jeffrey
University of Ottawa

Good Samaritan

The parable of the good Samaritan is told in Luke 10:30–35 in response to a lawyer's request for a definition of 'neighbour' in the second of the great commandments: 'Thou shalt love thy neighbour as thyself.' Jesus tells the story to make evident that a good neighbour comes sometimes from the least expected quarter and that true charity transcends the limits of community. A traveller is set upon by thieves, robbed, beaten, and left for dead. Two subsequent travellers, a priest and a Levite, observe his tattered body, but hasten on their way. A third, who would have been considered both an alien and a moral inferior, stops to give aid, then carries the man to a hospice where he pays for his recuperation expenses. The Samaritan was far from a *socius* to the Jew, and Jesus' story would have shocked his hearers, whose expectation would have been that such a 'reprobate' would more likely have finished off what the muggers had begun. The parable is intended to chasten self-righteousness.

The earliest allegorization of the parable is provided by Origen (*Homily*, 34, *Patrologia Graeca*, 13.1886), who may well be reflecting the exegesis of apostolic times. He writes:

> ...the man *who went down* is Adam; *Jerusalem* means Paradise; *Jericho,* the world; the *robbers*, the enemy powers; the *Priest* stands for the Law; the *Levite* for the Prophets; the *Samaritan* for Christ. The *wounds* stand for our disobedience; the *beast,* the body of the Lord. The common house, that is the *inn,* which receives all who wish to enter it, is interpreted as the Church. Furthermore, the *two denarii* are understood to mean the Father and the Son; the *innkeeper,* the Head of the Church, to whom the plan of redemption and its means have been entrusted. And concerning that which the Samaritan promises at his return, this was a figure of the Second Coming of the Saviour.

This teaching reached the West in St Jerome's Latin translation of Origen and is faithfully transmitted by St Ambrose (*Expositio Evangelii secundum Lucam*, *Patrologia Latina*, 15.1806), St Augustine (*Quaestiones Evangeliorum*, *Patrologia Latina*, 35.1340), and the

Venerable Bede (*In Lucae Evangelium Expositio, Patrologia Latina*, 92.469) among the most noteworthy.

As the Samaritan pericope came to be employed in the liturgy, its exegesis became even more widely known: portions of Bede's commentary on this passage were, for example, used in several lessons at Matins in the Roman and Sarum rites. Liturgical commentators such as Rupert of Deutz (*De Divinis Officiis, Patrologia Latina*, 170.322), Sicard of Cremona (*Mitrale, Patrologia Latina*, 213.396), and especially Guillaume Durandus (*Rationale Divinorum Officiorum*, 6.127), using the other scriptural texts of the proper of the Mass, explain the Samaritan's remedies in terms of the sacraments of baptism, penance, and the Eucharist.

It is in liturgical homilies rather than the poetry of the Old English period that one encounters the Samaritan parable and its traditional exegesis. Two homilies (ed. R. Morris, Early English Text Society old series 29 and 34, 1868) for Christmas Day use the Samaritan parable in a discussion of the incarnation and its place in salvation history. Striking use of the parable and its biblical and liturgical exegesis in Middle English occurs in Langland's *Piers Plowman* where Will, after meeting with Faith and Hope, encounters Charity in the person of the Samaritan. Passus 17 of the B text employs the Samaritan episode to sum up preceding developments in Will's quest for firsthand knowledge of Christ and salvation and to point the way to the poem's climax in Passus 18. There, Christ 'semblable to the Samaritan and some-del to Piers the Plowman' jousts with Death in Langland's depiction of the passion and harrowing of hell.

Although Spenser makes no extended use of the parable in *The Faerie Queene*, his wounded characters are generally treated in a manner sufficiently resembling the Samaritan's to lead critics to believe that he had Luke's text in mind (e.g. 1.5.17; 6.2.4.8; 3.28).

Fielding puts the parable to excellent satirical use in the twelfth chapter of *Joseph Andrews*. The cries of Joseph, lying wounded and bloody by the roadside, are heard by the passengers in a passing coach. A lawyer, a 'man of wit', a haughty lady, and several other characters are all anxious to pass by. When after much debate among the passengers Joseph is rescued, it is because the passengers fear some legal action if Joseph dies. A further debate follows about clothing the naked Joseph, and it is a postillion, 'a lad who hath been since transported for robbing a hensroost', who gives Joseph 'his only garment, at the same time swearing a great oath (for which he was rebuked by the passengers) that he would rather ride in his shirt all his life than suffer a fellow-creature to be in so miserable a condition'.

Brief sarcastic allusions to Samaritan-like behaviour or lack of it in certain characters are found in Byron's *Don Juan* (5.955–58) and 'Age of Bronze' (690–91), as well as Browning's 'Inn Album' (946–47). As is indicated in the full title of Thackeray's novel *The Adventures of Philip on His Way through the World; Shewing Who Robbed Him, Who Helped Him, and Who Passed Him By,* the Samaritan parable acts as the novel's framework for the various trials of Philip Firmin and as a model to test the charity and loyalty of those around him. In *The Way of All Flesh* (chapter 57), Samuel Butler describes Ernest Pontifex as having fallen 'among a gang of spiritual thieves', and Ernest himself feels 'as though if he was to be saved, a good Samaritan must hurry up from somewhere – he knew not whence'.

Raymond St-Jacques
University of Ottawa

Great Commandment

The Great Commandment, or 'Summary of the Law', as it is sometimes referred to in Western Christian liturgies, is found in the renewal document of the Torah, Deuteronomy 6:4–5. It reads: 'Hear, O Israel: the Lord our God is one Lord; and thou shalt love the Lord thy God with all thine heart, and with all thy soul, and with all thy might.' The *Shema,* as it is called in Jewish liturgy, is above all a call of the chosen to obedience: *shama* conveys the sense of the imperative 'obey' (cf. Numbers 27:20; Joshua 1:17; 1 Kings 2:42); hence the call to 'hear' this commandment and obey it implies obedience to the whole of the Law. Recited each morning and evening as a call to prayer, on a pattern ascribed to the angels themselves (Tannaim Bereshit 4.144–45; Liqqutim 4.70a–70b; Berakot 5a), the *Shema* is uttered also on joyous occasions. Talmudic midrashic sources regard it rather than the Ten Commandments as containing the substance of the entire Torah (e.g., Berakot 1.3c).

In the New Testament, when Jesus is asked 'which is the greatest commandment in the law?' he quotes the Deuteronomy passage, intensifying the last phrase by adding 'with all thy *mind*', and linking the *Shema* to a 'second' commandment in Leviticus 19:18: 'And the second is like unto it, Thou shalt love thy neighbour as thyself. On these two commandments hang all the law and the prophets' (Matthew 22:36–40; Mark 12:28–34; cf. Luke 10:25–37). The Great Commandment thus becomes foundational to Christian ethical life since, according to St Augustine, it is clearly a summary of both law and prophets as well as of Christian wisdom (*De sermone Domini in Monte*, 2.22.74–75; cf. *De consensu Evangelistarum*, 2.73.141–42). St Thomas Aquinas refers to this 'Law of Love' as the basis of 'perfection in the Christian life', observing in a famous passage that 'Christian perfection lies directly and essentially in charity, primarily in the love of God, secondarily in the love of our neighbour.' He continues: 'No measure is demanded in our loving, the reason being that "the end of the commandment is charity"' (1 Timothy 1:5), so that 'while nobody in this life may fully achieve this perfection' it is perfectly appropriate to our life's proper goal that the command should be given and obeyed (*Summa Theologica* 2a–2ae.184.3). In this vein Richard Rolle speaks of obedience to the Great Commandment as a willed motion of the heart towards God ('a wilful stiryng of owre thoght intil God'), so that it accepts nothing which opposes the love of Jesus Christ ('The Commandment').

The Ten Commandments themselves were often divided on the pattern of the twofold commandment of love, so that the first three were said to pertain to the love of God, the balance to the love of one's neighbours (e.g., Wyclif, *De Decem Precepta*). The Lollard Knight, Sir John Clanvowe, says in his devotional treatise *The Two Ways* that the Great Commandment thus simplifies one's approach to the Ten. To Chaucer's Parson, similarly, 'soothly the lawe of God is the love of God' (*The Parson's Tale*, 10.127) and 'the love of God principal, and lovyng of his neighebor as hymself' is the 'remedie agayns this foule synne of Envye' (10.514–30), but also intrinsic to the remedy, he adds, for each of the other Seven Deadly Sins. It is this fact which makes the poor Parson's brother the Plowman an ideal of the perfect Christian (*General Prologue*, 1.529–38).

The Great Commandment is a familiar element in Catholic, Anglican, and Calvinist catechisms but became less prominent in literary allusion after the Reformation. In the 19th century the second precept tended to predominate in theological and philosophical reflection and, where present, the 'first and great' commandment was often subsumed under duties to one's 'higher self', so that, for Carlyle, the personalized first commandment assumes its importance in terms of the second ('Characteristics'). During his debate over vocation in *A Portrait of the Artist as a Young Man,* Joyce has Stephen Dedalus reflect that it would be for him 'Idle and embittering, finally, to argue, against his own dispassionate certitude, that the commandment of love bade us not to love our neighbour as ourselves with the same amount and intensity of love but to love him as ourselves with the same kind of love' (chapter 4).

Peter C. Craigie (deceased)
University of Calgary

Hand to the Plow

In Luke 9:62 Jesus comments on the half-hearted commitment of those who say they would like to follow him after they have tended first to other duties: 'No man, having put his hand to the plow, and looking back, is fit for the kingdom of God.' The passage is widely referred by Christian commentators both to conversion and to spiritual vocation (e.g., St Jerome, *Epistle* 22.1; 71.1; 118.4; St Augustine, *Sermo,* 50.3).

Later Protestant commentary is reflected in Matthew Poole's *Annotations* (1635), which observes that the point of the figure is to compare a minister of the word or one who has a special calling to the

> Plough-man [who] is obliged to look forward to his Work, or he will never draw his furrows either strait enough, or of a just depth; so must a Minister of the gospel, if he be once called out of secular imployments to the service of God in the Ministry, he is bound to mind and attend that; that is enough, to take up the whole Man.

Walter Scott, in *Old Mortality*, has this connection in mind in his characterization of the theological polity of the Covenanters: 'When I put my hand to the plough, I entered into a covenant with my worldly affections that I should not look back on things I left behind me' (chapter 6). In Sinclair Lewis' *Dodsworth*, the titular character is lectured: 'I tell you Dodsworth, to me work is a religion. "Turn not thy hand from the plough." Do big things!' (chapter 3). In Hardy's *Tess of the D'Urbervilles*, Alec jokes about abandoning his preaching to court Tess again: 'I believe that if the bachelor-apostle, whose deputy I thought I was, had been tempted by such a pretty face, he would have let go the plough for her sake as I do' – apparently associating the phrase with St Paul rather than Jesus. The injunction is central to C.H. Spurgeon's popular *John Ploughman's Talk,* and maintains its connection to the idea of religious or spiritual vocation also in Shaw's *St Joan,* where Joan asks that a message be taken to the king: 'Tell him that it is not God's will that he should take his hand from the plough' (5.60).

David L. Jeffrey
University of Ottawa

House Divided Against Itself

When the aggrieved Pharisees suggested among themselves that Jesus cast out devils 'by Beelzebub, the prince of devils', Jesus perceived their thoughts and spoke to them directly, saying, 'Every kingdom divided against itself is brought to desolation; and every city or house divided against itself shall not stand' (Matthew 12:22–25). These words have become a watchword of political wisdom. In Shakespeare's *Richard II* the Bishop of Carlisle uses them in describing the looming Wars of the Roses (5.5.23–31). Thoreau speaks apprehensively about the division among Northerners over the slavery question, saying of his fellow citizens, 'There is hardly a house but is divided against itself, for our foe is all but the universal woodenness of both head and heart.' *A House Divided* (1935) is the title of a novel by Pearl Buck, and allusion to the text is pivotal to the action in chapter 18 of Thomas Wolfe's *Look Homeward, Angel*.

David L. Jeffrey
University of Ottawa

Judge Not

Matthew 7:1–5, taken as a whole, provides one of the most trenchant of biblical admonitions against hasty or ill-considered judgment: 'Judge not, that ye be not judged. For with what judgment ye judge, ye shall be judged: and with what measure ye mete, it shall be measured to you again. And why beholdest thou the mote that is in thy brother's eye, but considerest not the beam that is in thine own eye?...' This passage, like its parallel in Luke 6:36–38, points to the fact that all are culpable before God and as such should not be eager to condemn others. In short, it is a warning against self-righteousness. The conditional nature of the expression (which is elaborated in the Lucan passage) finds numerous analogues elsewhere in Jesus' teaching, one noteworthy example being the petition 'Forgive us our debts, as we forgive our debtors' from the Lord's Prayer (Matthew 6:12).

St Augustine, in his treatise *De sermone Domini in Monte,* interprets the injunction typically, arguing that it is not intended to enjoin against all judgment, since scripture elsewhere clearly advocates discriminating judgment. He sees it rather as a command against rash, pretentious, or uncharitable judgment, when the judge himself may be guilty of comparable offences. This interpretation, followed closely by later commentators (including Calvin in his *Gospel Harmony*) becomes important for Chaucer, who employs it as the explicit theme of *The Reeve's Tale* and makes it part of Prudence's counsel in *The Tale of Melibee* (7.2648–50); it is indeed an underlying concern of *The Canterbury Tales* as a whole.

By Shakespeare's day the phrase 'measure for measure' (or 'meed for meed') had acquired proverbial status and was applied in a variety of contexts with different meanings. As noted by M.P. Tilley, 'measure for measure' often carried the sense of a violent, exactly matching revenge: in *3 Henry VI,* 'measure for measure must be answered' refers to an order that Clifford's head be set upon the gates of York in reprisal for Clifford's having placed the Duke of York's head there (2.6.55). Similarly, at the end of *Titus Andronicus,* Lucio cries out, 'Can the son's eye behold his father bleed? / There's meed for meed, death for a deadly deed' as he kills Saturninus, who has just killed Titus (5.3.65–66). The proverb used in this sense is close to the Old Testament 'eye for eye, tooth for tooth' (Leviticus 24:20), bearing little relation to the Matthean injunction.

When the New Testament passage is quoted most directly, the phrase suggests not immediate revenge but a more general providential justice which brings eventual reward or punishment according to the individual's behaviour to others. Thus, when the expression 'measure for measure' is used by Shakespeare as the title of one of his major plays, the Matthew passage is central; integrated with a traditional Catholic exegesis of St Paul's Epistle to the Romans, it provides a lucid commentary on extravagant legal-mindedness of the 'old Law' sort, such as was evidently associated with certain Puritans in Shakespeare's day. (Seventeenth-century Puritan exegesis could indeed seem almost to reverse the sense of Matthew 7:1–2; see, e.g., Matthew Poole's *Annotations*.)

In *Measure for Measure* the words of the title occur in the dialogue during the last act (5.1.405–09), at a point where the Duke is pronouncing judgment on his corrupted deputy, Angelo:

> The very mercy of the law cries out
> Most audible, even from his proper tongue:
> 'An Angelo for Claudio; death for death.
> Haste still pays haste, and leisure answers leisure;
> Like doth quit like, and Measure still for Measure.'

The Duke's comment at this climactic moment has two functions: first to emphasize the exact justice which he apparently intends to exercise in the punishment of his deputy, an expected letter-of-the-law justice, which Angelo, now completely exposed, willingly embraces; and second to provide a trial or test for the attitudes of Mariana and Isabella: Is this the kind of justice they desire? Earlier in the play Shakespeare has Isabella remind Angelo of each individual's need for something more than mere judgment – indeed, for mercy: 'How would you be, if He, which is the top of judgment, should but judge you as you are?' (2.2.77). It is this larger and more merciful concept of justice, dependent not upon equally weighted retribution but upon recognition, self-awareness, and forgiveness, which prevails in the conclusion to the play.

In later literature the text devolves towards commonplace morality. For Donne, such human judgment as the text implies is invalid simply because it cannot be more than 'mere opinion' ('Progresse of the Soule', 520). Pope, who makes no explicit citation of the text, may perhaps intend an allusion in certain barbs at critics (e.g., *Essay on Criticism,* 18) or in warnings concerning the limited perspective in any human judgment: 'In Man, the judgment shoots at flying game' (*Essay on Man,* 1.96). Byron provides a representative instance of the encoded sentiment in *The Island:* 'And they / Who doom to hell, themselves are on the way' (4.353–54). In Aldous Huxley's *Eyeless in Gaza,* 'Mrs Foxe found herself suddenly thinking that there were also cripples of the spirit... John Beavis perhaps was one of them. But how unfair she was being! How presumptuous too! Judge not that ye be not judged. And anyhow, if it were true, that would only be another reason for feeling sorry for him' (chapter 9).

John Margeson
University of Toronto

Keys of the Kingdom

This figure, from Matthew 16:19, signifies the authority Jesus Christ confers on Peter as the foundation-rock of his future community of the faithful: 'I will give unto thee the keys of the kingdom of heaven: and whatsoever thou shalt bind on earth shall be bound in heaven: and whatsoever thou shalt loose on earth shall be loosed in heaven.' Behind this saying lies 'the key of the house of David' (Isaiah 22:22), which denotes the authority over the royal household vested by the king in his chief steward.

Matthew 16:19 has a history of interpretation and application long marked by far-reaching differences as to the nature, agent, and scope of the power of the keys. Among the Fathers of the Church, Tertullian and St Augustine broadly locate the power to loose and to bind – that is, to forgive and retain sin, to accept into the communion and to excommunicate – in the body of the faithful, which acts efficaciously as an intercessor only when it is at one with the Spirit of God from whom all forgiveness comes. St Cyprian and Pope Leo the Great, on the other hand, emphasize that the episcopate is the sole heir to the apostolic authority and is empowered to loose and to bind of its own accord. Of the efforts to integrate these readings in the late Middle Ages, the most sustained and influential is that of St Thomas Aquinas, according to whom priestly absolution is not simply an expression of the forgiveness granted by God, but a judicial act sacramental in nature. The teaching that solely the priest can absolve, and not only *in foro ecclesiae* but also *in foro Dei,* was officially proclaimed by the Council of Trent. For Luther, however, the keys of the kingdom mean 'nothing else than the authority or office by which the word is practised and propagated'; there is no distinction between the absolution of a layman and that of a priest (M'Clintock and Strong, 5.66–67).

In Middle English literature, the matter of the keys is understandably charged with a sense of urgency or foreboding. Langland's *Piers Plowman* (B text) repeatedly protests the abuses of apostolic power by an unworthy hierarchy, and ends with a nightmare of the coming Antichrist. Gower's *Confessio Amantis,* for example, responds to the ills of the Great Schism (1378–1417) with a plea for a return to genuine spirituality, to a time when 'the Church Key' did not stand in doubt ('Prologue', 211).

Later, after the breakup of European Christendom, Milton sounds a similar note in his pastoral elegy *Lycidas:* 'the Pilot of the Galilean Lake', bearing 'two massy keys' – 'the golden opes, the iron shuts amain' – answers a question about the fate of the shepherd who betrays his flock – that is, of an episcopacy which has become worldly. The reading privileged by dissenters is abridged in Bunyan's *Grace Abounding to the Chief of Sinners:* 'the keys of the kingdom of heaven' are 'the truth and verity' of Holy Writ; whom the scriptures favour 'must inherit bliss', whom they oppose 'must perish' (section 245). Both Dryden in *Religio Laici* (379) and Wordsworth in his *Ecclesiastical Sonnets* (1.39) criticize as tyranny and arrogation the Church of Rome's reading of its authority to loose and to bind. Later, in *The Hind and the Panther* (1687), Dryden tactfully relegates the question of the keys to a subtext; and Wordsworth, writing of the age of Fisher and More, subsequently refers to Roman Catholicism as the 'keystone' of Christendom, its 'supremacy from Heaven transmitted pure, / As many hold' (*Ecclesiastical Sonnets,* 2.26).

With Olympian assurance Gibbon declares in *The Decline and Fall of the Roman Empire* that the 'ecclesiastical governors' of the early Church, to whom 'the Deity had committed the keys of Hell and Paradise' (a conflation of Matthew 16:19 with Revelation 1:18), used that authority to keep their subjects in line and expand their political power (chapter 8). For Macaulay, it is 'a happy circumstance for the Protestant religion' that the conflict between Louis XIV and Innocent XI over 'secular rights' and 'the spiritual power of the keys' coincided with the moment of James II's accession to the throne of England (*History of England*, 1.4.463–64).

The several ironies intended by the reference to 'Trade's master-keys... / To lock or loose' in Newman's 'England' are absent from Henley's figure of the 'mailed hand [that] keeps the keys / Of... teeming destinies' in 'England, My England'. By contrast, Tennyson's reference to 'the Shadow cloak'd from head to foot, / Who keeps the keys of all the creeds' (*In Memoriam*, 23.4–5) conveys a lack of any assurance. The popular conception of Peter as *janitor coeli* is reworked in Kipling's cheerfully earnest 'Tomlinson'. There is a serious side as well to Joyce's running joke on 'the house of keys' in *Ulysses*. The figure of the 'two crossed keys' representing the house of Alexander Keyes, spirit merchant, has the 'innuendo of home rule' (122). In T.S. Eliot's *Murder in the Cathedral,* Thomas à Becket is tempted to presume upon the power of the keys conferred on him by the Pope (1.378, 510).

Camille R. La Bossière
University of Ottawa

Kingdom of God

The Zealots and others of Jesus' time expected a messianic political deliverance from the tyranny of Roman occupation. When such persons asked Jesus when the 'kingdom of God' should come, they were therefore discomposed by his answer: 'The kingdom of God cometh not with observation: Neither shall they say, Lo here! or lo there! For, behold, the kingdom of God is within you' (Luke 17:20–22). On another occasion, when Pilate put a similarly political question to Jesus ('Art thou King of the Jews?'), Jesus answered, 'My kingdom is not of this world: if my kingdom were of this world, then would my servants fight' (John 18:36).

This central idea of Jesus makes spiritual self-governance rather than political power the goal of moral and ethical endeavour. It provided Tolstoy with his criticism of mistaken materializations of Christianity in *The Kingdom of God is Within You* (1893), a book of essays on non-violent resistance to oppression. Francis Thompson's poem 'The Kingdom of God' begins with a series of paradoxes such as are central also to Jesus' so-called 'kingdom parables':

> O world invisible, we view thee,
> O world intangible, we touch thee,
> O world unknowable, we know thee,
> Inapprehensible, we clutch thee!

Part of the object of Matthew Arnold's criticism of institutional Christianity in *Essays in Criticism, Final Series* is its tendency to materialize, to offer external reward when it should be saying, 'The kingdom of God is within you.' In *Culture and Anarchy* he comments further, 'Religion says: *the kingdom of God is within you,* and culture, in like manner, places human perfection in an internal condition, in the growth and predominance of our humanity proper' ('Sweetness and Light'). In Tennyson's *Becket,* when the Archbishop is warned by John of Salisbury that his return to England has occasioned angry political opinion against him, Becket responds with Jesus' words: 'Why John, my kingdom is not of this world.' Salisbury replies with the worldly wisdom suitable to one who authored the *Policraticus* and a history of the Popes: 'If it were more of this world, it might be / More of the next. A policy of wise pardon / Wins here as well as there.' When Mr Pontifex goes 'the way of all flesh' in Butler's novel of that title, Butler observes that some persons find their happiness in having a higher moral standard than others: 'If they go in for this, however, they must be content with virtue as her own reward, and not grumble if they find lofty Quixotism an expensive luxury, whose rewards belong to a kingdom that is not of this world' (chapter 19).

David L. Jeffrey
University of Ottawa

Labourers in the Vineyard

In Matthew 20:1–16, Jesus tells a parable concerning a householder who hires five groups of labourers – at the first, third, sixth, ninth, and eleventh hours – to work in his vineyard. When at the end of the day everyone receives the same wages of one denarius (KJV 'a penny'), the first group accuse the proprietor of unfair treatment. Although they agreed to work for a denarius, they feel that by bearing the burden and heat of the day they have earned more than the latecomers. The householder maintains that he may freely dispose of his property and that what seems an injustice done to them actually is a sign of his goodness towards the others. The parable ends with the words, 'So the last shall be first, and the first last: for many be called, but few chosen' (v. 16; cf. Matthew 19:30; Mark 10:31; Luke 13:30). Most modern interpreters see the parable as a defence of Jesus' welcome of sinners into the kingdom of God.

In the early Church, the text was understood allegorically. St Irenaeus (*Adversus haereses* 4.36.7) interprets the various hours at which the workers are called as periods of history: morning: Adam – Noah; third hour: Noah – Abraham; sixth hour: Abraham – Moses; ninth hour: Moses – Jesus; eleventh hour: Jesus – world's end. Origen, by contrast, took the hours to signify the stages of human life: childhood, youth, adulthood, old age, extreme old age (*In Matthaeum*). These renderings were repeated and sometimes combined by later exegetes (e.g., St Jerome, *In Matthaeum*; St Gregory, *Homily in Evangelia*, 19; the Venerable Bede, *In Matthaei Evangelium Expositio*; St Thomas Aquinas, *Summa contra Gentiles*, 58.8). The workers were often understood as representing the clergy, and the vineyard the Church (e.g., Gregory, Bede), while the denarius, paid equally to all, was generally thought to signify eternal life (Tertullian, *De monogamia*; St Augustine, *De sancta virginitate* and *Sermons on New Testament Lessons*) or the contemplation and enjoyment of God (Aquinas). The 'burden and heat of the day' (v. 12) in such readings was sometimes seen as the knowledge that divine retribution at the end of the world is still far away (Aquinas, *In Matthaeum*), or the heat of the flesh during the greater part of one's life (Gregory).

Wyclif (*In Omnes Novi Testamenti Libros*, 36c–37a) still holds to

Irenaeus' reading, while Luther dismisses it as 'idle talk'. For the latter, the first workers signify those who want to go to heaven proudly on account of their good works (the Jews and the clergy of Luther's time), whereas those who are humble and do not look for pay may rejoice about God's mercy (*Fastenpostille*, 1525, *Weimarer Ausgabe*, 17.2). Calvin concludes from the text that 'men are created in order to do something' and that 'according to the decree of God everybody is placed in his special province so that he sit not around idle' (*Harmony of the Gospels*).

For Latimer, the parable teaches 'that all christian people are equal in all things appertaining to the kingdom of Christ' (Sermon 43). American Puritan Jonathan Edwards, on the other hand, used the text to argue that the Great Awakening signalled God's purpose to begin his renewal of the earth in America, the 'utmost, meanest, youngest and weakest part of it' (*Some Thoughts Concerning the Present Revival of Religion*, 2.2).

St Thomas More's Anthony in *A Dialogue of Comfort Against Tribulation* (2.5) warns those who procrastinate in turning to God: 'Now he that in hope to be callid towards night, will slepe out the mornyng, & drinke out the day, ys full likely to pass at night vnspoken to / & than shall he with shrewid rest go souperlesse to bedd.' Shakespeare makes a more veiled reference to the parable by having Guiderius say in his dirge for the dead Cloten:

> Fear no more the heat o' the sun
> Nor the furious winter's rages;
> Thou thy worldly task hast done,
> Home art gone, and ta'en thy wages.
> (*Cymbeline*, 4.2.259–62)

In the 17th century, the parable was often alluded to in discussions of predestination. Robert Burton quotes verse 16 in his *Anatomy of Melancholy* (3.4.2.6), where he warns against a fatalistic understanding of predestination and reminds the reader: 'Thou mayest in the Lord's good time be converted; some are called at the eleventh hour.' In Michael Wigglesworth's apocalyptic poem *The Day of Doom*, God uses Matthew 20:15 to justify his unconditional election. The phrase 'the chosen few' came to acquire proverbial status, evidenced by Lord

Byron's 'Answer to Some Elegant Verses' (37), which applies it to those sensible lovers of his poetry who are 'to feeling and to nature true' (for a similar reference cf. Wordsworth, 'Written in a Blank Leaf of MacPherson's "Ossian"'). In Charlotte Brontë's *Jane Eyre* (chapter 38), St John Rivers, the stern missionary, is finally vindicated as one of those 'who are called, and chosen, and faithful' (a description which also echoes Matthew 25:21).

While Christina Rossetti follows Origen's exegesis in her poem 'How long?' John Ruskin makes the 'penny' a symbol of any wages and suggests it be convertible into bread, cloth, etc. (*Fors Clavigera*, 8.86.8; cf. also his use of vv. 13 and 14 as a motto for his essays on political economy, *Unto This Last*).

The traditional equation of labourers and clergy occurs in Mark Twain's satire 'Important Correspondence'. An avaricious and ambitious bishop, hungry for money and fame, calls himself one of the 'poor labourers in the vineyard' and refers to San Francisco as a 'pleasant field for the honest to toil in'. Similar ironic (and often incidental) applications can be found in modern works such as Thornton Wilder's *Heaven's My Destination* (chapter 7), where the obnoxious evangelist Dr Bigelow has been 'in the vineyard' for twenty-five years, does not belong to any church, but tries to help his 'labouring brothers'. In *Go Tell It on the Mountain* James Baldwin applies the parable repeatedly to the situation in the 'Temple of the Fire Baptized', as when Gabriel and the elders are dining upstairs, and 'the less-specialized workers in Christ's vineyard' are being fed at a table downstairs.

Emily Dickinson (in poem 1720) draws a somewhat hedonistic conclusion from verse 16:

Had I known that the first was the last
I should have kept it longer.
Had I known that the last was the first
I should have drunk it stronger.

Edwin A. Robinson uses 'Many Are Called' as a title for a poem on the inscrutability and the arbitrary ways of the 'Lord Apollo'. The last group of labourers becomes the Unemployed in T.S. Eliot's choruses from *The Rock*. In having them complain: 'In this land / No man has hired us,' Eliot expresses the plight of the jobless of Britain. At the same time he seems to give an answer in the chant of the workmen building a church: 'Each man to his work.'

Manfred Siebald
Johannes Gutenberg Universität, Mainz, Germany

Last Shall Be First

In the parable of the vineyard told in Matthew 20:1–16, even the workers hired at the 'eleventh hour' are paid the stipulated wages which those who laboured from daybreak received. To the grumbling of those first hired the lord of the vineyard replies, 'I will give unto this last, even as unto thee' (v. 14). Jesus then adds, 'So the last shall be first, and the first last: for many be called, but few chosen' (v. 16). When the disciples dispute among themselves concerning 'who should be greatest' in the kingdom of heaven, Jesus rebukes them, saying, 'If any man desire to be first, the same shall be last of all, and servant of all' (Mark 9:33–37; cf. Mark 10:31; Matthew 19:30). This principle is stressed again in reminding the disciples that the order of pre-eminence in the kingdom of God will respect divine judgment concerning due reward, not any contemporary sense of who is eminent in religious life: 'there are last which shall be first, and there are first which shall be last' (Luke 13:30). This principle of divine preference echoes the theme of the younger son being 'preferred' over the elder in Old Testament narrative: Abel and Seth over Cain, Jacob rather than Esau, Ephraim rather than Manasseh, David rather than any of his older brothers – a feature notably reflected in the genealogy of Jesus appearing in Matthew 1 and Luke 3.

The dominant emphasis placed upon this theme in early Christian and medieval exegesis regards it as expressing a principle of humility to be observed in the kingdom of God in the present, since it will be a certain principle in heaven. St Jerome illustrates this admirably in his memorable letter to Marcella (AD386) on behalf of Paula and Estochium, inviting her to join them in Bethlehem, which was by now to be Jerome's home for the remainder of his life. After describing the beauties of the city, past and present, the letter goes on to celebrate the strikingly diverse and harmonious character of Christian community assembled there:

In speaking thus we do not mean to deny that the kingdom of God is within us, or to say that there are no holy persons elsewhere; we merely assert in the strongest manner that those who stand first throughout the world are here gathered side by side. We ourselves are among the last, not the first; yet we have come hither to see the first of all nations... Yet amid this great concourse there is no arrogance, no disdain of self-restraint; all strive after humility, that greatest of Christian virtues. Whosoever is last is here rewarded as first.

Calvin, in a contrast of both tone and application, sees the words (Matthew 19:30; 20:16) as 'added to take away the laziness of the flesh', and Christ's purpose as exhortation to run the race of spiritual life effectively: 'He tells them that to have begun the race fast will do no good if they break down in the middle... Therefore,' he concludes, 'so often as we think of the heavenly crown, it should prick us with ever new incitements so that we should be less slack in future' (*New Testament Commentaries*, 2.263–64, 266).

Bunyan's Christian, in *Pilgrim's Progress*, echoes a Calvinist appropriation when, after Faithful refuses to heed his call to wait until he could catch up with him, 'putting to all his strength, he quickly got up with Faithful, and did also overrun him, so the last was first.' In the first of Donne's Holy Sonnets, 'La Corona', the biblical theme is central to both content and design. A song of prayer and praise in seven stanzas, it owns that 'The ends crown our workes, but thou crown'st our ends, / For, at our end begins our endlesse rest; / The first last end, now zealously possest.' The last line of each stanza is repeated as the first line of the stanza following, as the poem traces the life and ministry of Christ as prime model – the King of Glory in an ox's stall, the child in the Temple confounding the scholars, God on the cross, the dead raised to life – all instancing the divine principle in both aspects. So instructed, the poet can see that he now need have no 'Feare of first or last death', and may by grace 'Salute the last and everlasting day.'

In Sterne's *Tristram Shandy* (1760), the theme is stated on the first and last pages. In Tennyson's *Rizpah,* a despondent recollection is made by the mother of a young man hanged on the gallows. When she picks up his bones and secretly buries them she thinks of God's forgiveness, and in that context tells herself: 'He'll never put on the black cap except for the worst of the worst, / And the first may be last – I have heard it in church – and the last may be first.' G.K. Chesterton, in his *George Bernard Shaw*, reflects the texts more closely: 'That reversal is the whole idea of virtue; that the last shall be first and the first last' ('The Dramatist'). Last but not least, John Galsworthy wrote a story entitled 'The First and the Last' (1915), which he then adapted as a play (1921).

David L. Jeffrey
University of Ottawa

Let the Dead Bury Their Dead

One of Jesus' disciples (identified by St Clement of Alexandria as Philip), wishing perhaps to withdraw for a season, asked: 'Lord, suffer me first to go and bury my father. But Jesus said unto him, Follow me; and let the dead bury their dead' (Matthew 8:21–22; Luke 9:60). This verse has occasioned divergent commentary, but the usual sense in patristic and medieval exegesis has to do with the soul rather than the body. In his discussion of Christian belief in the resurrection St Ambrose speaks of the first death as 'when we die to sin but live to God'. The second is 'departure from this life', in which 'the soul is set free from the fetters of the body'.

> The third death is that of which it is said: Leave the dead to bury their own dead. In that death not only the flesh but also the soul dies... through the weakness not of nature, but of guilt. This death is not then a discharge from this life, but a fall through error. Spiritual death [i.e., to the 'old man'], then, is one thing, natural death another, a third is the death of punishment. (*De excessu fratris Satyri*, 2.36–37)

For St Augustine the 'dead' who are to bury their own are those 'dead in the soul' (*Sermo*, 88.3), as 'all who are under sin are dead, dead servants, dead in their service, servants in their own death,' only seeming to be alive (*Sermo*, 134.3). For such, the only means of resurrection is the Word of God; hence Jesus' admonishment to the disciple about to leave the presence of the Word in which alone, Augustine says, 'is the resurrection of hearts, the resurrection of the inner man, the resurrection of the soul' (*Sermo*, 127.7). Matthew Henry reads the passage in terms of a pattern of challenges to vocational single-mindedness in which purity of heart is to will one thing: 'The meaning of *Non vacat* is, *Non placet* – *The want of leisure is the want of inclination*,' he observes, whereas the principal obligation of discipleship is almost self-evident:

> Piety to God must be preferred before piety to parents, though that is a great and needful part of our religion. The Nazarites, under the law, were not to mourn for their own parents, because they were *holy to the Lord* (Numbers vi.6–8); nor was the high priest to *defile himself for the dead*, no, not for *his own father*, Leviticus xxi.11, 12. And Christ requires of those who would follow him, that they *hate father and mother* (Luke xiv.26); love them less than God; we must comparatively neglect and disesteem our nearest relations, when they come in competition with Christ, and either our doing for him, or our suffering for him. (*Commentary on the Whole Bible*, 5.109)

Calvin's *New Testament Commentaries* (1.255) had already suggested that Jesus' intent was to encourage focus on the future rather than the dead past. This notion seems to have been broadly adapted by the 19th century, enough to be reflected in Longfellow's 'A Psalm of Life', which contains the injunction 'Trust no Future, howe'er pleasant! / Let the dead Past bury its dead.' In Thoreau's 'A Plea for Captain John Brown' he says that Harpers Ferry confronted him with the cold fact of death, yet he concludes that there was in some sense really 'no death in the case, because there had been no life; they merely rotted or sloughed off... Let the dead bury their dead' – an attitude which bears disturbing resemblance to that expressed by Lord Henry to Dorian after the suicide of Sibyl Vane in Oscar Wilde's *The Picture of Dorian Gray* (1891). Exemplifying the proverbial sense, Somerset Maugham's Kitty, in *The Painted Veil*, resists depression after defeat in love, saying, 'I have hope and courage. The past is finished; let the dead bury their dead. It's all uncertain, whatever is to come to me, but I enter upon it with a light and buoyant heart' (chapter 80). The older Catholic sense seems ironically present, however, in Joyce's *A Portrait of the Artist as a Young Man,* even where it is being most obviously contested. Writing about his rejection of faith and apostolic vocation, Stephen writes in his journal: '*March 21, night.* Free. Soul free and fancy free. Let the dead bury the dead. Ay. And let the dead marry the dead' (chapter 5).

David L. Jeffrey
University of Ottawa

Light under a Bushel

In the Sermon on the Mount (Matthew 5:14–16; cf. Mark 4:21; Luke 11:33) Jesus said to his followers:

> Ye are the light of the world. A city that is set on a hill cannot be hid. Neither do men light a candle and put it under a bushel, but on a candlestick; and it giveth light to all those that are in the house. Let your light so shine before men, that they may see your good works, and glorify your Father which is in heaven.

This passage has been a keynote for Christian discussions of vocation and practical obedience. St Jerome comments that 'God's motive for lighting the fire of his knowledge in the bishop is that he may shine not for himself only but for the common benefit' (*Adversus Luciferianos* 5). St Augustine relates the passage to the commendation of John the Baptist, that 'he was a burning and a shining light' (John 5:35; *De consensu Evangelistarum,* 4.10.17), and to the vocation of every follower of Christ, which is 'to be fervent and shine in good works, that is, to have our lights burning' (*Sermo,* 108.1).

The passage was important also in Puritan writing: hence the bite in Shakespeare's *Measure for Measure* (1.1.33–36), where the Duke ironically admonishes the Puritan Angelo for not showing his virtue in community life:

> Heaven doth with us as we with torches do.
> Not light them for themselves; for if our virtues

Did not go forth of us, 'twere all alike
As if we had them not.

By the same token, the traditional companion phrase from John 5:35 becomes widely applied in the 18th century, especially by figures in the Methodist movement, to those exemplary in the practice of the virtues mentioned in Matthew 5:14–16. George Whitefield and others thus speak of Lady Selina Hastings, Countess of Huntingdon and guiding spirit of the Great Revival, as 'a burning and a shining light'. The same phrase comes also to be related to the image of the virtuous Christian life as a beacon or lighthouse (cf. the hymn, 'Let the Lower Lights Be Burning'). Thoreau, speaking of the lighthouse at Provincetown (*Cape Cod*), says, 'What avails it though a light be placed on top of a hill, if you spend all your life directly under the hill? It might as well be under a bushel.'

Nineteenth-century liberal theology readily transferred the light imagery of the Bible, following 18th-century precedents, to the sphere of reason and knowledge. In James Fenimore Cooper's *The Pioneers*, 'knowledge is not to be concealed, like a candle under a bushel' (chapter 29). In Hardy's *Far from the Madding Crowd* the covered candle is identified with personal gifts: when Joseph Poorgrass is praised he reluctantly owns to hidden virtues, and is chided: 'But under your bushel, Joseph! Under your bushel with 'ee! A strange desire, neighbours, this desire to hide, and no praise due' (chapter 33). Joyce uses the familiar conjunction of Matthew 5:15 and John 5:35 in *A Portrait of the Artist as a Young Man*: 'Is he the shining light now? Well I discovered him... Shining quietly under a bushel of Wicklow bran' (chapter 5). A more obverse inflection is found in Gissing's 'A Poor Gentleman': 'It had come to be understood that he made it a matter of principle to hide his light under a bushel, so he seldom had to take a new step in positive falsehood.' In an unusual allusion in Aldous Huxley's *The Olive Tree*, modern translations of scripture are contrasted with the Codex Sinaiticus: 'the five-shilling Bible is comprehensive and available; whereas the Codex is kept locked up in a box and can be read only by experts. Its light is permanently under a bushel' ('Modern Fetishism').

David L. Jeffrey
University of Ottawa

Lilies of the Field

In the Sermon on the Mount Jesus stressed the relative impropriety of worry over material things, including food, personal appearance, and clothing: 'And why take ye thought for raiment? Consider the lilies of the field, how they grow; they toil not, neither do they spin: And yet I say unto you, that even Solomon in all his glory was not arrayed like one of these. Wherefore, if God so clothe the grass of the field, which today is and tomorrow is cast into the oven, shall he not much more clothe you, O ye of little faith?' (Matthew 6:28–30; cf. Luke 12:27–31).

St Augustine insists that the plain character of the comparison be taken at face value and not allegorized; the meaning, he says, is simply stated by Jesus himself: 'Seek ye first the kingdom of God and his righteousness, and all these things shall be added unto you' (v. 33). Most commentators have heeded his advice.

George Herbert alludes to the passage as one of a number which illustrate the correspondences of natural to special revelation. 'God's generall providence extended even to lillyes' makes the book of Nature mnemonic of scripture so that 'labouring people (whom he chiefly considered) might have everywhere monuments of his Doctrine, remembring in gardens, his mustard-seed, and lillyes; in the field his seed-corn, and tares; and so not be drowned altogether in the works of their vocation, but sometimes lift up their minds to better things, even in the midst of their pains' (A Priest to the Temple, 15, 23). The passage comes gradually to be a byword for perspective on overwork: the motto for Keats' 'Ode on Indolence' is 'They toil not, neither do they spin.' Felicia Hemans in her reflection on the passage concludes: 'The great ocean hath no tone of power / Mightier to reach the soul, in thought's hushed hour, / Than yours, ye lilies! chosen thus and graced' ('The Lilies of the Field').

For John Keble they are 'Sweet nurslings of the vernal skies', but he laments that

> Alas! of thousand bosoms kind,
> That daily court you, and caress,
> How few the happy secret find

Of your calm loveliness!
'Live for today!' tomorrow's light
Tomorrow's cares shall bring to sight.
('Consider the Lilies')

In Aldous Huxley's *Point Counter Point* the rejection of preoccupation with 'tomorrow's cares' is also expressed: 'I can't tell you how much I enjoy not being respectable. It's the Atavismus coming out. You bother too much, Mark. Consider the lilies of the field' (chapter 9). For Somerset Maugham the 'lilies of the field' are idealists who 'took it as a right that others should perform for them these menial offices' (*The Narrow Corner,* chapter 19). For P.G. Wodehouse they are aristocrats, as in his *Indiscretions of Archie:*

> 'I always looked on you as one of our leading lilies of the field,' he said, 'Why this anxiety to toil and spin?' to which comes the answer, 'Well, my wife, you know, seems to think it might put me up with the jolly old dad if I did something.' (chapter 4; cf. *Uncle Fred in the Springtime,* chapter 11)

In his essay on 'Providence and the Guitar', Robert Louis Stevenson quips that while a 'commercial traveller is received' and may even 'command the fatted calf' (cf. Luke 15:23), 'an artist, had he the manners of an Almaviva, were he dressed like Solomon in all his glory, is received like a dog and served like a timid lady travelling alone.' Ruskin alludes to the passage in a similar context in his essay 'Grass,' and a delayed performance occasions from the hard-pressed impresario in Henry James' 'The Madonna of the Future' a brusque retort: 'O ye of little faith!'

Among the more subtle allusions in American literature is that found in Edith Wharton's *The Custom of the Country* (1913), a novel about the decline of New York culture: 'If Undine, like the lilies of the field, took no care, it was not because her wants were as few but because she assumed that care would be taken for her by those whose privilege it was to enable her to unite floral insouciance with Sheban elegance' (chapter 11; cf. 1 Kings 10:1–13).

Anthony Hecht's 'Behold the Lilies of the Field' is a horrifying narration of a delirious torture victim being admonished to 'take it easy. Look at the flowers there in the glass bowl,' while in his poem 'Envy' he refers to 'the holy sloth of the lily'. In Rudy Wiebe's *The Blue Mountains of China* the horrors of a Stalinist labour camp in Siberia are thrown into stark relief for some of its victims by a night spent waiting out a blizzard in the ruins of a cloister; on the wall is a fresco of a vase of lilies – symbol of the Virgin Mary as well as a reminder of the pre-revolutionary peacefulness of the convent. To Jacob Friesen the whole passage, 'Think of the lilies... Take therefore no thought for the morrow' filters through his fatigue and misery in cruel parody of the prisoners' situation ('Cloister of the Lilies').

Allusion to the 'lilies' often implies or directly incorporates reference also to the subsequent verses in Matthew: 'But seek ye first the kingdom of God and his righteousness; and all these things shall be added unto you. Take no thought for the morrow: for the morrow shall take thought for the things of itself. Sufficient unto the day is the evil thereof' (vv. 33–34). In Butler's *The Way of All Flesh* verse 33 is quoted in an ironic context in a sermon (chapter 24), but verse 34 has typically prompted a more varied pattern of allusion. Galsworthy's *The Patrician* 'was a man who did not go to meet disturbance... He temperamentally regarded the evil of the day as quite sufficient to it' (1.1).

In Trollope's *Barchester Towers* the phrase 'sufficient unto the day' is quoted by Bertie in facing up to the prospect of her deprivation (chapter 15). D.H. Lawrence turns the same phrase in *Lady Chatterley's Lover*: 'Where should there be anything in them, why should they last? Sufficient unto the day is the evil thereof. Sufficient unto the moment is the appearance of reality' (chapter 2). Aldous Huxley applies the verse in sobering fashion in *Eyeless in Gaza,* where he opines that, in the wake of 19th-century secularized reading, the whole passage is an injunction simply to take life as it comes without much reflection: 'Like Jesus' ideal personality, the total, unexpurgated, now carnalized man is... like a little child, in his acceptance of the immediate datum of experience for its own sake, in his refusal to take thought for tomorrow, in his readiness to let the dead bury their dead' (chapter 11; cf. Matthew 8:22).

David L. Jeffrey
University of Ottawa

Lord's Prayer *see* Our Father

Lost Sheep

Jesus' parable of the lost sheep is recorded in two different forms, in Matthew 18:12–14 and Luke 15:4–7. J. Jeremias sees Matthew's version as secondary, reflecting a change of emphasis from Jesus' original *apologia* for his association with sinners to an exhortation to Christian leaders to seek out apostates. In both forms the parable derives its power from the basic human experience of being lost and found, especially as this is symbolized by the plight of a gregarious animal cut off from the herd which gives it identity and life.

Matthew 18 as a whole concerns the community's care for its members, who are not to be offended against in their weakness (18:1–9) and should be corrected and forgiven when they have erred (18:15–35). The parable of the lost sheep serves as conclusion and example of the former theme as well as introduction to the latter. The value of 'little ones', already stated in the introduction (v. 10), is exemplified by the actions of the shepherd seeking the lost and forcefully reiterated as the 'lesson' of the parable: 'It is not the will of your Father... that one of these little ones should perish' (v. 14).

In Luke's version the author does not 'introduce' the meaning of the parable but allows readers to discover it in their own experience. The Pharisees complain about Jesus' practice of receiving and eating with sinners. Abruptly Jesus confronts them with a parable which traps them in their own expectations. The parable's power resides in the imaginative shock of a shepherd abandoning his whole flock in the steppes to seek out the one lost sheep 'until he finds it' (v. 4). (A Palestinian shepherd would ordinarily drive his remaining flock into a pen or natural enclosure, or turn it over to a neighbouring shepherd lest it scatter or be ravaged.) This figure, then, illustrates the extravagant action of God himself, who rejoices more over one sinner who repents than over ninety-nine who need no repentance (v. 7). Jesus not only reveals the value of sinners but challenges his hearers to re-evaluate their conception of their own 'righteousness'. This two-pronged truth is repeated in the three subsequent parables of the lost coin (15:8–10), the prodigal son (15:11–32), and the unjust steward (16:1–13).

According to St Irenaeus the gnostics connected the straying of the sheep with the enfleshment of the aeons. Within the Church the parable was used sparingly, to vindicate reconciliation of Christians who had sinned (*Apostolic Constitutions*, 2.13–14) and reception of those lapsed in the Decian persecution (St Cyprian, *Epistle* 46, 51). Tertullian, in his *De poenitentia* (chapter 8), uses Luke 15:4–7 to vindicate the Church's practice of a second repentance for Christians; later, however, in his Montanist treatise *De pudicitia* (chapter 7), he denies this practice, there taking the wandering sheep to represent the heathen.

St John Chrysostom, the first to treat the parable exegetically, notes (with reference to Luke 15:7) that the righteous are imperilled for the sake of the lost (*Homily* 59, on Matthew). St Augustine interprets the parable as manifesting the Lord's extravagant zeal in seeking the lost, whom he identifies as all of humanity implicated in original sin (*De peccatorum meritis et remissione*, 1.40). For St Thomas Aquinas (following St Gregory, *Homily 34 on the Gospels*), the flock represents all rational creatures and (following St Hilary's commentary on Matthew) the lost sheep the human race, strayed through Adam and redeemed by Christ, the Good Shepherd (*Super Evangelium Sancti Mattaei Lectura*, 1509–13).

The Reformers also used the parable rarely (Luther refers to it only twice). Calvin explains the angels' greater joy as caused by God's mercy shining more brightly in the liberation of a sinner (*Harmony of the Gospels*).

An extended literary parody occurs in the opening scene of Shakespeare's *Two Gentlemen of Verona*, where Speed and Proteus trade witticisms about Speed's relationship with his absent master Valentine. Speed responds to Proteus' calling him a sheep by countering: 'The shepherd seeks the sheep, and not the sheep the shepherd; but I seek my master, and my master seeks not me. Therefore I am no sheep.' Proteus replies: 'The sheep for fodder follow the shepherd; the shepherd for food follows not the sheep. Thou for wages followest thy master; thy master for wages follows not thee. Therefore thou art a sheep.' 'Such another proof will make me

cry "baa",' exclaims Speed, who then identifies himself as 'a lost
mutton' (1.1.69–110).

Byron, who makes a comic allusion to Luke 15:7 in the
dedication to *Don Juan* (41–43), elsewhere refers to the same passage
straightforwardly, observing: 'He who repents... occasions more
rejoicing in the skies / Than ninety-nine of the celestial list' (*Morgante
Maggiore*, 466–67). Ira D. Sankey, while touring Scotland with
American evangelist Dwight L. Moody, composed a musical setting for
an obscure, posthumously published poem by Elizabeth Clephane,
'The Ninety and Nine' (1874). In this well-known hymn the
shepherd's suffering in seeking the lost is implicitly connected to the
passion:

> 'Lord, whence are those blood drops all the way
> That mark out the mountain's track?'
> 'They were shed for one who had gone astray
> Ere the Shepherd could bring him back.'
>
> 'Lord, whence are thy hands so rent and torn?'
> 'They are pierced tonight by many a thorn,·
> They are pierced tonight by many a thorn.'

George Eliot, in her *Scenes from Clerical Life*, observes that for one who
'has learned pity through suffering'

> the old, old saying about the joy of angels over the repentant
> sinner outweighing their joy over the ninety-nine just, has a
> meaning which does not jar with the language of his own
> heart. It only tells him... that for angels too the misery of
> one casts so tremendous a shadow as to eclipse the bliss of
> ninety-nine. ('Janet's Repentance')

In Galsworthy's *Flowering Wilderness*, the misery of the penitent
somewhat outweighs any attendant joy: 'There was no rejoicing as
over a sinner that repenteth. All were too sorry for her, with a sorrow
nigh unto dismay' (chapter 31). Allusion to the parable takes a sinister
twist in Shaw's *St Joan* when Ladvenue, handing Joan's recantation to
Cauchon, exults: 'Praise be to God, my brothers, the lamb has
returned to the flock; and the shepherd rejoices in her more than in

ninety and nine just persons.' Luke 15:7 provides the title for Morley Callaghan's novel *More Joy in Heaven* (1937).

L. John Topel, SJ
Seattle University
Katherine B. Jeffrey
Spencerville, Ontario

Love Your Enemies

One of the most striking injunctions in Jesus' Sermon on the Mount is his challenge to normal definitions of love: 'Ye have heard that it hath been said, Thou shalt love thy neighbour, and hate thine enemy. But I say unto you, Love your enemies, bless them that curse you, do good to them that hate you, and pray for them which despitefully use you, and persecute you' (Matthew 5:44). This commandment of Jesus, recollected by many Christians of the early centuries in times of dire persecution, was stressed as central to Christian obedience by bishops such as St Ambrose (e.g., *De officiis clericorum,* 1.48), who says that it is characteristic of divine justice that it asks of us charity and not vengeance (*Epistle* 63.84). A popular Yorkshire tract of the 14th century, incorporated by Walter Hilton into his *Ladder of Perfection,* cites St Stephen praying for those who stoned him to death even as he was dying (an analogy with Jesus' 'Father, forgive them, for they know not what they do', Luke 23:34) as one example of what such love in practice means. The other he adduces in Jesus' treatment of Judas who, even though known by Jesus to be a betrayer, was given all the intimacy and privilege accorded the other disciples. This, says the author, can be regarded as a corollary of Jesus' commandment to his disciples, 'that ye love one another, as I have loved you' (John 15:12). It thus marks the extent of 'love of neighbour' enjoined in the Great Commandment.

American literary examples often serve to show how this commandment is more honoured in the breach than the observance. Thoreau, for example, comments on the irony in stoical Indians being burned at the stake by 'missionaries': 'the law to do as you would be done by fell with less persuasiveness on the ears of those... who loved their enemies after a new fashion' (*Walden*, 'Economy'). Mark Twain writes in *Innocents Abroad*, in a more humorous vein, of the challenge of the standard: 'I know it is my duty to "pray for them that despitefully use me", and therefore, hard as it is, I shall still try to pray for these fumigating, macaroni-stuffing organ grinders' (chapter 20).

David L. Jeffrey
University of Ottawa

Mammon

Mammon appears in Matthew 6:24 and Luke 16:9–13, where it is a transliteration of a Semitic word meaning 'wealth', 'riches', 'property'. The term was untranslated in the Greek text of these two gospels, suggesting that it was familiar enough to require no explanation for the original readers. There are other occurrences of the term in ancient Jewish and Christian writings (Sirach 31:8, Hebrew; 1 Enoch 63:10; 2 Clement 6:1). In the gospels mammon is personified as a master, service to whom is incompatible with service to God (Matthew 6:24; Luke 16:13). In Luke 16:9–11, mammon is described as 'unrighteous', reflecting a view of wealth as obtained by injustice, coercion, trickery, and similar measures. These passages warn against preoccupation with obtaining wealth and pose the same stark alternative between hoarding riches and service to God that is reflected in other gospel passages (e.g., Mark 10:17–27).

In subsequent tradition 'mammon' came to be taken as the name of the demon of covetousness. Robert Burton observes in *The Anatomy of Melancholy*, 'Yet thus much I find, that our School-men and other Divines make nine kinds of bad spirits, as Dionysius hath done of Angels... The ninth are those tempters in several kinds, and their Prince is Mammon' (1.2.1.2). Mammon does not appear among the devils or vices in medieval morality plays, though there are many personified characters of a similar nature: Lucre, Avarice, Mundus, and Money.

There are three notable Renaissance examples of Mammon as a personification of avarice and worldliness. In *The Faerie Queene* (2.7), Spenser describes Guyon's encounter with Mammon as the first great temptation of his career. Wandering through a forest, Guyon stumbles upon 'an uncouth savage, an uncivil wight' counting his gold in a dark glade, the traditional medieval figure of Avarice. But as Mammon announces his rank as 'greatest god below the sky' and leads Guyon to the underworld, he takes on a certain fearsome majesty. He leads Guyon to the very gate of Hell, where lies the 'House of Richesse'. Guyon's three-day ordeal is linked with Christ's temptation in the wilderness, Mammon taking the place of Satan as prince of this world and offering Guyon unlimited wealth and power if he will but serve him. Like Christ, Guyon is tempted three times and returns to the ordinary world sinless but in a state of exhaustion.

Milton's version of Mammon appears in the first two books of *Paradise Lost*. His description of Mammon as one of the fallen angels derives from the medieval tradition. From Spenser's vivid account of the fiends mining and smelting gold under Mammon's direction, Milton may have drawn his similar picture of Mammon and a crew of fallen angels digging out gold from a mountain in Hell for the building of Pandemonium. Original with Milton is the comic account of Mammon before the Fall as

> ... the least erected spirit that fell
> From Heav'n, for even in Heav'n his looks and thoughts
> Were always downward bent, admiring more
> The riches of Heav'n's pavement, trodd'n gold,
> Than aught divine... (1.679–84)

In the diabolical council in book 2, Mammon speaks after Belial, advising that the devils accept their lot, 'preferring / Hard liberty before the easy yoke / Of servile pomp.'

In Ben Jonson's satiric comedy *The Alchemist* (1610), the most important of the clients who come to Subtle, the alchemist, is Sir Epicure Mammon. The play presents a realistic view of contemporary London, and yet the morality tradition survives in that the three rogues – Face, Dol Common, and Subtle – suggest that unholy trio, the World, the Flesh, and the Devil. Their clients make up a kind of corporate Mankind. Sir Epicure Mammon represents not only the lust for wealth implied by his surname but also all the appetites. Jonson pictures him as exuberant in his desires and extravagant in his projects. He becomes bloated with expectation, and the pricking of the balloon as alchemical apparatus explodes is one of the great comic moments in Jacobean drama.

Jack Drum's Entertainment (1601), a weakly plotted romantic comedy attributed to John Marston, presents a character called Mammon, a 'yeallow toothd sunck-eyde, gowtie shankt Vsurer'. He attempts to win Katherine, the daughter of Sir Edward Fortune, as his bride, turns villain, and is eventually discomfited by Katherine's lover, Pasquil.

In the late 19th and early 20th centuries, Mammon becomes a symbol of commercial, materialist society, as in E.F. Benson's novel Mammon & Co. (1899) and in essays by Upton Sinclair (Mammon Art: An Essay in Economic Interpretation, 1925) and Robert Graves (Mammon and the Black Goddess, 1965). However, John Davidson (1857–1909) presents a Mammon of a very different kind in his two blank-verse dramas, The Triumph of Mammon (1907) and Mammon and His Message (1908), two parts of a projected trilogy. This Mammon is an allegorical character on a large scale engaged in a struggle against traditional moral and religious codes and proclaiming a society based on science and human will. Though denying the influence of Nietzsche and disapproving of Darwin's theory of natural selection, Davidson creates a world-view owing much to their ideas. Traditional concepts of good and evil are transcended by a dictator-like leader for whom: '...our watchword shall be still, / "Get thee behind me, God; I follow Mammon."' Davidson's Mammon is a version of Milton's Satan transformed into a prophet and leader of the coming age.

John Margeson
University of Toronto

Marriage Feast

The parable of the marriage feast (Matthew 22:1–14) contains one of Christ's principal statements about the kingdom of God. Its main features are the king's two sets of invitations, each refused; the murder of the king's messengers and subsequent punishment of the murderers; the invitation to strangers from the highways; and the arrival and expulsion of the guest who is not in his wedding garment. The moral of the parable, that 'many are called, but few are chosen,' may apply to the parable as a whole or specifically to the expulsion of the improperly attired guest. Luke 14:15–24 gives what may be another version of the same parable, in which a man sponsoring a great supper invites guests who turn him down with various excuses. He then extends an invitation to the poor, maimed, and blind; and when still there is room at the banquet he invites – indeed compels – people from the highways and hedges with the words, 'for I say unto you, that none of those men which were bidden shall taste of my supper' (Luke 14:24). The two parables are treated interchangeably.

Throughout Christian history, and with greater or lesser elaboration, the version in Matthew is interpreted as an allegory of the Church Militant. The kingdom of heaven is the Church; the king is God, who invites the Jews to celebrate the coming of Christ. When they refuse, killing his prophets and apostles, God sends the Romans to conquer the Jews, and invites the Gentiles. But some approach him lacking works of charity, and these are cast into hell. (See, e.g., St Jerome, *Commentary in Matthaeum*, 3.22, *Patrologia Latina*, 26.165–68; Cornelius à Lapide, *Commentary in Scripturam Sacram*, ed. A. Crampon, 1872, 15.474–75; Calvin, *Harmony of the Gospels*, trans. W. Pringle, 1845, 2.168–69; Matthew Poole, *Synopsis Criticorum Aliorumque Sacrae Scripturae Interpretum*, 1674, 4.521–24.) The Lucan version is considered an allegory of the Church Triumphant. God offers eternal life to all; the worldly scorn God's invitation, while those scorned by the world accept it. (See, e.g., Bede, *In Lucam Expositio*, 4.14, *Patrologia Latina*, 92.514–16; Cornelius à Lapide, 16.196–200; Poole, 4.1036–38. On the currency of these interpretations, see C.H. Dodd, *Parables of the Kingdom*, 1936, 122.) The image of the wedding garment is related to the image of the soul's clothing, which has penitential and baptismal significance in sermon literature (e.g., *Mirk's Festial*, Early English Text Society extra series 96, 1905, 130; *Middle English Sermons*, Early English Text Society, old series 209, 1940, 167). The condition of the soul's clothing generally marks the distinction between the old and new man.

Some of the few literary adaptations of the parables follow the allegorical and homiletic traditions as well as the biblical text. In such works, the image of the soiled garment of the soul is prominent, and the message is to cleanse one's soul while there is still time. A similar integration of the two parables is achieved in *Cleanness*, in which the parable serves as the introduction for the theme from Matthew 5:8 ('Blessed are the pure in heart: for they shall see God'). Like Langland, the *Cleanness*-poet freely combines both parables and changes the guest's inappropriate clothing into tattered, dirty clothing which represents the sinful soul. Unlike Langland, the *Cleanness*-poet provides a full retelling of the parable plus a moralizing gloss (25–192). The same image for the soul occurs in Francis Quarles' 'My Glass is Half Unspent', in which the poet begs God for more time to prepare for the heavenly banquet: 'Behold these rags; am I a fitting guest / To taste the dainties of thy royal feast, / With hands and feet unwash'd, ungirt, unblest?'

Other uses are diverse. Browning's churlish narrator in *Christmas-Eve*, apparently remembering the exhortations to communion in the Book of Common Prayer, thinks to himself as he returns the suspicious stares of a poor congregation entering a chapel for services:

> I prefer, if you please, for my expounder
> Of the laws of the feast, the feast's own Founder;
> Mine's the same right with your poorest and sickliest
>   Supposing I don the marriage vestment:
> So, shut your mouth and open your Testament,
> And carve me my portion at your quickliest! (117–22)

Instead of being cast into outer darkness, the speaker falls asleep during the service and dreams a vision of divine love which provides him his figurative marriage garment. Tennyson's Becket acquires a Christlike dimension by deliberately re-enacting the Lucan parable (*Becket*, 1.4); when the beggars arrive from the streets, Becket waits on them himself. In the Sirens episode of Joyce's *Ulysses*, Ben Dollard recounts his efforts at finding a pair of trousers for his first concert with Molly Bloom, saying that he had 'no wedding garment'; the allusion invites a significant comparison to Bloom, who must, if he is ever to collaborate successfully with Molly, put on what Virginia Moseley has called 'the proper garment of faithfulness' (*Joyce and the Bible*, 1967, 103).

M.W. Twomey
Ithaca College

Meek Shall Inherit the Earth

The phrase 'the meek shall inherit the earth' is found in Psalm 37:11 and Matthew 5:5. In both cases the passage ties into the themes of poverty and oppression and God's eventual vindication.

Meekness in scripture is the quality of humility, self-effacement, or gentleness which accepts personal abuse without retaliation or harshness. In this Moses in Numbers 12:3 is the archetypal example in that he remains silent in the face of Aaron's and Miriam's accusations. Such non-retaliation may be due to inner restraint (as with Moses) or it may be due to external weakness, for the meek are the oppressed, the poor sufferers who are the victims of others' exploitation (Job 24:4; Psalms 37:14; Isaiah 32:7). Since the meek cannot defend themselves, God will defend them (Exodus 22:21–24; Deuteronomy 24:14–15; Psalms 25:9; 34:2; 149:4; Proverbs 31:9, 20; Amos 2:7). This declared readiness of God to stand up for the meek (so evident in Moses' case) meant that those pious people in trouble or suffering who humbly hoped in God's deliverance appropriated this title for themselves as a favourite self-designation and claim upon God (Psalms 40:17; 102, title; Isaiah 41:17; Zephaniah 2:3). The basis of all this behaviour is a confident expectation that *God* will bring salvation; thus it is not a product of human violence and scheming.

There is one direction in which this concept expands, namely the meekness of Christ. In Zechariah 9:9 the messianic king is seen as a person of peace and gentleness rather than violence and war. This was picked up in the New Testament as a characteristic of Jesus, whose kingdom comes through peace, not violence (Matthew 11:29; 21:5; 2 Corinthians 10:1), and thus a virtue to be imitated by his followers, who should likewise be characterized by gentleness and non-retaliation (Galatians 5:23; 1 Timothy 3:3; James 3:13, 17; 1 Peter 3:4, 16).

The meek, then, are those who are oppressed or despised, the dispossessed physically or socially. They have only God to trust in, and they look to him for vindication as they live humbly and gently in the world. These 'shall inherit the earth'. The image is that of possessing the land of Israel (as in Deuteronomy 4:1; 16:20; Psalm

68:36), but now the old image of God's giving Palestine to Israel has been transformed into a gift of the messianic kingdom (in Psalm 37) or the kingdom of God (Matthew 5). The message to the sufferer is that his or her humble dependence on God and obedience to God's commands (which is the message of the Sermon on the Mount) will not go unrewarded. God will deliver them from their oppression and reward their gentle non-retaliation, for theirs is his coming kingdom.

Patristic tradition for the most part simply confirms the obvious sense of the biblical writers. St Augustine is typical: 'The meek are those who yield to acts of wickedness, and do not resist evil, but overcome evil with good. Let those, then, who are not meek quarrel and fight for earthly and temporal things; but "blessed are the meek, for they shall by inheritance possess the earth", from which they cannot be driven out' (De sermone Domini in Monte, 2.4). Fourteenth-century English spiritual writer Walter Hilton devotes a substantial portion of his Ladder of Perfection to defining meekness as the opposite of pride. Essentially, meekness is neither extreme, abject humility nor ostentation, but candid reflection on the truth about oneself (pt. 1). Hilton then distinguishes two types of meekness: one is obtained by the 'operation of intellect' in examination of conscience, the other as 'a special gift of love'. It is the latter which is ultimately to be preferred, arising not merely from the necessity of an honest self-assessment but from a true 'self-forgetfulness', that higher wisdom which comes when the mind is fully preoccupied with God's magnificence and eternal glory. Meekness is, in effect, the good sense of those who know that this world is not their home. In this respect, Hilton's 'inheritance' is more spiritualized than that of Augustine. Chaucer's Knight in the General Prologue to The Canterbury Tales is described as a valiant warrior who, 'though that he were worthy, he was wys, / And of his port as meeke as is a mayde' (1.68–69). His chaste meekness is an attribute or function of his wisdom, and similarly declares his ultimate love and pilgrim spirit.

Matthew Henry, in his Commentary on the Whole Bible (5.50), defines the 'meek' as those who are truly obedient to God, and

> gentle towards all men (Titus 3:2); who can bear
> provocation without being inflamed by it; are either silent, or
> return a soft answer; and who can show their displeasure

> when there is occasion for it, without being transported into
> any indecencies; who can be cool when others are hot; and
> in their patience keep possession of their own souls when
> they can hardly keep possession of anything else.

Henry argues that the meek are blessed even in this world, for like
Jesus himself they have learned to bear a mild yoke (Matthew 11:29).
As to their inheriting the earth, which Henry notes is an echo of Psalm
37:11 and 'the only express temporal promise in all the New
Testament', he observes: 'Meekness, however ridiculed and run
down, has a real tendency to promote our health, wealth, comfort,
and safety, even in this world. The meek and quiet are observed to live
the most easy lives, compared with the froward and turbulent' (ibid.).
Few biblical precepts, nonetheless, have gone down less well with
modern intellectuals from Blake to Joyce, among whom Nietzsche and
his admirers have been notably prominent.

Among American writers Theodore Dreiser articulates the
objection succinctly: 'Unless one acted for oneself, upon some stern
conclusion nurtured within, one might rot and die spiritually. Nature
did not care. "Blessed be the meek" – yes. Blessed be the strong,
rather, for they made their own happiness' ('Free'). G.B. Shaw's Eve
(echoing parodically Homer's Athena) in *Back to Methuselah* remarks
sardonically: 'The clever ones were always my favourites. The diggers
and the fighters have dug themselves in with the worms. My clever
ones have inherited the earth. All's well.' J.B. Priestley, however, in
Midnight on the Desert, attempts to recover the meaning of the virtue
for a modern context: 'Rationalist critics have always seemed to me to
miss the profound psychological truth of such observations as "The
meek shall inherit the earth", for the meek, that is, those who are
modest but hopeful in heart and mind, continually inherit the earth,
for it is theirs to enjoy' (chapter 14). Arnold Bennett offers a variation
upon the sentiment in his novel about a miser's daughter, *Anna of the
Five Towns:* 'Blessed are the meek, blessed are the failures, blessed are
the stupid, for they, unknown to themselves, have a grace which is
denied to the haughty, the successful, and the wise' (chapter 6).

Peter H. Davids
Langley, British Columbia

Millstone about His Neck

When Jesus' disciples wanted to know 'who is the greatest in the kingdom of heaven' Jesus called a little child to him, and set him in the midst of them. He then said, 'Except ye be converted, and become as little children, ye shall not enter into the kingdom of heaven. Whosoever therefore shall humble himself as this little child, the same is greatest in the kingdom of heaven' (Matthew 18:1–4). Having thus disposed of the implicit question of personal merit or, as St Augustine puts it, their 'agitated dissension about pre-eminence' (*Sermo*, 145.6), Jesus continued, 'And whoso shall receive one such little child in my name receiveth me. But whoso shall offend one of these little ones which believe in me, it were better for him that a millstone were hanged about his neck, and that he were drowned in the depth of the sea' (Matthew 18:5–6; cf. Mark 9:42; Luke 17:2). Jesus' condemnation is aimed not only at child abuse *per se* (Vulgate, *Qui autem scandalizaveret*) but at the dissuasion of children from faith.

Patristic commentary generally passes over Jesus' assertion of the simplicity of children, and even neglects his equation of caring for a little child with receiving him, preferring instead to universalize 'little ones' as any of the humble faithful. This bias is evident also in Calvin's *Commentary* on the passage, where he argues (the actual child in the incident notwithstanding) that the word 'children' ought here to be understood metaphorically. The passage is thus read strictly as an injunction to humility. According to Matthew Poole (*Annotations*, on Matthew 18:4), Christ is not enjoining his followers to become 'as little Children in all things (which was the *Anabaptists* dream in *Germany*, upon which they would run about the streets, playing with Rattles, etc.)'. He nevertheless goes on to observe that children are, in their characteristic disposition, worthy of imitation:

> 1. Little Children know not what dominion means, and therefore affect it not, are not Ambitious. 2. They are not given to Boast and Glory, and to prefer themselves before others. 3. They are ready to be taught and instructed. 4. They live upon their Father's Providence, and are not over Sollicitous. 5. They are not Malitious, and Vindictive.

Poole's view of little children, echoed in countless post-Reformation sermons on this passage, might seem to such as William Golding (*Lord of the Flies*) to evidence a striking lack of familiarity with the young of the species, which Christopher Smart, for one, cannot suppose Jesus to have shared. Smart's 'children' are, like their medieval predecessors, still adult *in potentis*. Hence, in his *Hymns for the Amusement of Children*, he appeals to the child's simplicity in accepting the gospel at face value, even while his children's hymns make clear his expectation that the actual behaviour of children is proleptic of adult sinfulness. The interpretation he offers in 'Parable 36: The Kingdom of Christ compared to a Little Child' –

> The man, who e'er shall not receive;
> (In strict attention to believe)
> Christ's kingdom, as 'tis preach'd by me,
> With all a child's simplicity,
> Shall in that kingdom find no place

– in this sense accords with the children's prayer in his 'Charity':

> Make me, O Christ, tho' yet a child,
> To virtue zealous, errors mild,
> Profess the feeling of a man,
> And be the Lord's Samaritan.

Keble's somewhat more misty view of 'child-like hearts' (e.g., 'Palm Sunday') applies the passage to a defence of the authenticity of children's response to faith in the fourth stanza of his 'Catechism', a poem which begins,

> Oh! say not, dream not, heavenly notes
> To childish ears are vain
> That the young mind at random floats,
> And cannot reach the strain.

In the 19th century the millstone itself was frequently lifted from its context to become a term for any impediment or noxious burden. Thackeray's allusion in *The Newcomes* is typical: 'He was anxious to break the connexion: he owned it had hung like a millstone round his neck and caused him a great deal of remorse' (chapter 30). In

Melville's *White-Jacket* there is a trivialized reference with respect to the unfortunate reception of a pudding: 'They beat down my excuses with a storm of criminations. One present proposed that the fatal pudding should be tied round my neck, like a millstone, and myself pushed overboard' (chapter 15). In a singularly apt (though ironic) borrowing, Ernest Pontifex in Butler's *The Way of All Flesh* thinks his readiest access to Mr Holt to effect his conversion might be by way of first winning over his children: 'Ernest felt that it would indeed be almost better for him that a millstone should be hanged about his neck, and he cast into the sea, than that he should offend one of the little Holts.'

D.H. Lawrence affords an ironically perverse allusion in one of his *Letters,* where he opines that 'the old Moses wouldn't have valued the famous tablets if they hadn't been ponderous, and millstones around everybody's neck' (615). In Joyce's *A Portrait of the Artist as a Young Man,* in the famous Christmas dinner scene, Dante charges that the credibility of Parnell has been undermined by his being a 'public sinner'. When Parnell is defended by Mr Casey, Mrs Riordan takes up Dante's point (quoting the Vulgate translation of Matthew 18:6): 'Woe be to the man by whom the scandal cometh! It would be better for him that a millstone were tied about his neck and that he were cast into the depth of the sea rather than that he should scandalize one of these, my least little ones. That is the language of the Holy Ghost' (chapter 1).

David L. Jeffrey
University of Ottawa

Mote and Beam

After his admonishment against unjust judgment, 'Judge not that ye be not judged,' Jesus adds the emphasis: 'And why beholdest thou the mote that is in thy brother's eye, but considerest not the beam that is in thine own eye?' (Matthew 7:3). The person who is blind to his own vices Jesus calls a hypocrite. While to complain against sin is the duty of good and benevolent persons, says St Augustine, 'there is in fact a class of troublesome pretenders much to be guarded against, who even while motivated to complain against all manner of others' faults merely from hatred and spite, wish to present themselves as counsellors.' Therefore, he observes, 'if on reflection we find ourselves involved in the same fault as one whom we are beginning to censure we should neither censure nor rebuke but mourn deeply over the case, and rather than invite that person to obey us, rather urge them to join us in a common effort' (*De sermone Domini in Monte*, 2.19.64). 'Rarely, therefore, and only in a case of great necessity, are rebukes to be administered,' he concludes, 'yet in such a way that even in these very rebukes we make it our earnest endeavour, not that we, but that God should be served.' One's first task, in any case, is to remove from one's own eye 'the beam of envy, malice, or pretence' (2.19.66). For Calvin, Christ's words suggest that 'we should not be too eager or ill-natured or malicious, or even over-curious in judging those nearest to us' (*Commentary*, on Matthew 7:1–3).

Chaucer's Reeve, insulted by *The Miller's Tale*, which lampoons an old carpenter whose life circumstances bear considerable relationship to his own, exclaims in the Preface to his own tale: 'I pray to God his nekke mote to-breke; / He can wel in myn eye seen a stalke, / But in his owene he kan nat seen a balke' (*Canterbury Tales*, 1.3918–20). He then commences, predictably, to tell a tale about a miller. In Shakespeare's *Love's Labour's Lost*, Berowne reproves his three friends:

> But are you not ashamed? Nay, are you not,
> All three of you, to be thus much o'ershot?
> You found his mote, the king your mote did see;
> But I a beam do find in each of three. (4.3.156–59)

The saying is often paraphrased, as in John Newton's lines, 'Ere you remark another's sin, / Bid your own conscience look within' (*Olney Hymns*), and frequently misapplied, as in Charles Lamb's definition of a poor relation as 'a mote in your eye' ('Poor Relations'). A.M. Klein directs the saying against anti-Semitism in Germany in his poem 'Johannus, Dei Monachus, Loquitur', in which the sinister narrator exclaims, 'Before you cast the beam from Palestine / Pick out the mote from Mainz; perish the Jews!'

David L. Jeffrey
University of Ottawa

Mustard Seed

In one of his parables Jesus compared the kingdom of heaven to 'a grain of mustard seed, which a man took, and sowed in his field: which indeed is the least of all seeds: but when it is grown, it is the greatest among herbs, and becometh a tree, so that the birds of the air come and lodge in the branches thereof' (Matthew 13:31–32; cf. Mark 4:32; Luke 13:19). The particular type of mustard intended may be the *sinapis nigra,* the cultivated black mustard (commonly 4 ft, but capable of reaching 15 ft). The parable suggests, nonetheless, deliberate hyperbole: rabbinic commentary made reference to the mustard seed as an example of minuteness, a commonplace echoed in Jesus' observation that if the disciples had 'faith as a grain of mustard seed' they would move mountains (Matthew 17:20; Luke 17:6).

Carlyle was fond of the mustard seed parable, using it in his essay 'Boswell's Life of Johnson' to describe the fertility and power of Johnson's prose, and again in *Sartor Resartus* to describe the growth of an idea into an institution (2.10). Hardy, of whom Phelps in his *Essays on Modern Novelists* observes that 'after a time he ceased to have even the faith of a grain of mustard seed,' writes of another aspiration in *Far from the Madding Crowd:* 'This fevered hope had grown up again like a grain of mustard seed during the quiet which followed the hasty conjecture that Troy was drowned' (chapter 49). And in another description of a writer's power Alexander Anderson echoes Carlyle as well as St Matthew in his *Aldous Huxley,* 'He has only to note an idea, and it proliferates rapidly into a vast foliage, like the Biblical seed of mustard sprouting into a lodging for the fowls of the air' (243).

David L. Jeffrey
University of Ottawa

My Yoke is Easy

In Matthew 11:28–30 Jesus invites sin-weary hearers: 'Come unto me, all ye that labour and are heavy laden, and I will give you rest. Take my yoke upon you, and learn of me, for I am meek and lowly in heart: and ye shall find rest unto your souls. For my yoke is easy, and my burden is light.' This text was especially popular among preachers in the 18th-century Great Revival (e.g., John Newton, *Sermons in Olney*, 1767, nos. 10, 11, 12, and 13), and on into the Victorian era. In Victorian times the 'weary and heavy-laden' were identified typically with the poor (e.g., Carlyle, *Sartor Resartus*, 3.4; Thoreau, *Walden*, 'Sounds'), though the original sense is reckoned with by Stephen in Joyce's *A Portrait of the Artist as a Young Man* (chapter 4): 'It was easy to be good. God's yoke was sweet and light. It was better never to have sinned.'

David L. Jeffrey
University of Ottawa

Not Peace but a Sword

In the context of Jesus' instruction to his disciples concerning the message of the kingdom of heaven which they were to profess, he said, 'Think not that I am come to send peace on earth, but a sword' (Matthew 10:34; cf. Luke 12:51–53). He then went on to outline the uncompromising commitment and self-denial required of his followers, and the inevitable opposition they would face from even within their own households.

St Augustine identifies the 'sword' with Jesus' word, which some obey, some resist, and some resist others obeying (*Enarrationes in Psalmos* 45.10; 68.5): 'the sword of his own word hath in salutary wise separated us from evil habits... and separated every believer either from his father who believed not in Christ, or from his mother in like manner unbelieving; or at least, if we were born of Christian parents, from our ancestors... among the heathen' (*Enarrationes in Psalmos* 97.7). This basic interpretation is followed by Calvin and other Reformation commentators, Calvin observing that from reading the Prophets the disciples might well have expected the reign of Christ to be one of peace. Such peace could only be realized, however, if 'all the world were to subscribe to the authority of the gospel. But as the majority is not only opposed, but actually in bitter conflict, we are not able to profess Christ without the strife and hatred of many' (*Harmony of the Gospels,* on Matthew 10:32–35).

In English literature, the phrase 'not peace but a sword' is typically turned against its source, or at least its context. Swinburne's 'Hymn of Man' champions the liberation of persons from religious orthodoxy, and addresses Jesus: 'Ah, thou that darkenest heaven – ah thou that bringest a sword – / By the crimes of thine hands unforgiven, they beseech thee to hear them, O Lord.' In Montague's *A Hind Let Loose,* 'Thither, as a Christian publicist, each brought not peace but a sword, or, where a sword would not have been in place, a squirt of weed-killer' (chapter 1). Of a character in Somerset Maugham's *Catalina* it is observed that 'the people approved his strictness... and did what was in their power to support him. There had been in consequence unfortunate occurrences, and the authorities had been obliged to intervene. He had brought not peace to the city, but a sword' (chapter 34).

David L. Jeffrey
University of Ottawa

Our Father

The *Pater Noster* ('Our Father') Prayer was taught by Christ to his disciples (Matthew 6:9–13; cf. Luke 11:2–4). From apostolic times it has been regarded as the most important 'common' prayer for Christians. In the 2nd-century manual *The Didache* (8.2–3), the longer version of the prayer is prescribed for use thrice daily, and the importance of teaching the prayer to the laity was stressed uniformly by the Fathers and by successive church councils. The Lord's Prayer has a central place in Christian liturgies in Latin and in the vernaculars. There are about ten extant Old English versions – both verse and prose – in translation, gloss, and paraphrase. Middle English versions and expositions are also very common, though there seems to have been no authorized English translation until 1541. One form of exposition for the laity was the Paternoster Play, of which there were versions (now lost) at Lincoln, Beverley, and York. The York play was performed as late as 1572, when the Protestant Archbishop Grindal confiscated the text. One of the strangest commentaries on the Pater Noster is in Old English, a poetic *Dialogue of Salomon and Saturn* together with a prose piece from the same manuscript (ed. by R.J. Menner, 1941), in which the Pater Noster is represented as a huge creature which fights the devil in various guises. In the poem, Salomon instructs Saturn on the powers of the Pater Noster and of every letter or rune in it. The characters (given in both Roman and runic) are personified as warriors who defeat the devil. Such letter mysticism was known among the Greeks and Hebrews, but the presence of the runes here suggests also the old pagan Germanic association of runes with magic. In fact, the Pater Noster was used in some periods as something of a magic formula in charms, medicine, and exorcism (cf. the 'white paternoster' in Chaucer's *Miller's Tale*, 1.3485).

The seven petitions of the Lord's Prayer were regarded from patristic times as a compendium of the things for which the Christian should pray; to these petitions a good deal else in Christian doctrine could be and was related, frequently in parallel heptamerologies. St Augustine associated the seven petitions with the seven gifts of the Holy Ghost and with seven of the eight Beatitudes. Later writers added the association with the seven deadly sins, seven virtues, seven works of mercy, etc. Recitation was thought, in the Middle Ages, to be sufficient for the daily remission of venial sins. Hugh Latimer, in a sermon preached in 1552, makes the Paternoster 'a prayer above all prayers', to prayer in general what the 'law of love' (Matthew 22:37) is to 'all the laws of Moses' (ed. G. Corrie, 1844, 327). Latimer's point is that the Paternoster is not only a model for every kind of prayer, but that it is the précis of a rounded, prayerful life. Hence it is to be taken most seriously, 'for it is better once said deliberately with understanding, than a thousand times without understanding: which is in very deed but vain babbling, and so more a displeasure than pleasure unto God' (329). The doxology 'For thine is the kingdom, the power, and the glory for ever and ever' (based on 1 Chronicles 29:11–12) was also in early liturgical use (with variations), although in the West its use has until recently been confined to Protestant churches. It has provided the title for several books, most notably Graham Greene's novel *The Power and the Glory*. References to the Lord's Prayer in English literature are, of course, numerous (e.g., Dickens, *Bleak House*, where Alan Woodcourt tries unsuccessfully to teach the prayer to Jo), as are parodic revisions, such as Steinbeck's in *Cannery Row* ('Our Father who art in nature, who has given the gift of survival to the coyote, the common brown rat, the English sparrow, the house fly and the moth...') and Hemingway's in 'A Clean Well-Lighted Place' ('Our nada who art in nada, nada be thy name thy kingdom nada thy will be nada in nada as it is in nada'). The term *Pater Noster*, or its shorter form, *Pater*, is not in much use among writers of English after the Reformation except in sardonic or anti-Catholic contexts. Joyce plays with the Latin form of the word 'Patrecknocksters' in *Finnegans Wake*.

Michael Murphy
Brooklyn College and City University of New York

Pearls before Swine

In the Sermon on the Mount Jesus admonishes his hearers: 'Give not that which is holy unto the dogs, neither cast ye your pearls before swine, lest they trample them under their feet, and turn again and rend you' (Matthew 7:6). St Augustine applies this verse to the study and teaching of scripture and spiritual matters:

> By pearls... are meant whatever spiritual things we ought to set a high value upon, both because they lie hid in a secret place, as it were brought up out of the deep, and are found in wrappings of allegory, as it were in shells that have been opened.

He goes on to say that the 'holy' understanding should not be offered to those spiritually unprepared to receive it, either assailants of the truth (dogs) or despisers of it (swine), both of which animals, he notes, are 'unclean' (*De sermone Domini in Monte*, 2.20.68–69).

This application became standard not only for scriptural interpretation (e.g., John Scotus Erigena, *Expositiones super Ierarchiam Caelestem*, *Patrologia Latina*, 122.151–52, 170) but also for the high purposes of medieval secular poetry. The preface to the influential *Anticlaudianus* of Alain of Lille is representative:

> For in this work the sweetness of the literal sense will caress the puerile hearing, the moral instruction will fill the perfecting sense, and the sharper subtlety of the allegory will exercise the understanding nearing perfection. But may the

approach to this work be barred to those who, following only the sensual motion, do not desire the truth of reason, lest a thing holy be defouled by being offered to dogs, or a pearl trampled by the feet of swine be lost, and the majesty of these things be revealed to the unworthy. (ed. Bossuat, 43; cf. *De Planctu Naturae, Patrologia Latina*, 210.445)

This sentiment is echoed by Boccaccio in his *De Genealogia Deorum Gentilium.*

In his 'Sonnet 12' Milton writes about hostile reaction to his liberal views on divorce: 'But this is got by casting Pearl to Hoggs', a secularized employment of the phrase which was to become general in the century following. The gospel context is still in Cowper's mind, however, when he writes of those who 'live in pleasure, dead ev'n while they live', that '...truth, propos'd to reasoners wise as they, / Is a pearl cast – completely cast away' ('Hope', 230, 258–59). In his poem 'Sir John Oldcastle' Whittier imagines Wyclif defending his translation of the Bible by turning a charge of his attackers back on them: 'The gospel, the priest's pearl, flung down to swine – / The swine, laymen, lay-women, who will come, / God willing, to outlearn the filthy friar.' In Sarah Orne Jewett's 'The Dulham Ladies' Miss Dobbin prides herself on trying always 'to elevate people's thoughts and direct them to higher channels'. When it comes to 'that Wolden woman', however, her principles fail her: 'there is no use casting pearls before swine.' In *Music at Night* Huxley adapts the phrase in judging that Lucretius' aim was to see that religion was 'put underfoot and trampled on in return' ('And Wanton Optics Roll the Melting Eye').

David L. Jeffrey
University of Ottawa

Poor with You Always

In Matthew 26:6–14, after an unnamed woman (identified in John's account as Mary, sister of Martha and Lazarus, John 12:1–10) had poured out a costly ointment, using it to anoint Jesus' head, the disciples rebuked her, saying that the ointment might have been sold and the money given to the poor (cf. Mark 14:3–10). Jesus defended her gesture, saying, 'Why trouble ye the woman? For she hath wrought a good work upon me. For ye have the poor always with you; but me ye have not always. For in that she hath poured this ointment on my body, she did it for my burial. Verily I say unto you, Wheresoever this gospel shall be preached in the whole world, there shall also this, that this woman hath done, be told for a memorial of her.' In both Matthew's and Mark's accounts, Judas' anger at this response prompted his going immediately to the chief priests to offer to betray Jesus.

In classical Greek two terms are used to designate the poor: *penes*, the working poor who own little or no property, and *ptochos*, the beggar or destitute who is totally dependent upon others for survival. While the Septuagint uses both terms to translate the various Hebrew words, the New Testament uses *ptochos* in all but two instances (2 Corinthians 9:9 uses *penes* in a quotation of Psalm 112:9; and Luke 21:2 describes the poor widow who offered her 'two mites' as *penichros*). In the New Testament the term *ptochos* refers to both the person entrapped by the consequences of sin (Luke 4:18; 6:20; 7:22) and those who are the politically or economically downtrodden. In this latter broad sense, Jesus is said to be anointed by the Spirit 'to preach good news to the poor' (Hebrews 4:18), who are also the 'captives', the 'blind', and the 'oppressed' (Luke 7:22; Matthew 11:15), recalling Old Testament prophecies of messianic liberation (cf. Isaiah 61:1ff.; Leviticus 25; Deuteronomy 15). Such expectations apparently contributed to Judas' growing anger as he realized the degree to which the 'kingdom' announced by Jesus was to be, pro tem, a spiritual kingdom rather than a political utopia. Care of the poor was a cardinal point in the ethics commanded in Mosaic law (Leviticus 25:38, 42, 55; Deuteronomy 25:18, 22). According to Ezekiel, Sodom was condemned not only for its sexual immorality but also because it 'did not aid the poor and the needy' (16:49). By contrast, those who distribute freely and give to the poor will endure for ever (Psalm 112:9; cf. Deuteronomy 24:13).

What then does Jesus, who had earlier been at pains to encourage the rich young ruler to divest himself and distribute all to the poor (Luke 18:18–30), and who received as authentic the repentance of a tax collector who resolved to give half his goods to the poor (Luke 19:8), mean in this exchange? For most commentators, his phrase 'the poor ye have always with you' should be seen in the light of firm Mosaic commitment to assist the poor, who are always to be found because of human sin. The ideal state, when 'there shall be no poor among you' (Deuteronomy 15:4), was to come to pass 'only if thou hearken unto the voice of the Lord thy God, to observe to do all these commandments which I command thee this day' (v. 5). But as long as the people do not obey, 'the poor shall never cease out of the land' (v. 11). Poverty is therefore a continuing axiomatic condition of the sinful world. And those who are obedient will always have ample opportunity to fulfil their obligations by ministering to the poor until poverty, like other products of sin, vanishes under God's judgment. Mary's action is thus seen as an extravagant exception which proves the rule: in a kind of celestial irony, she contributes to the preparation for Jesus' atoning death (Matthew 26:12; Mark 14:8), even as in diabolical irony Judas prepares for the triumph that death will achieve in making the ultimate kingdom possible.

The account in John, which identifies the woman as Mary, has her anointing Jesus' feet with her hair, and it undercuts any possible moral validity in Judas' reaction by pointing out that his motives, as treasurer, were in fact pecuniary and corrupt (v. 6). St Augustine reconciles the accounts by seeing them as describing two separate incidents, since Judas is not in John's Gospel made to run out to the chief priests, but believes the woman was in both instances Mary (*De consensu evangelistarum*, 79.154–55). He sees her actions as exemplary of devotion, and while 'good are the ministrations done to the poor, and especially the due services and the religious offices done to the saints of God' (*Sermo*, 103.5), he nevertheless inclines to an analogy suggested by the Martha/Mary incident in Luke 10, to aver that 'Mary hath chosen that better part.' This analogy has been reiterated by many later commentators.

Calvin observes that 'Christ's defence of the anointing is not for our imitation but to teach us the reason for its earning favour.' In a rejection of Catholic tendencies to see in Mary's extravagance a precedent for 'incense, candles, splendour in vestment, and like ceremonial' (cf. *Glossa Ordinaria*, *Patrologia Latina*, 114.167), he insists on the exceptional nature of the incident:

Since he says the poor will always be in the world he is distinguishing between the daily services whose practice should flourish among the faithful, and the exceptional which ceased at his ascension into heaven. Do we want to lay out our money on true sacrifices? Let us expend it upon the poor: for Christ says that he is not with us, to receive the service of external ceremonies. (*Harmony of the Gospels*, 3.123)

Matthew Henry takes a strikingly different view, seeing the anointing 'as an act of faith in our Lord Jesus, the Christ, the Messiah, the anointed', and her action as exemplary for all those who would make Christ King over their own hearts. 'When there is true love in the heart to Jesus Christ, nothing will be thought too good, no, nor good enough, to bestow upon him.' He cites Deuteronomy 15:11 to observe that we cannot help but 'see some in this world who call for our charitable assistance'; nevertheless, 'sometimes special works of piety and devotion should take the place of common works of charity' (*Commentary* 5.385–86).

In English literature the passage generally excites less controversy than it does among the theologians; George Herbert refers matter-of-factly to the 'poor box', a common feature of churches of the day ('Praise'; *A Priest to the Temple*) and, as in Cowper's 'Charity', it is generally held by English poets that 'to smite the poor is treason against God' (217). On the other hand, Jesus' words provide a caution for Cowper against misestimation of the high place of charity among Christian obligations ('Charity', 447–52):

Some seek, when queasy conscience has its qualms,
To lull the painful malady with alms;
But charity, not feigned, intends alone
Another's good – their centres in their own;
And too short liv'd to reach the realms of peace,
Must cease for ever when the poor shall cease.

In *Walden* Thoreau observes that in America the tables have been turned and one of the burdens of his readers is that of owning superfluous property: 'What mean ye by saying that the poor ye have always with you...?' He then quotes Ezekiel (18:3) and alludes to

Jeremiah (31:29) that 'ye shall not have occasion any more to use this proverb in Israel.' In Longfellow's *Evangeline,* however, the emphasis falls upon continuing obligation to the poor: the humble almshouse surrounded by the city's splendour has walls which 'seem to echo / Softly the words of the Lord: – "The / poor ye have always with you"' (2.5). The phrase, lifted out of context, as in a Depression era union song or the rhetoric of the Fabian socialists at the turn of the century (cf. G.B. Shaw's *Major Barbara*), becomes an attack on the instability of Christian commitment to really solving 'once and for all' the 'problem of poverty'. Dickens anticipates this use of the phrase in *Our Mutual Friend.* Podsnap, whose perversion of Christianity includes a red-letter edition of 'the gospel according to Podsnappery' (3.8), appropriates Jesus' words (1.11) to put down 'the meek man' (i.e., citizen of the kingdom of heaven) who has dared to suggest that something may possibly be wrong with the economic system. When Podsnap insists that 'Providence has declared', says Dickens' narrator, he is merely using an 'absurd and irreverent conventional phrase', to declare what he himself means and wants.

David L. Jeffrey
University of Ottawa

Prodigal Son

One of Jesus' major parables, the story told in Luke 15:11–32 unfolds in three phases: the rebellion and subsequent repentance of the prodigal son who, having squandered his inheritance in 'riotous living' in a far country, returns home in abject poverty; the unconditional forgiveness and welcome of the father; and the refusal, on the part of the elder and more 'responsible' son, to participate in his brother's homecoming festivities.

In its context, the last phase of the story carries its central message; Jesus painted the satiric portrait of the elder brother as a rebuke to the Pharisees, who occasioned the parable by criticizing Jesus for his association with 'sinners' (Luke 15:2). The most significant part of the story for most commentators, however, is the portrait of the forgiving father, which captures the gospel in miniature.

St Ambrose sets the dominant tone of early exegesis in his

treatise against the Novatian heresy, *De poenitentia*, where he argues from the example of the forgiving father that no one, on proof of authentic repentance, should be denied reconciliation:

> Therefore most evidently are we bidden... to confer again the grace of the heavenly sacrament on those guilty even of the greatest sins, if they with open confession bear the penance due to their sin.

Chaucer's Parson uses the story in much the same way, to teach that no one should needlessly despair because of sin, but rather turn to God in penitence (*Parson's Tale*, 10.700). The narrative of the prodigal became, in fact, a staple of penitential teaching in the Middle Ages (cf. Bishop John Fisher's *Treatyse Concernynge the Seven Penytencyall Psalmes*, which contains both a paraphrase and exposition of the parable).

Although Calvin and other later commentators returned to a consideration of the older brother as an example of the 'inhumanity [of] those who want maliciously to restrict God's grace, as if they grudged poor sinners their salvation' (Calvin, *Harmony of the Gospels*), exegetical and homiletical emphasis tended still to fall elsewhere. Ruskin, in his autobiographical *Praeterita* (3.1.16), complained that in a certain Puritan study group the parable was expounded to the utter exclusion of the elder son, since 'the home-staying son was merely a picturesque figure introduced to fill the background of the parable agreeably, and contained no instruction or example for the well-disposed scriptural student...'.

Widespread literary interest in the story begins in the 16th century, during which time a number of didactic continental plays were written on the subject – among them Burkart Waldis' German drama *De Parabell vam verlorn Szohn* (1527), Guilielmus Gnaphaeus' Latin *Acolastus* (1528; trans. into English by John Palsgrave in 1540), Georgius Macropedius' *Asotus* (1537), Jörg Wickram's *Schönes und evangelisches Spiel von dem verlorenen Sohn* (1540), and Lope de Vega's *El hijo pródigo* (1604).

In England, in the decades to follow, a multitude of plays, now commonly designated 'Prodigal Son Plays', were fashioned. The tendency of these plays was to emphasize moral teaching and to portray the excesses of the prodigal's 'riotous living'. Among the better known of these dramas are the morality-like *Lusty Juventus* by R. Wever (c. 1550), the anonymous *Nice Wanton* (c. 1550), Thomas Ingeland's *The Disobedient Child* (c. 1560), *Misogonus* (c. 1570, of uncertain authorship), George Gascoigne's *The Glasse of Government* (1575), John Marston's *Histriomastix* (1599), the anonymous (Pseudo-Shakespearean) *The London Prodigal* (1604), Thomas Middleton's *A Mad World My Masters* (1606), and Francis Beaumont's *The Knight of the Burning Pestle* (1607).

Shakespeare alludes more often to this parable than to any other. There are references to the prodigal's departure from home and his loose living (*The Merchant of Venice*, 2.6.14–19), his waste of resources in trivial pursuits (*Love's Labour's Lost*, 5.2.64; *Twelfth Night*, 1.3.24), his prodigal spending (*Timon of Athens*, 4.3.278), his poverty and his swinekeeping (*As You Like It*, 1.1.38–42; *1 Henry IV*, 4.2.36–38; *King Lear*, 4.7.38–40), and his eventual return (*Comedy of Errors*, 4.3.18–19; *Winter's Tale*, 4.3.103). Pictorial renderings of the parable are mentioned in *Merry Wives of Windsor*, 4.5.8, and *2 Henry IV*, 2.1.56. There is clowning on its theme by Launce in *The Two Gentlemen of Verona* (2.3.1–35): 'I have receiv'd my proportion, like the Prodigious Son...' The invention of such puns became a favourite pastime for later writers (e.g., Dickens: 'a reg'lar prodigy son', *Pickwick Papers*, chapter 43; Maxwell Anderson: 'I'd fiddle these prodigies back home to Sunday school', *Winterset*, 1.2).

Ben Jonson elaborates the plot in the career of Asotus (Latin for 'prodigal') in *Cynthia's Revels, or The Fountain of Self-Love*, and later in the equally allegorical *The Staple of News* (cf. the allusions in 4.2.123; 5.6.18–19; 5.6.60–66); Jonson also uses the parable in a more specifically religious context in his poem 'The Pleasures of Heaven'. Equally close to the original content of the text are Robert Southwell's poem 'The prodigall childs soule wracke', describing the prodigal's career in terms first of a sea voyage and then of imprisonment, and William Drummond of Hawthornden's sonnet 'For the Prodigal'. George Herbert's poem 'Love (3)' presents the thoughts and doubts of the homecoming prodigal and the father's (Love's) unperturbed words of welcome.

Robert Burton uses the first part of the parable to declare that times of sinful pleasure are frequently followed by a 'cruel reckoning in the end, as bitter as wormwood' and the second part to show that repentance cures despair (*Anatomy of Melancholy*, 3.4.2.3–6). The prodigal's resolution to return is referred to in Francis Quarles' poem 'The New Heart' and in Bunyan's *The Pilgrim's Progress*. When Christian is asked whether he is really determined to leave the City of Destruction, he answers, in the words of the prodigal, that where he goes there is 'enough and to spare'. Defoe's Robinson Crusoe, having acted against his father's counsel by going to sea, resolves during a terrible storm that he will 'like a true repenting prodigal' go home to his father, who, being 'an emblem of our blessed Saviour's parable had even killed the fatted calf for me'. In the end, however, Robinson is ashamed to return.

When, in Fielding's *Joseph Andrews,* Parson Adams witnesses the encounter of Joseph and his father, he cries out, '*Hic est quem quaeris, inventus est etc.*' (4.15). His combination of the angel's address to the two Marys at the empty grave (John 20:15) with the father's words in Luke 15:24 gives the reunion the quality of a resurrection. Goldsmith's *Vicar of Wakefield* echoes the situation and the atmosphere of the parable, when the vicar tries to reclaim 'a lost child to virtue' (chapters 17–18).

Alexander Pope's 'Epistle to Richard Boyle, Earl of Burlington' aims at philistine prodigals in general. Before him, the older Samuel Butler had already satirized a prodigal as someone whose 'Life begins with keeping of Whores, and ends with keeping of Hogs' (*Characters*). Laurence Sterne colourfully embroiders the parable in *The Sermons of Mr Yorick* (20) only to launch into a discussion of young people's 'love of variety'.

In the sixth book of Wordsworth's *Excursion* (275–375), the priest tells the story of a Prodigal, a gifted young fortune hunter, who returns home only to depart again after a while – a pattern which is repeated three times, until his parents witness his 'last, repentant breath'. In Byron's drama *Werner, or the Inheritance,* the impoverished protagonist, who is fighting incognito for his inheritance, is called

A prodigal son, beneath his father's ban
For the last twenty years: for whom his sire

Refused to kill the fatted calf; and therefore,
If living, he must chew the husks still. (2.1; cf. also 2.2)

When, in Dickens' *Martin Chuzzlewit* (chapter 6), Mr Pecksniff invites the protagonist to make himself at home in the Pecksniff house, he offers him 'the fatted calf' – using it as a symbol of complete liberty; 'but as no such animal chanced at that time to be grazing on Mr Pecksniff's estate, this request must be considered rather as a polite compliment than a substantial hospitality'. In *Dombey and Son* (chapter 22), Rob Toodle is several times called a 'prodigal son'. He prefers to be welcomed by his mother rather than his father, since '*she* always believes what's good...'. Miss Wren, in a 'dire reversal of the places of parent and child,' scolds her father and calls him a 'prodigal old son' (*Our Mutual Friend*, 2.2).

Elizabeth Gaskell describes a prodigal's return that fails, when, in *Mary Barton* (chapter 10, 'Return of the Prodigal'), John Barton flings the returning 'long-lost Esther', his sister-in-law, away from him and refuses to forgive her for causing his wife's death. Charles Kingsley devotes chapter 27 ('The Prodigal's Return') of his novel *Hypatia* to Raphael Aben-Ezra's account of his conversion to Christianity after a long preoccupation with various philosophies. In Thackeray's novel *The Newcomes,* both Clive Newcome and Reverend Charles Honeyman are called prodigal sons – the latter because he has lived beyond his means and yet is to be treated kindly (chapter 26), the former on account of his thoughtless ingratitude towards his father, who 'lay awake, and devised kindnesses, and gave his all for the love of his son; and the young man took, and spent, and slept, and made merry'. The moral conclusion is that 'Careless prodigals and anxious elders have been from the beginning: – and so may love, and repentance, and forgiveness endure even till the end' (chapter 20).

Little Maggie Tulliver, in George Eliot's *The Mill on the Floss,* encounters a remarkable series of pictures representing the Prodigal Son in the costume of Sir Charles Grandison. 'In the Prison', chapter 45 of Eliot's early novel *Adam Bede,* shows Dinah Morris, the Methodist preacher, exhorting and comforting Hetty Sorrel, convicted of murdering her child. Dinah's fervent prayer for the Lord's mercy on Hetty, which culminates in the words '...make her cry with her whole soul, "Father, I have sinned"', leads to Hetty's confession of her past action (cf. George Macdonald's novel *Robert Falconer*, 2.3; 3.14).

John Ruskin offers a lengthy interpretation of the parable in *Time and Tide* (25.174–77), stressing its literal sense. His two main conclusions are that the love of money is the root of all evil, and that true repentance begins when a man 'complains of nobody but himself'. But in his second monologue, Robert Browning's Count Guido (*The Ring and the Book*, 11.760–63) tries to justify himself by pointing to the iniquities of others:

> Each playing prodigal son of heavenly sire,
> Turning his nose up at the fatted calf,
> Fain to fill belly with the husks, we swine
> Did eat by born depravity of taste!

While Christina Rossetti's poems (e.g., 'I Will Arise', 'A Prodigal Son') closely reflect the original intent of the parable, Rudyard Kipling's 'The Prodigal Son (Western Version)' shows a basically unrepentant son who, disappointed by the moralism and narrowness of the home he has returned to, leaves again for the Yards. This prodigal foreshadows André Gide's narration 'Le retour de l'Enfant prodigue', in which the returning son's younger brother leaves the father's house in order to attempt all the things the prodigal was not able to achieve. In Gide's wake, German poet Rainer Maria Rilke tells the story of a prodigal who leaves the parental home because he does not want to be loved (*Die Aufzeichnungen des Malte Laurids Brigge*, 938–46; cf. also his poem 'Der Auszug des verlorenen Sohnes'). Other continental versions of the time are Franz Kafka's short prose piece 'Heimkehr' and Swiss writer Robert Walser's 'Die Geschichte vom verlorenen Sohn'.

Thomas Hardy alludes to the parable in his tragic story 'The Grave by the Handpost' (in *A Changed Man and Other Tales*), in which the protagonist has the words 'I am not worthy to be called thy son' inscribed on his father's gravestone. Yeats, in 'The Lake Isle of Innisfree', invests the speaker's choice of nature over civilization with moral depth by echoing the prodigal's moment of epiphany: 'I will arise and go...' In James Joyce's *Ulysses*, Stephen in a drunken mood echoes and at the same time significantly mutilates the same words when he says, 'I will arise and go to my' – deliberately omitting the word 'father'.

There are several references to the parable in Alan Paton's *Cry, the Beloved Country,* most obviously in the conversation between Stephen and John Kumalo about Stephen's prodigal son Absalom, who has been found 'not as he was found in the early teaching', but arrested for the murder of a white man (1.14; cf. also 1.2, 1.5, 2.12). Graham Greene's *Monsignor Quixote* offers a communist reading of the 'pretty parable', presented by Mayor Enrique Zancas. In it, the prodigal feels stifled by his bourgeois surroundings, gets rid of his wealth in the quickest way possible ('perhaps he even gave it away'), and 'in a Tolstoyian gesture' becomes a peasant. Another peasant tells him about the capitalist subjection of the working class and the class struggle, and when the young man returns home for a week, he is so disillusioned that he returns to the peasant, who offers a welcome similar to that of the father in verses 20–21.

In America, the first literary treatments of the parable were imported from England or had English settings. Thus, an often-reprinted chapbook entitled *The Prodigal Daughter, or The Disobedient Lady Reclaimed* presents a cautionary tale about an English girl who tries to poison her parents, falls in a deathlike trance, but is reformed through a vision. In Washington Irving's tale 'The Spectre Bridegroom' (from *The Sketch Book*), the 'fatted calf' is killed for the wedding of the heroine and the fake bridegroom. After the couple has run away and returned, the bride's father, who has 'lamented her as lost' and rejoices 'to find her still alive', pardons them. Poe alludes to the prodigal's 'riotous living' in his stories 'Thou art the Man' and 'Never Bet the Devil your Head'. In Harriet Beecher Stowe's novel *Dred,* Nina Gordon's dying words are 'Good-by! I will arise and go to my Father!' (chapter 36). Another prodigal comes home in Edward Eggleston's *The Circuit Rider,* chapter 18.

After having been 'numbered with the dead', Herman Melville's Israel Potter is welcomed by his father like the prodigal son (*Israel Potter,* chapter 2), but he leaves his home again – this time for fifty years. During his years at sea, he works as one of the waisters, who are 'sea-Pariahs, comprising all the lazy, all the inefficient, all the unfortunate and fated, all the melancholy, all the infirm, all the rheumatical scamps, scapegraces, ruined prodigal sons, sooty faces, and swineherds of the crew' (chapter 20). The Prodigal in Melville's *Clarel* (4.26) by his conduct represents an earlier stage of the biblical son's career: he is still occupied with amorous adventures and riotous living.

In his humorous sketch 'The Scriptural Panoramist', Mark Twain describes a 'moral-religious show' accompanied by a pianist's ill-matched playing. When a picture of the prodigal son's arrival at home is shown, the pianist plays, 'Oh we'll all get blind drunk / When Johnny comes marching home.' W.D. Howells refers to Luke 15:32 in a homecoming scene in *The Rise of Silas Lapham*. He identifies both Silas and young Tom Corey as prodigal sons – the one because in his youth he 'cleared out West' and his return was a 'Fatted-calf business', and the other because, upon returning from Texas, he has to learn that 'the prodigal must take his chance if he comes back out of season.'

When Stephen Crane's Maggie has left home, her mother anticipates triumphantly how 'deh beast' will return. She corrects Maggie's brother when he talks of 'dis prod'gal bus'ness': 'It wa'n't no prod'gal daughter, yeh fool... It was prod'gal son, anyhow' (chapter 13). Though her vocabulary is 'derived from mission churches', her complaint, 'Ah, what a ter'ble affliction is a disobed'ent chile' (chapter 19), only serves to illustrate Crane's insight into 'the abandonment of Christian love by his culture' (Stein, 'New Testament Inversion in Crane's *Maggie*', 270).

Bret Harte's short story 'Mr Thompson's Prodigal' (a plot later expanded into the drama *The Two Men of Sandy Bar*) presents a well-to-do father in search of his runaway son, and an imposter who takes advantage of this situation. When the real son appears, he turns out to be a drunken tramp. Mary Hallock Foote's *The Prodigal* tells the story of the reformation of a rich man's son in San Francisco. In Jack London's 'The Prodigal Father', Josiah Childs runs away to California from his domineering New England wife and when, upon returning after eleven years, he finds her unchanged, he persuades his son to run away with him again.

Eugene O'Neill alludes to the parable several times (e.g., *Dynamo*, 2.1; *Days Without End*, 1), usually with an ironic refraction of the parable's message. In *The Rope,* the returning son Luke is welcomed by a scripture-chanting father who uses the exact words of verses 22–24; but Luke soon turns out to be concerned only for the rest of his father's money. His unrepenting attitude is punished, however, by his niece's squandering the gold pieces before he can find them. In *Desire under the Elms* the role of the elder brother is given to Eben (3.1), but Eben is at the same time the real father of the son who has arrived.

Sinclair Lewis reverses the character constellation of the parable in his light-hearted novel *The Prodigal Parents,* in which parents refuse to be exploited by their greedy grown-up children and flee to Europe. In the end, the sobered daughter tries to comprehend the new distribution of roles, observing that her father is 'Prodigal Son, obviously, with Mother as Assistant Prodigal, and I'm the forgiving parent and I'm afraid Howard is the swine, with Cal for husks, but who's the fatted calf, and who's the elder son that got sore?' (chapter 38).

The parable looms large in the works of Thomas Wolfe, as evidenced in such titles as *You Can't Go Home Again,* 'The Lost Boy', 'O Lost', and, most conspicuously, 'The Return of the Prodigal'. In his *Look Homeward, Angel,* Eugene is 'not safe, not sound' (chapter 32), he is 'like a man who had died, and had been re-born' (chapter 33), and he wants to pay his way to Harvard from his share in his father's estate (chapter 39).

In Morley Callaghan's *They Shall Inherit the Earth,* Michael Aikenhead, estranged from his father for ten years, hates being greeted upon his return by his half-brother Dave Choate, whom he later lets drown (chapter 4). Callaghan's *More Joy in Heaven* tells the story of a paroled criminal who is welcomed loudly by society, because 'After all, they did a little feasting and celebrating for the prodigal son...' (chapter 5). The promise inherent in the parallel does not prove to be true: overburdened by society's expectations, the prodigal fails in his new life. Another returning prisoner is young Tom Joad, in Steinbeck's *The Grapes of Wrath.* His former preacher Jim Casy speculates that maybe old Tom Joad will 'kill the fatted calf like for the prodigal in scripture' (chapter 4).

Edwin Arlington Robinson's poem 'The Prodigal Son' is a dramatic monologue spoken by the returned prodigal to his elder brother. It leaves out the forgiving father altogether and is not much more than a plea for human sympathy. Stephen Vincent Benét's 'The Prodigal Children' describes the attitudes of the prodigal generation which left their ideals of peace behind and 'got the world in a mess' – that of the Second World War. Elizabeth Bishop's poem 'The Prodigal' evokes the sensations of the prodigal's degrading experience as an exile working among the swine and ends on the unspoken question of why it takes him so long to make up his mind to go home.

The 1970s saw the production of a number of 'prodigal-son plays' revolving around the generation conflict and about particular problems of modern society. The troubles the prodigals of these plays run into are teenage pregnancy (J.E. Franklin and M. Grant, *The Prodigal Sister*), abortion (D. Turner, *The Prodigal Daughter*), and drugs and imprisonment (D. Evans, *The Prodigals*).

When in *The Fixer*, a novel by Bernard Malamud, protagonist Yakov Bok's wife Raisl is called 'dead' by the rabbi because she has left her family, the saying reflects Jewish belief, particularly the ceremony of *ketsatsah*, which has been claimed to be the frame of verse 24 (cf. Rengstorf, *Die Re-Investitur des verlorenen Sohnes*). In Malamud's novel *God's Grace*, the gorilla George is an outsider who disrupts the seder celebration. The protagonist Calvin Cohn tries to assure him that he is forgiven by relating the story of the Prodigal Son. The gorilla listens 'with tears flowing' (p. 124).

Manfred Siebald
Johannes Gutenberg Universität, Mainz, Germany
Leland Ryken
Wheaton College

Prophet is Not without Honour

When Jesus returned to his own place of upbringing, and there 'taught them in their synagogue', his former townspeople were put off by his 'wisdom' and 'mighty works', leading Jesus to observe that 'a prophet is not without honour, save in his own country, and in his own house' (Matthew 13:57; John 4:44). This saying is modified in logion 6 of the 2nd-century Oxyrhynchus *Sayings of Our Lord* to read 'A prophet is not acceptable in his own country, neither doth a physician work cures upon them that know him.' Proverbial in status, by the 19th century this saying of Jesus was susceptible to inversion. Thus, Lytton Strachey says in his *Portraits in Miniature* of Carlyle's ambitions that 'he had higher views: surely he would be remembered as a prophet. And no doubt he had many of the qualifications for that profession – a loud voice, a bold face, and a bad temper. But unfortunately there was one essential characteristic that he lacked – he was not dishonoured in his own country.' In Butler's *The Way of All Flesh,* when Ernest's father is irresponsible to his new commitment to the spiritual life, 'He said to himself that a prophet was not without honour save in his own country, but he had been lately getting into an odious habit of turning proverbs upside down, and it occurred to him that a country is not without honour save for its own prophet' (chapter 40). John Dos Passos' celebration of an avant-garde architect, itself prophetic, is more straightforward: 'His plans are coming to life… His blueprints, as once Walt Whitman's words, stir the young men.' Yet this architect-prophet Frank Lloyd Wright, 'patriarch of the new building', is 'not without honour except in his own country' (*The Big Money,* 'The Architect').

David L. Jeffrey
University of Ottawa

Render to Caesar

Each of the synoptic gospels tells the story of Jesus' response to the messengers sent by the Pharisees and members of Herod's party to test him with a question concerning the lawfulness of paying taxes to the Roman emperor (Matthew 22:15–22; Mark 12:13–17; Luke 20:20–26). A 'yes' would find no favour with a people resentful of their subjugation to infidel Rome; a 'no' would put him in defiance of the secular authority. Seeing through their flattery and dissimulation, Jesus turned the tables on his inquirers. 'Whose is this image and superscription?' he asked them with reference to a silver piece, the coin of tribute. From their answer, 'Caesar's', followed his own: 'Render therefore unto Caesar the things which are Caesar's; and unto God the things that are God's' (Matthew 22:21).

Romans 13:17 and 1 Peter 2:13–17 require obedience to the

civil authority as the securer and minister of mankind's temporal welfare, a position characteristic of early Christianity. This principle informs St Augustine's *De civitate Dei*, where the task assigned to the state is the maintenance of that good order required by both the wicked and the just in this world, and it is reiterated in the political theory of St Thomas Aquinas (Copleston, *A History of Philosophy*, 1962, 2.2.132–42; cf. J. Maritain, *Man and the State*, 1951, 108). The argument for ecclesiastical sovereignty in temporal matters such as Giles of Rome advances in his 13th-century *De Ecclesiastica Potestate* is exceptional, even in the late Middle Ages, and runs counter to the traditional teaching. It is in large measure the medieval effort to tease out a detailed legal code from Matthew 22:21 that led to the repeated conflicts between church and state which come to a head in the Reformation.

Langland's *Piers Plowman* is the first major work of English literature explicitly to take 'Render unto Caesar...' as its ruling text. According to Lady Holy Church Christ's words are intended to warn against luxury or an inordinate love of 'the money of this world' and to counsel thrift (B.1.50–55). The application of Matthew 22:21 in Shaftesbury's *Characteristics* conforms to the usage made traditional by three centuries of Reformation polemics, picturing the Church of Rome's hierarchy in embrace with the Caesars (2.6.2.3). Blake's application is more comprehensive. His vision of all the established churches as inimical to Christ and friendly to Caesar leads him to an ironic inversion in annotating Dr Thornton's 'New Translation of the Lord's Prayer': 'God is only an Allegory of Kings.' Thoreau's 'Civil Disobedience' effectively responds to the affluent citizen who would be exempt from taxation: 'If you use money which has the image of Caesar on it and which he has made current and valuable, that is, *if you are men of the State*, and gladly enjoy the advantages of Caesar's government, then pay him back some of his own when he demands it.' In Joyce's *Ulysses*, the fact that 'To Caesar what is Caesar's, to God what is God's' appears to Stephen 'a riddling sentence' does not allow him clearly to distinguish between these authorities; nor does his perception of himself as 'the servant of two masters... an English and an Italian' encourage him to prefer one to the other. The abbot who argues against euthanasia in Walter M. Miller, Jr's *A Canticle for*

Leibowitz urges obedience to Caesar's law, but not when it contravenes God's (chapter 27).

Camille R. La Bossière
University of Ottawa

Rich Fool

This parable, which appears in the noncanonical Gospel of Thomas as well as in Luke 12:16–21, forms part of Jesus' response to a man who asks him to become involved in the matter of a disputed inheritance. Jesus pointedly refuses to become 'a judge or divider' (v. 14). He warns against 'all covetousness' and admonishes the man that 'a man's life consisteth not in the abundance of the things which he possesseth' (v. 15). The parable which follows illustrates these teachings.

Jesus speaks of a rich farmer whose all-consuming concern is preserving and enjoying his wealth. He contemplates a future time when his 'ample goods' (v. 19) are securely stored and he will be free to 'eat, drink, and be merry' (v. 19) with self-indulgent abandon.

Abruptly, God enters the scene to disrupt the wealthy man's plans. God addresses the farmer as 'fool' (v. 20), a term applied to one who does not give God proper acknowledgment and reverence (Psalm 15:1). The fool is informed that his soul is at God's disposal; indeed, it is required by God 'this night' (v. 20). God reminds the fool that at his death he will not even have the power to give away the goods he has worked to acquire and keep for himself: 'Whose will they be?'

The parable ends with the warning that the rich fool's fate awaits all those who rely on material goods as their ultimate form of security instead of putting their lives and possessions at the disposal of God: 'So is he that layeth up for himself and is not rich towards God.'

Although it has lent itself to two modern books entitled *A Certain Rich Man,* one by W. Allen White (1909) and the other by Vincent Sheehan (1949), this parable is better recognized in literature for two of its sayings than for its use as a model for narrative. The rich fool's smug 'eat, drink, and be merry' has become proverbial, and is applied trenchantly by William Hazlitt, for example, in his 'Merry

England'. G. K. Chesterton, in a similar context, in his book on *George Bernard Shaw*, quips: 'Let us endure all the pagan pleasures with a Christian patience. Let us eat, drink, and be serious' ('The Philosopher'). The divine response, 'Thou fool, this night thy soul shall be required of thee' (v. 20), has also found its way into literary idiom, as in Butler's *The Way of All Flesh*: 'And there is not one of us can tell but what this day his soul may be required of him' (chapter 49). The basic structure of the parable has been employed repeatedly in didactic literature, from the medieval play *Everyman* to a modern dramatization by Mary Moncure Parker, *The Soul of the Rich Man: A Morality Play* (1908).

Lenore Gussin
New York, New York

Salt of the Earth

In his Sermon on the Mount, Jesus calls his listeners the 'salt of the earth' (Matthew 5:13) and adds, as a warning, that savourless salt is 'good for nothing but to be cast out, and to be trodden under foot of men' (cf. parallels in Mark 9:50 and Luke 14:34–35).

While some modern scholars believe that Jesus' words about savourless salt originally referred to the 'state of Judaism' in his time (Dodd, 111; cf. Hunter, 21), the Fathers took Jesus' exhortation and warning as addressed to the disciples (e.g., St John Chrysostom, *Homily on Matthew*, 15.10) and more especially the bishops, prelates, and preachers of the Word (e.g., St Jerome, *Dialogus adversus Luciferianos*, 5; cf. St Thomas Aquinas, *In Matthaeum*; St Thomas More, *A Dialogue of Divers Matters*, 1.18). This interpretation was then reinforced by spiritualizing the theories of the origin of salt: its origin from the water of the ocean – tribulation – and the heat of the sun – love (Aquinas, *In Matthaeum*; cf. Wyclif, *In Omnes Novi Testamenti Libros*).

The function of salt as a preservative was emphasized by many of the Fathers (e.g., St Augustine, *De sermone Domini in Monte*, 1.6). Its effect was said to be felt both in the Church and in the world, since 'society is held together as long as the salt is uncorrupted' (Origen, *Contra Celsum*, 8.70). The importance of salt in healing, purifying, and seasoning was also stressed, as was the fact that salt makes the soil barren; hence the apostles' teaching suppresses carnal desires and vices in their listeners (Bede, *In Matthei Evangelium Expositio*; Aquinas, *In Matthaeum*). The loss of the salt's savour can, according to these same exegetes, be brought about by the fear of temporal persecutions, by wealth and worldly entanglements, or by deviation from the truth.

Following the application of Jesus' word to teachers of the gospel, the Reformers used the text to criticize the Pope, clergy, and monks. They read it as a serious warning for the Church not to become savourless (Calvin, *Harmony of the Gospels*), accusing monks of staying in their 'dens' instead of 'salting' their neighbours (Tyndale, *Exposition of Matthew*) and clergy of shying away from preaching the 'biting' message that 'everything born and living on the face of the earth is unworthy before God, rotten and corrupted' (Luther, *Weimarer Ausgabe* 32.343–54). For John Wesley, Matthew 5:13 underscores the practical implications of the gospel, indicating that 'Christianity is essentially a social religion' (*Standard Sermons*, 19.1).

In the 19th century, John Ruskin made ironic use of the metaphor in referring to the salt Swiss Catholics needed in the making of their cheeses, but which over-eager Protestants denied them in order to convert them (*Time and Tide*, 9.45). Equally ironic is Dickens' reference to the presumptuous mayor Thomas Sapsea: 'Of such is the salt of the earth' (*The Mystery of Edwin Drood*, chapter 12). Gerard Manley Hopkins ('The Candle Indoors') makes a connection between the liar who is 'cast by conscience out, spendsavour salt' and the 'beam-blind' man of Matthew 7:1–5.

In Flannery O'Connor's short story 'Good Country People', a fake Bible salesman calls himself a 'country boy', and Mrs Hopewell remarks that 'good country people are the salt of the earth!' Her ignorance blinds her to the fact that he is an imposter and an atheist.

Having acquired proverbial status, the metaphor is frequently deprived of any spiritual content. The salt of Swinburne's poem 'The Salt of the Earth', for example, is childhood, without which 'This were a drearier star than ever / Yet looked upon the sun.' D.H. Lawrence's poem 'Salt of the Earth' likewise secularizes the passage: 'the wisdom of wise men, the gifts of the great' are salt of the earth which becomes salt of the ocean of the afterward. Yet the younger generations would be better without such 'pickling'. In *Ulysses,* James Joyce makes the salt an epithet of military efficiency when he calls the royal Dublins 'the salt of the earth, known the world over'.

Manfred Siebald
Johannes Gutenberg Universität, Mainz, Germany

Seek and Ye Shall Find

Jesus' invitation to his hearers in the Sermon on the Mount is 'Ask, and it shall be given to you; seek, and ye shall find; knock, and it shall be opened unto you: For every one that asketh receiveth; and he that seeketh findeth; and to him that knocketh it shall be opened' (Matthew 7:7–8). St Augustine says that

> the asking refers to the obtaining by request soundness and strength of mind, so that we may be able to discharge those duties which are commanded; the seeking, on the other hand, refers to the finding of truth. For inasmuch as the blessed life is summed up in action and knowledge, action wishes for itself a supply of strength, contemplation desires that matters should be made clear: of these therefore the first is to be asked, the second is to be sought; so that the one may be given, the other found.

He adds, 'The possession itself... is opened to him that knocks' (*De sermone Domini in Monte*, 2.21.71), and concludes that 'there is need of perseverance in order that we may receive what we ask, find what we seek, and that what we knock at may be opened' (2.21.73). Calvin follows Augustine in this emphasis. Bunyan, in *Pilgrim's Progress,* exhibits the faithful pilgrim Christian as an essay in perseverance; when Christian finally reaches the strait gate he finds written over it 'Knock and it shall be opened unto you.' John Wesley follows the main lines of traditional exegesis, but understands 'asking' to mean the study of Christian doctrine and 'seeking' to be 'searching the scriptures' – hearing them expounded and participating in the Eucharist; 'knocking' involves the disciplines of prayer (*Sermon* 30, Sermon on the Mount, no. 10, 1747). Christopher Smart's *A Song to David* gives Wesley's emphasis poetic form:

But stronger still, in earth and air,
And in the sea, the man of pray'r;
   And far beneath the tide;
And in the seat to faith assign'd
Where ask is have, where seek is find,
   Where knock is open wide.

David L. Jeffrey
University of Ottawa

Separate Sheep from Goats

In Matthew 25 Jesus describes to his disciples the scene to take place at the Last Judgment 'when the Son of man shall come in his glory… And before him shall be gathered all nations: and he shall separate them one from another, as a shepherd divideth his sheep from the goats: And he shall set the sheep on his right hand, but the goats on the left' (vv. 31–33). The 'goats', in this instance, are sent 'into everlasting fire prepared for the devil and his angels' because of their lack of charity. 'For I was an hungered, and ye gave me no meat: I was thirsty, and ye gave me no drink' (vv. 41–42). In Jesus' own exposition, distinguishing between those who have acted in unselfish charity towards the needy stranger and those who have not, the former are counted as having acted charitably towards Christ himself, albeit unwittingly, while the latter are seen to have deprived and neglected Christ himself.

Subsequent Western exegesis makes the sheep a figure of the faithful, the goats of schismatics (e.g., St Augustine, *Sermo,* 146, on John 21:16). St John Chrysostom follows the text more closely, noting that while all are 'mingled together' in the world, 'the division then shall be made with all exactness', but on the basis not of doctrinal purity but of charity or lack of charity to those in need. Chrysostom observes that the poor are said by Jesus to be his 'brethren' (v. 40), 'because they are lowly, because they are poor, because they are outcast', and should be received by us as brethren too (*Homily,* 79.1, on Matthew 25:31–41). The principle is given memorable fictional form in Tolstoy's 'What Men Live By' and is discussed in his book of essays *The Kingdom of God is Within You.*

Michael Wigglesworth's *The Day of Doom* (1662) commences with the midnight coming of Christ to a sinful world and the separation of goats, including people who have performed good works and lived moral lives, from the sheep, the repentant and humble sinners. Carlyle's *Inaugural Address,* 'The Reading of Books', adapts the text to the purposes of his own judgment: 'In short... I conceive that books are like men's souls – divided into sheep and goats.' In *Culture and Anarchy* Arnold inveighs against the Victorian predilection for large families, sarcastically upbraiding the 'British Philistine' who imagines that he 'would have only to present himself before the Great Judge with his twelve children, in order to be received among the sheep as a matter of right!' ('Sweetness and Light'). In modern literature the phrase often appears in humorous contexts. P.G. Wodehouse's *Uncle Fred in the Springtime* offers an example: '"I wish I had a brain like yours," said Lord Ickenham. "What an amazing thing. I suppose you could walk down a line of people, giving each of them a quick glance, and separate the sheep from the goats like shelling peas"' (chapter 8).

David L. Jeffrey
University of Ottawa

Seven Last Words

Known also as the Passion Sayings, Words (Sayings, Seven Words) from the Cross, and the Last Words of the Redeemer, the Seven Last Words are the utterances of Christ on the cross, as reported in the four gospels: (1) 'Father, forgive them; for they know not what they do' (Luke 23:34); (2) 'Verily I say unto thee, Today shalt thou be with me in paradise' (Luke 23:43); (3) 'Woman, behold thy son!... Behold thy mother!' (John 19:26–27); (4) 'Eli (Eloi), Eli, lama sabachthani?... My God, my God, why hast thou forsaken me?' (Matthew 27:46 and Mark 15:34); (5) 'I thirst' (John 19:28); (6) 'It is finished' (John 19:30); and (7) 'Father, into thy hands I commend my spirit' (Luke 23:46). This harmonized arrangement, now almost universally the focus of Good Friday observances, is a recent development, although public reading during the Easter 'octave' of the gospel narratives concerning the sufferings of Christ began early.

The 'Seven Last Words' are the subject of many noteworthy musical settings, including those of Graun (*Der Tod Jesus*, 1755), Haydn (*Seven Last Words,* first published in Vienna as *Seven Sonate*, c. 1802), Beethoven (*Mount of Olives*, 1803), Spohr (*Calvary*, 1833), Dubois (*The Seven Words of Christ*, 1867), Williams (*Gethsemane*, c. 1880), Gounod (*Redemption*, 1882), Stainer (*Crucifixion*, 1887), and Somervell (*The Passion of Christ*, 1914). Saverio Mercadante's oratorio *The Seven Last Words of Our Saviour,* published the year of James Joyce's birth, 1882, achieved literary prominence by occurring several times in Leopold Bloom's stream of consciousness during *Ulysses*.

Probably because of the comparatively late focus on the Seven Last Words themselves, English writers turned for inspiration before the last century to the entire passion, the crucifixion, the cross itself, Good Friday, or to specific words – mainly the second, third, sixth, and seventh. One of the earliest extant uses of an individual word is a 10th-century frontispiece of an Old English psalter manuscript, a drawing of Christ on the cross with his mother and John below (third word). Medieval poetry in general favoured the potentially dramatic second and third words, the only two mentioned in Rolle's 'Meditations on the Passion', but both the alliterative *Morte Arthure* and *Everyman* use the seventh word in Latin, *In manus tuus*, as the last words of their hero. The crucifixion passage of *Piers Plowman* alludes to the sixth word but differs from most other medieval works in referring also to the fifth word ('I thirst'), the first to be self-directed and the one Clemence Dane said in *Will Shakespeare* (1922) caused Queen Elizabeth to exclaim, 'This was a God for kings and queens of pride, and Him I follow.' The Wakefield Mystery Cycle's inclusion of all but the second word, substituting torturers for thieves, is significant (cf. Masefield's *Good Friday,* 1912, one of his five biblical plays modernizing the mystery plays). Marlowe's Faustus uses the sixth word blasphemously when signing away his soul, and Congreve's *Love for Love* employs it parodically to indicate the consummation of marriage.

Structural influences may appear in the seven-stress line of Thomas Halles' 'Passion of Our Lord', Milton's seven-line stanza in his unfinished ode on the passion, and Coleridge's seven-part design in *The Rime of the Ancient Mariner.*

Since the Reformation and the Counter-Reformation it has been the spirit rather than the format of the Seven Last Words which has caused theological debate, a controversy whose influence can be traced not only in literature but also in church music, architecture, and decoration. The emphasis of the Church during the Middle Ages was increasingly on the desolation and darkness of the Words from the Cross, the first three being interpreted as petition, penitence, and piety, and the last four as desolation (although not despair). An atmosphere of mystery was provided by the medieval cathedral for the continual re-enactment of the sacrifice of Christ's passion in the Mass, and the power of the priest to effect transubstantiation of the bread and wine to absolve the meditating laity was stressed. But Luther, in an attempt to recapture aspects of primitive Christianity, opposed the 'theology of the cross' to the established 'theology of glory' (phrases he coined), arguing that the hiddenness of God lies in the reversal of values the cross revealed – life through death, light through darkness, power through weakness. Calvin thought the desolate cry of the fourth word, interpreted by the early Church as a meditation on Psalm 22, to be a cry of dereliction consistent with the sense of abandonment by God felt by one assuming the sins of the world.

The Reformers read the 'Words from the Cross' as words of love summarizing the whole gospel, their sequence reflecting the gradual unfolding of God's will and purpose for the redemption of mankind in the seven stages of Jesus' life: incarnation, intercession, blessing, suffering, thirsting, reconciliation, and triumph. Picturing Christ's life as 'a continual Passion', Donne wrote in his last sermon (1630), entitled 'Death's Duel or a Consolation to the Soule, against the Dying Life, and Living Death of the Body'. 'That which we call life is but *Hebdomada mortium,* a weeke of deaths, seaven dayes, seaven periods of our life spent in dying, a dying seaven times over.'

Not until Good Friday observances instituted the harmonized arrangement of the Seven Last Words in the late 19th century does the direct influence of the whole sequence become noticeable again in English literature. During the 1880s Hopkins, by then a Jesuit priest, composed seven 'terrible' sonnets, which plumb the emotional depths of each utterance. Soon after, the Jesuit-trained Joyce wrote *Stephen Hero,* an early version of *A Portrait of the Artist as a Young Man,* in which Stephen, after hearing the 'Three Hours' Agony', a Good Friday liturgy in which the Seven Last Words figure prominently, wanders for three hours in agonized silence before deciding to 'regard himself seriously as a literary artist' (cf. Alice Munro's 'Age of Faith' episode in *Lives of Girls and Women*, 1971). At the end of his career Joyce characterized the artist in *Finnegans Wake* as a 'first to last alchemist... writing in seven divers stages of ink'.

Dylan Thomas, in Sonnet 8 of his sequence on the artist, 'Altarwise by Owl-light' (1953), paraphrases all the words (although not in order), beginning 'This was the crucifixion on the mountain, / Time's nerve in vinegar' and ending with 'Suffer the heaven's children through my heartbeat'. Echoing Thomas' last line in his own ('the year packs up / Like a tatty fairground, / That came for the children'), Ted Hughes adds to the poignancy of his ostensibly secular picture of the 'destructive reality we inhabit' in 'The Seven Sorrows' (1976) with a dim recollection of the Seven Last Words in their traditional order. Geoffrey Hill's 'LACHRIMAE or *Seven tears figured in seven passionate Pavans*' (*Tenebrae*, 1978) blends musical and literary tradition in a sonnet sequence: 'Lachrimae Verae', 'The Masque of Blackness', 'Martyrium', 'Lachrimae Coactae', 'Pavana Dolorosa', 'Lachrimae Antiquae Novae', 'Lachrima Amantis'.

Samuel Beckett seems indebted to the Seven Last Words in his insistence upon Good Friday as his birthday and his declaration that his 'birthmark' is his 'deathmark'. In the 'single sentence' of the spiritual biography gradually unfolding in his magnum opus, 'flesh becomes word' only to degenerate through a series of 'last words' into sound, 'a stain upon the silence'.

Virginia Moseley
University of Ottawa

Sower

Jesus' parable of the sower is found in all three synoptic gospels (Matthew 13:3–8; Mark 4:3–8; Luke 8:5–8; cf. also The Gospel of Thomas 82:3–13), and each time it is followed by an allegorical interpretation. Using the sowing metaphor common in the Old Testament prophets (e.g., Isaiah 55:10), Jesus describes in three steps how portions of the seed cast by a sower fall into places (by the wayside, on rocky ground, among the thorns) where they cannot yield grain. A fourth portion, which falls into good soil, is divided into three categories, yielding a hundredfold, sixtyfold, and thirtyfold. (Mark has the reverse order; Luke, only the hundredfold.) The interpretation identifies the seed as the word of the kingdom, which is received in the world in four ways: some do not understand it, some are superficial in accepting it, some are too occupied by worries and material desires to accept it, and some, the fourth group, accept it and bear fruit.

That Jesus himself here uses a figurative device, so making the parable effectively the 'literal' meaning of the text, seems to have made further allegorizations unnecessary to most Church Fathers – with the exception of the assignment of meaning to the various numbers given in Matthew 13:8 and 23. Numerous allegorical readings for the hundredfold, sixtyfold, and thirtyfold fruit appeared – for example, perseverance, perfection of good works, and belief in the Trinity respectively (Bede, *In Matthaei Evangelium Expositio*); or life in quiet peace, victory over minor temptations, and strong resistance against strong temptations (St Augustine, as cited in St Thomas Aquinas, *Expositio in Evangelium S. Matthaei*). The most popular interpretations were those of St Cyprian (who saw the hundredfold fruit realized in the martyrs and the sixtyfold in the virgins, *De habitu virginum*, 21), and St Jerome (who attributed the hundredfold to virginity, the sixtyfold to widowhood, and the thirtyfold to matrimony, *Adversus Jovinianum* 1.3). Jerome's view was adopted by many exegetes throughout the Middle Ages, and Wyclif still adhered to it (*In Omnes Novi Testamenti Libros*, 27d). Augustine, on the other hand, had his doubts (*Of Holy Virginity*, 46), and Martin Luther flatly called it 'utterly unchristian' (*Fastenpostille*, 1525; *Weimarer Ausgabe* 17.2, 154–61).

In his *Harmony of the Gospels,* Calvin warned against any contempt for the less excellent fruit – 'since the Lord himself in his mercy praises the inferior ones as being good soil'. Latimer used the parable to refute the Anabaptists (who denounced Anglican preaching as fruitless), explaining that 'the word of God, though it be most sincerely and purely preached, yet it taketh little fruit; yea, scant the fourth part doth prosper and increase' (Sermon 44; cf. a similar emphasis on the loss of much of the seed in Thomas Shepard, *The Sincere Convert,* 5).

Treatment of the parable in English literature seems to begin with the Middle English dialogue *Vices and Virtues* (Early English Text Society old series 89, 69), which uses it to illustrate Mark 10:17–27. Other works, for example, Dan Michel's *Ayenbite of Inwit* (Early English Text Society old series 23, 234), follow Jerome's allegorization. In Chaucer's *The Parson's Tale* Chaucer likewise refers to a girl's virginity as to 'thilke precious fruyt that the book clepeth the hundred fruyt' (*Canterbury Tales,* 10.869).

A brief reference is found in Shakespeare's *King John* (4.3.141), where the Bastard thinks he loses his way 'Among the thorns and dangers of this world'. Milton's sonnet 'On the Late Massacre in Piemont' commemorates the fate of the slain Waldenses by merging elements of the parable with Tertullian's image of the martyrs' blood being the seed of the Church (*Apology,* 50). He asks God to sow their blood and ashes over the Italy of the Pope (the 'triple Tyrant'), 'that from these may grow a hunder'd-fold...'. Thus he echoes Cyprian's interpretation.

John Bunyan's protagonist Christian, in *The Pilgrim's Progress,* elaborates, during a conversation with his companion Faithful, on the difference between talking and doing. Referring to the parable, he compares the sowing to the hearing of the gospel, which then has to result in fruit, not in talking only.

Jonathan Swift illustrates Matthew 13:22 by showing that a 'Man of Business' cannot even be reached by telling him the words of the parable: 'his Faculties are all gone off among Clients and Papers, thinking how to defend a bad Cause, or find Flaws in a good one; or, he weareth out the Time in drowsy Nods' (sermon 'Upon Sleeping in Church'). There are rather remote echoes of the parable in *Robinson Crusoe* ('The Journal: I Throw Away the Husks of Corn') and in Keats' 'Sleep and Poetry' (245, 255).

Washington Irving produced a secularized, Romantic version of the parable's action in his sketch 'Roscoe', in which a writer of genius is depicted as one of Nature's chance productions: 'She scatters the seeds of genius to the winds, and though some may perish among the stony places of the world, and some be choked by the thorns and brambles of early adversity, yet others will now and then strike root even in the clefts of the rock, struggle bravely up into sunshine, and spread over their sterile birthplace all the beauties of vegetation' (for other poetic twists of the parable cf. Byron, *Don Juan*, 16.6, and Ruskin, *The Bible of Amiens*, 1.30).

For Ruskin the good fruit is like charity which does not fail – after the blade of fresh religious feeling and the ear of well-formed purpose have passed away (*Letters*, 21 June 1861). Anthony Trollope, in *The New Zealander*, a book of social criticism, refers to the parable in suspecting that the seed sown in churches is one of religious hatred (chapter 6). When Donald Farfrae, in Hardy's *The Mayor of Casterbridge* (chapter 24), comments on a new seed drill, he contrasts this innovation with the traditional agricultural methods described in the parable: 'No more sowers flinging their seed about broadcast, so that some falls by the wayside and some among thorns, and all that. Each grain will go straight to its intended place, and nowhere else whatever!'

In an early sonnet ('See how Spring opens with disabling cold') G.M. Hopkins uses the parable's imagery to lament the belatedness of his learning the truth. In 'New Readings' (11–15) he leaves Christ's explanation of the parable aside and instead praises him by applying the rocks, thorns, and birds of the parable to episodes in Christ's life:

> From wastes of rock He brings
> Food for five thousand: on the thorns He shed
> Grains from His drooping Head;
> And would not have that legion of winged things
> Bear Him to heaven on easeful wings.

The song of the fairy people in Yeats' drama *The Land of Heart's Desire* describes how 'the lonely of heart is withered away' – which reflects the futile attempts of Father Hart to save Mary Bruin's soul. Gabriel in Baldwin's *Go Tell It on the Mountain* would have 'fallen by the wayside' had it not been for the support of Deborah.

The parable furnishes the 'central dramatic metaphor' in Flannery O'Connor's novel *The Violent Bear It Away* (J. May, *The Pruning Word*, 137). Protagonist Tarwater's granduncle has planted the seed of the word in his nephew Rayber and his grandnephew, neither of whom believes the granduncle has succeeded. The novel shows that Tarwater is not the 'rock' he believes himself to be, nor is Rayber successful in keeping the seed 'under control' (2.9). In John Updike's novel *Couples* (chapter 1), the seed fallen among the thorns – recognized by Piet Hanema in a freckle on Georgena's (his lover's) face – serves as an image of the fallen world of the town of Tarbox. The leader of the 'post-pill Paradise' created by the couples is Freddy Thorne, whose name may allude both to the parable and to Genesis 3:18 ('Thorns also and thistles shall it bring forth to thee') – the world after Eden.

Manfred Siebald
Johannes Gutenberg Universität, Mainz, Germany

Sparrow's Fall

Jesus, warning his disciples that they, like himself, would be persecuted, encouraged them not to lose heart: 'And fear not them which kill the body, but are not able to kill the soul: but rather fear him which is able to destroy both soul and body in hell. Are not two sparrows sold for a farthing? and one of them shall not fall on the ground without your Father. But the very hairs of your head are all numbered. Fear ye not therefore, ye are of more value than many sparrows' (Matthew 10:28–31).

In commentary by the early Fathers of the Church emphasis is placed upon the general injunction to trust in God's provident care. Calvin and other Reformation commentators pick up the image of the sparrow, Calvin adducing Luke's variant ('Are not five sparrows sold for two farthings?', Luke 12:6) to make the point that

> Christ asserts that each single creature is distinctly under God's hand and protection, that nothing may be left open to chance. For the will of God is opposed to contingency... In the nature of things itself, I agree there is contingency, but I say that nothing occurs by the blind turn of fortune where God's will holds the cords. (*Harmony of the Gospels*, 1.307)

In Shakespeare's *Hamlet*, when Horatio suggests postponing the duel with Laertes because of evil omens, Hamlet overrules him: 'Not a whit, we defy augury: there's a special providence in the fall of a sparrow. If it be now, 'tis not to come; if it be not to come, it will be now; if it be not now, yet it will come' (*Hamlet*, 5.2.221–24). This parody of Calvinist theological formulation on predestiny is prepared for earlier in the scene: 'There's a divinity that shapes our ends, / Rough-hew them how we will' (5.2.10–11), and relates the scene to ongoing theological debate about the operations of Providence.

In Alexander Pope's *Essay on Man* a view more like that of St Thomas Aquinas is reflected. According to Aquinas, 'All events that take place in this world, even those apparently fortuitous or casual, are comprehended in the order of divine Providence, on which fate depends.' To the question, 'If divine Providence be the direct cause of everything that happens in the world, at least of the good things, does it not then seem that everything must come about because of necessity?' Aquinas answers in the negative: 'The divine will cannot fail, but we cannot therefore ascribe necessity to all its effects' (Expositio, *Perihermenias*, 1.14). In Pope's theodicy:

> Heav'n from all creatures hides the book of Fate,
> All but the page prescrib'd, their present state;
> From brutes what men, from men what spirits know:
> Or who could suffer Being here below?...
> Oh blindness to the future! kindly giv'n,
> That each may fill the circle mark'd by Heav'n;
> Who sees with equal eye, as God of all,
> A hero perish, or a sparrow fall,
> Atoms or systems into ruin hurl'd,
> And now a bubble burst, and now a world.
> (*Essay on Man*, 1.3.77–80, 85–90)

In later tradition, as in Mark Twain's *The Mysterious Stranger*, the figure is usually employed in the context of special providence, personally conceived. When the poor old widow Ursula tells Satan that God will help her find the means to care for the stray kitten she wants to keep, Satan sarcastically asks, 'What makes you think so?' Ursula retorts heatedly, 'Because I know it. Not a sparrow falls to the ground without his seeing it.' In one of Emily Dickinson's poems, 'Mame never forgets her birds', her dead aunt is presented as an omniscient viewer of the mortal life of her children, noticing 'with cunning care' (her ongoing maternal scrutiny) 'if either of her "sparrows fall"'. David Jones simply adduces the passage as an instance of God's compassion for his creatures: 'They say he cared / when sparrows fall' (*Anathemata*, 8.240).

David L. Jeffrey
University of Ottawa

Strait and Narrow

Jesus indicated to his hearers in the Sermon on the Mount that the way of life he commanded was one of self-scrutiny and moral discernment: 'Enter ye in at the strait gate: for wide is the gate, and broad is the way, that leadeth to destruction, and many there be which go in thereat. Because strait is the gate, and narrow is the way, which leadeth unto life, and few there be that find it' (Matthew 7:13–14). This portion of the Sermon on the Mount is among the best known in Christian literary tradition. Commentary upon it in the *Sayings of the Fathers* of the Egyptian desert (6.81) pertains to vocation as a solitary, but in other respects differs little from that of St Benedict in his *Rule*:

> It is for the sake of obedience that they [i.e., those who love Christ] enter into the narrow way of life of which the Lord said: 'Narrow is the way that leads unto life' (Matthew 7:14, Vulgate). The 'narrowness' of the way is opposite to the broad way suggested by self-will and desire and pleasure: and they follow it by delighting to dwell in a community, to be subject to their abbot, and to follow the judgment of another. Such men live up to the practice of our Lord, who tells us: 'I come not to do mine own will, but the will of him that sent me' (John 6:36). (*Regula Magistri*, 5)

While such words reflect the typical orientation of monastic interpretation, St Augustine reads the passage with an eye to Christians in secular occupations, yet who desire spiritual progress in 'searching for and possessing wisdom, which is a tree of life'. In the contemplation of such wisdom the 'eye is led through all that precedes to a point where there may now be seen the narrow way and strait gate'. Augustine observes that Jesus does not say that 'his yoke is rough or his burden heavy'; it is in fact because 'few are willing to bring their own labours to an end', and instead spurn 'this easy yoke and light burden,' that they cannot squeeze through the 'narrow way which leads to life and the strait gate by which it is entered upon' (*De sermone Domini in Monte*, 2.33.77). The appeal of the broad road, suggests Augustine, is the appeal of popular and conventional 'wisdom'.

Sir John Clanvowe, a friend of Chaucer and sympathizer with Wyclif, takes up this point in his spiritual treatise *The Two Ways,* which draws its title and first section from Matthew 7:13–14. The broad way is attractive to many, says Clanvowe, because it maintains the illusion that all those set upon the broad way are part of a grand consensus, even as it promotes a contradiction, that each person is a law unto himself. Clanvowe defines the 'narghwe wey' as simply the keeping of God's commandments, 'which is wisdom', and the 'strait gate' which leads into this way as the fear of God, through which one is prompted to abandon sinful appetites and self-will. The broad way, conversely, is the breaking of God's laws, and leads to hell; the wide gate through which one enters it is a kind of studied carelessness about God's law in deference to self-will or pride (1–2).

In Shakespeare's *All's Well That Ends Well,* the clown Lavatch jokes about serving 'The Black Prince, sir, alias the Prince of Darkness, alias, the Devil', one who is 'sure, Prince of the world'. But he prefers another domicile: 'Let his nobility remain in —'s Court. I am for the house with the narrow gate, which I take to be too little for pomp to enter. Some that humble themselves may, but the many will be too chill and tender, and they'll be for the flowery way that leads to the broad gate and the great fire' (4.5.42–55). After the murder scene in *Macbeth*, a series of loud knocks at the gate of Macbeth's castle is responded to slowly by the thickheaded porter. Hearing the insistent knocking, he quips: 'But this place is too cold for Hell. I'll devil-porter it no further. I had thought to have let in some of all professions that go the primrose way to th' everlasting bonfire' (2.3.15–20; hence the phrase 'led down the primrose path').

Reformation writers tend to elaborate the main line of commentary but with particular emphasis falling on the carnal appetite and the emotions as they pertain to the 'way that leads to destruction'. Calvin, influenced by ascetic spiritual writers, finds that

Christ's teaching is at no point more opposed to the flesh; no-one ever makes any headway on this until he has learned to get a real grip on his emotions and on all his desires, so as to keep them in that narrow way which the heavenly Teacher prescribes for the restraint of our cravings. Men are so permissive towards themselves, so uncontrolled, and lax, that Christ here tells his disciples to get themselves onto the narrow and thorny road... That we should not be trapped by the delights of a licentious and dissolute life, and drift along at the impulse of the desire of the flesh, he declares that men are rushing to their death, when they prefer to enter by the spacious way and broad gate, rather than negotiate the straits which lead to life. How is it that men knowingly and willingly rush on, carefree, except that they cannot believe that they are perishing, when the whole crowd goes down at the same time. Contrarily, the small numbers of the faithful make many cowards, for it is hard to induce us to renounce the world, and to pattern our life upon the ways of a few. We think it unnatural to be forced out of the generality, as if we were not part of the human race. (*Harmony of the Gospels*, on Matthew 7:13–14)

Calvin's exegesis offers a pertinent introduction to Bunyan's *Pilgrim's Progress,* in which, though almost dissuaded by Mr Worldly Wiseman in the 'Town of Carnal Policy', Christian arrives at last at the 'Strait' or 'Wicket-gate' over which is written: 'Knock and it shall be opened unto you' (Matthew 7:8). Good-Will bids Christian enter, and because he is contrite for his sins, he is able to set upon the 'narrow way... cast up by the Patriarchs, Prophets, Christ, and his Apostles, and... is as straight as a Rule can make it'. He finds many temptations to leave this path for ways 'Crooked, and Wide' but eventually arrives at the gate of his destination, that of the Celestial City, over which is written in gold letters 'Blessed are they that do his commandments, that they may have right to the Tree of Life; and may enter in through the Gates into the City' (cf. Revelation 22:14).

Although George Herbert identifies 'the narrow way and little gate' with his baptism as an infant ('H. Baptisme 2'), the typical usage of evangelical and Puritan writers is to identify the strait gate with adult conversion. For Matthew Henry, 'Conversion and regeneration are *the gate,* by which we enter into this way, in which we begin a life of faith and serious godliness; out of a state of sin into a state of grace we must pass, by the new birth, John iii.3, 5. This is a strait gate, hard to find, and hard to get through; like a passage between two rocks, 1 Sam. xiv.4.' Once through the gate and set upon the narrow way, Henry says, 'we must be strict and circumspect in our conversation' and expect that 'we must swim against the current', for 'it is easier to set a man against all the world than against himself, yet this must be in conversion' (*Commentary* 5.92–93). This is the theme also of John Wesley's address on the passage (Sermon 31 in the 1747 *Sermons on Several Occasions*), in which he defines the 'inseparable properties' of each way, underscoring the need to strive for a 'separated' life in pursuit of the narrow way.

Such striving itself could take on carnal forms, and in the 19th century Dickens indicates in *Little Dorrit* something of the abuse of the distinction which had come about in hypocritical and moralizing preaching, when Clennam proves to have profited little from the rigid reiterations of a woman ('strait', 'narrow', 'far straiter and narrower') who herself had been 'brought up strictly, and straitly' on a Bible bound in the 'straitest boards' (1.3.30; 2.30.753). It is this kind of exposition as much as Wesley's which Samuel Butler reflects when, in *The Way of All Flesh,* he has the Rev. Gideon Hawke preach to the followers of Charles Simeon at Cambridge: 'My dear young friends, strait is the gate, and narrow is the way which leadeth to Eternal Life, and few there be that find it. Few, few, few, for he who will not give up ALL for Christ's sake, has given up nothing.'

The phrase has become a cliché in modern literature and as such appears in diverse contexts. For Ruskin there is no value in 'grumbling provided always you have entered in at the strait gate' (*Praeterita*, 3). Dean Inge says in 'The Idea of Progress' – conversely to his source, one suspects – that 'there will never be a crowd gathered round this gate; "few there be that find it"'. Theodore Dreiser, on the other hand, offers self-conscious reflection on the theme in revivalist preaching in both *American Tragedy* and *The Financier;* the protagonist of the latter novel 'in his younger gallivantings about places of ill repute, and his subsequent occasional variations from the straight and narrow path... has learned much of the curious resources of immorality' (chapter 20). In England, Aldous Huxley complains of a residue of Puritan morality associated with contemporary social values: 'Today a man is free to have any or no religion; about the Established Church and its divinities he can say almost anything he likes. But woe to him if he deviates from the narrow path of sexual orthodoxy' (*Music at Night*, 'To the Puritan All Things are Impure'). Upton Sinclair's *Wide is the Gate* (1943) is one of an eleven-volume series of novels warning of the drift of modern political ethics and destiny.

David L. Jeffrey
University of Ottawa

Suffer the Little Children

Once when Jesus was teaching the multitudes, several of his audience brought him little children to bless, asking that he 'put his hands on them and pray'. The disciples rebuked them for what they regarded as an intrusion, perhaps, as Calvin suggests, because they thought it was 'beneath his dignity to receive children' (*Harmony of the Gospels*, 2.251). But Jesus intervened, saying, 'Suffer the little children to come unto me, and forbid them not: for of such is the kingdom of God. Verily I say unto you, Whosoever shall not receive the kingdom of God as a little child, he shall not enter therein' (Mark 10:14–15; cf. Matthew 19:13–15; Luke 18:15–17).

Calvin saw the text as a ground for opposing the Anabaptists on the issue of infant baptism. Matthew Henry draws the inference that 'little children may be brought to Christ as needing, and being capable of receiving, blessings from him, and having an interest in his intercession'. 'We cannot do better for our children,' he adds, 'than to commit them to the Lord Jesus, to be wrought upon, and prayed for, by him.' Yet 'we can but beg a blessing for them, it is Christ only that can command the blessing' (*Commentary*, 5.271–72). Henry, while he does not mention baptism, sees in the narrative the basic principle of covenant theology: 'The promise is to you and to your children. I will be a God to thee and thy seed.' W.M. Hutchins' hymn (1850), 'When mothers of Salem their children brought to Jesus', is a sentimentalized rendering of the passage, with 'suffer little children to come unto me' as a recurrent refrain.

In his essay 'Jonathan Edwards', Oliver Wendell Holmes represents Edwards as saying that children who are 'out of Christ' are 'young vipers'. Holmes asks: 'Is it possible that Edwards read the text mothers love so well, "Suffer the little *vipers* to come unto me, and forbid them not, for of such is the kingdom of God"?' Swinburne's poem 'Of Such is the Kingdom of Heaven' concludes sarcastically:

> Earth's creeds may be seventy times seven
> And blood have defiled each creed:
> If such be the kingdom of heaven,
> It must be heaven indeed.

In general the text has suffered more than been suffered by 20th-century writers. Aldous Huxley has little patience with the catechetical sensibility: 'Dear priceless creatures! Of such is the kingdom of our anglican heaven' (*Music at Night,* 'Foreheads Villainous Low'). In Joyce's *A Portrait of the Artist as a Young Man,* Stephen reflects in his temporary agony of conscience that 'It was better never to have sinned, to have remained always a child, for God loved little children and suffered them to come to Him. It was a terrible and a sad thing to sin' (chapter 3). Later, however, when his sadness has been banished by other emotions and his choice, *'non serviam',* declared, Stephen, Temple, and Cranly can only disdain the use of the passage by Glynn the teacher, who says, 'I suffer little children to come unto me.' Temple, recurring to the New Testament source of the phrase, retorts, 'If Jesus suffered the children to come why does the church send them all to hell if they die unbaptized?' (chapter 5).

David L. Jeffrey
University of Ottawa

Treasures Upon Earth

The phrase 'treasures upon earth' derives from Christ's Sermon on the Mount: 'Lay not up for yourselves treasures upon earth, where moth and rust doth corrupt, and where thieves break through and steal' (Matthew 6:19). 'Treasures upon earth' is often contrasted with the parallel phrase 'treasures in heaven', which is somewhat more common in English. In addition to several direct allusions, many authors refer indirectly to 'treasures upon earth' by citing the phrases following it – 'where moth and rust doth corrupt' or 'where thieves break through and steal'.

St Augustine, in his *Sermo*, 60.7, emphasizes that the passage affords counsel 'for keeping, not for losing', and ensures 'not a wasting, but a saving'. He draws an analogy with prudent husbandry:

> Thou puttest wheat in the low ground; and thy friend comes, who knows the nature of the corn and the land, and instructs thy unskilfulness, and says to thee, 'What hast thou done? Thou hast put the corn in the flat soil, in the lower land; the soil is moist; it will all rot, and thou wilt lose thy labour.' Thou answerest, 'What then must I do?' 'Remove it,' he says, 'into the higher ground'... Behold the Lord thy God when he giveth thee counsel touching thine heart... Lift up, saith he, thine heart to heaven, that it rot not in the earth. It is his counsel, who wisheth to preserve thy heart, not to destroy it.

Although St Thomas More mentions 'treasures in earth' in *Dialogue of Comfort* (3.15.1232E), Spenser is the first English poet to refer frequently to the phrase. He writes in 'An Hymne in Honour of Beautie' of 'That wondrous paterne, wheresoere it bee, whether in earth layd up in secret store' (37) and refers indirectly to earthly treasure three times in *The Faerie Queene*:

> The second was as Almner of the place...
> The grace of God he layd up still in store...
> And had he lesse, yet some he would give to the pore.
> (1.10.38.1, 6, 9)

> What secret place (quoth he) can safely hold
> So huge a masse, and hide from heavens eye?
> Or where hast thou thy wonne [riches], that so much gold
> Thou canst preserve from wrong and robbery? (2.7.20.1–4)

> For feare least Force of Fraud should unaware
> Breake in, and spoile the treasure there in gard. (2.7.25.3–4)

Marlowe writes in *The Massacre at Paris* of 'all the wealth and treasure of the world' (1163). Pericles in Shakespeare's play of that name contemplates his demise and bequeaths 'My riches to the earth from whence they came' (1.1.52). Herbert hymns in his *Valdesso* the 'word of God, as their Joy, and Crowne, and their Treasure on earth' (34). Milton, in *The Reason of Church Government*, writes of his determination to speak freely about his religious opinions: 'For me, I have determined to lay up as the best treasure and solace of a good old age... the honest liberty of free speech from my youth' (1.804.9).

The 19th century saw several uses of the 'treasures upon earth' theme. Blake asks in 'Visions of the Daughters of Albion'. 'Does not the eagle scorn the earth and despise the treasures beneath?' (149). Wordsworth writes in 'Ode 1815', 'And well might it beseem that mighty Town / Into whose bosom earth's best treasures flow' (46–47).

The phrase has become common enough that a biblically oriented poet such as Christina Rossetti can allude to the passage in at least four places: 'Three Nuns' begins by quoting the verse from Matthew, then laments that 'With foolish riches of this world / I have bought treasure where / Nought perisheth.' In 'Testimony' Rossetti puts the verse in metre: 'Our treasures moth and rust corrupt, / Or thieves break through and steal.' 'Days of Vanity' includes the lines

> A scanty measure,
> Rust-eaten treasure,
> Spending that nought buyeth,
> Moth on the wing,
> Toil unprofiting.

There is a further indirect reference in 'Old and New' in the lines 'Rust in thy gold, a moth is in thine array.'

In America Thoreau focused the allusion on the burden of owning property. Those who devote their lives to acquiring wealth, he says, 'are employed, as it says in an old book, laying up treasures which moth and rust will corrupt and thieves break through and steal' (*Walden*, 51). Melville's *Moby Dick* includes a more extensive allusion which plays on the multiple meanings of one of the words in the biblical verse. Captain Bildad offers Ishmael a very small share of the whaling profits, called a 'lay'; mumbling from his Bible, Bildad says,

'"Lay not up for yourselves treasures upon the earth, where moth...
and rust do corrupt, but lay –" Ishmael thinks to himself, "Lay
indeed... and such a lay! The seven hundred and seventy-seventh!
Well, old Bildad, you are determined that I, for one, shall not lay up
many lays, here below, where moth and rust do corrupt."'

In the 20th century, Shaw twists Matthew's verses ironically in
his preface to *Major Barbara*: 'Let the deserving lay up for himself, not
treasures in heaven, but horrors in hell upon earth' (215). Father
Arnall alludes to the earth–heaven contrast in a passage from his
famous sermon in *A Portrait of the Artist as a Young Man*: 'How they will
rage and fume to think that they have lost the bliss of heaven for the
dross of earth' (chapter 3).

Steven C. Walker
Brigham Young University

Turn the Other Cheek

In his Sermon on the Mount Jesus reminded his audience of the *lex
talionis* provisions of Mosaic law – 'an eye for an eye, and a tooth for
a tooth' (Matthew 5:38), and then added,

> But I say unto you, That ye resist not evil: but whosoever
> shall smite thee on thy right cheek, turn to him the other
> also. And if any man will sue thee at the law, and take away
> thy coat, let him have thy cloak also. And whosoever shall
> compel thee to go a mile, go with him twain. Give to him
> that asketh thee, and from him that would borrow of thee
> turn not thou away. Ye have heard that it hath been said,
> Thou shalt love thy neighbour and hate thine enemy. But I
> say unto you, Love your enemies, bless them that curse you,
> do good to them that hate you, and pray for them which
> despitefully use you and persecute you. (vv. 39–44)

The basic precepts of Christian non-violent resistance and
'overcoming evil with good' are in this passage set over against not
only Mosaic law but also universal notions of revenge and justice.

St Augustine observes that here the 'incomplete but by no
means severe, but rather comparatively merciful [Mosaic] justice is

carried to perfection by him who came to fulfil the law, not to destroy it'. He goes on to say that 'there are still two intervening steps which he has left to be understood': the first of these would be a system of retribution in which the punishment was more modest than the crime, the second in which there would be no retribution at all. Not even the second of these, however, reaches the quality of mercy which Jesus teaches: 'Therefore he does not say "But I say unto you that you are not to return evil for evil", though even that would be a great precept. Rather he says "that ye resist not evil," so that not only are you not to pay back what may have been inflicted on you, but you are not even to resist other inflictions' (*De sermone Domini in Monte,* 1.19.57). Similarly, to 'go the second mile' is for Augustine a metaphor for bearing twice the weight of an imposition, and to bear the burden 'with tranquil mind' (1.19.61).

All through the history of Christian literature these words have been found a 'hard saying', obtaining evasive commentary from theologians and sometimes trivializing quotations from others. In the 14th century, however, a brief anonymous epistle, paraphrased in Walter Hilton's *Ladder of Perfection* and possibly authored by him, reiterates the challenge of the passage straightforwardly, insisting that Jesus' standard for dealing with enemies is made most clear in his own relationship with Judas. Despite his knowledge that Judas would betray him, says the writer, Jesus loved him and privileged him as much as any of the other disciples (1.69); Christians ought to do likewise. In his version of 'The Lamentations of Jeremy', Donne's free translation of Tremellius is 'He gives his cheekes to whosoever will / Strike him, and so he is reproched still' (3.221–22); there is no guarantee of temporal reward for Christlike forbearance.

In later times it may be, as Thoreau suggests in *Walden,* that 'the law to do as you would be done by [cf. Matthew 7:12] fell with less persuasiveness on the ears of those who, for their part, did not care how they were done by, who loved their enemies after a new fashion' ('Economy'). In his 'Former Inhabitants' chapter the intrepid outdoorsman reduces the allusion to a quip: 'When the frost had smitten me on the cheek, heathen as I was, I turned to it the other also.' In Ambrose Bierce's *Can Such Things Be?* an entrepreneurial gambler recounts his victory over a 'mulish' opponent: '...after

turning the other cheek seventy and seven times [cf. Matthew 18:22]
I doctored the dice so he didn't last forever' ('The Haunted Valley').
Goldsmith's observation that 'it was more than human benevolence
that first taught us to bless our enemies' (*The Vicar of Wakefield*,
chapter 17) indicates something of the difficulty of authentic
Christian behaviour. 'I know it is my duty "to pray for them that
despitefully use me,"' writes Twain with tongue in cheek in *The
Innocents Abroad*; 'and therefore, hard as it is, I shall still try to pray for
those fumigating, macaroni-stuffing organ grinders' (chapter 20). The
experience of a practical demonstration – even if fleeting – comes as
a shock in Wells' *Tono-Bungay*:

> 'You sneak!' I said, and smacked his face hard forthwith.
> 'Now then,' said I.
> He started back, astonished and alarmed. His eyes met
> mine, and I saw a sudden gleam of resolution. He turned his
> other cheek to me.
> ''It it,' he said; ''it it. I'll forgive you.' (1.2)

David L. Jeffrey
University of Ottawa

Unpardonable Sin

Of the three gospel texts which speak of the unpardonable sin –
Matthew 12:31–32; Mark 3:28–29; Luke 12:10 – the first has been
the focus of most exegetical and literary commentary:

> Wherefore I say unto you, All manner of sin and blasphemy
> shall be forgiven unto men: but the blasphemy against the
> Holy Ghost shall not be forgiven unto men. And whosoever
> speaketh a word against the Son of man, it shall be forgiven
> him: but whosoever speaketh against the Holy Ghost, it shall
> not be forgiven him, neither in this world, neither in the
> world to come.

This hardest of Christ's sayings is directed at the Pharisees, who have
ascribed to Beelzebub's power Jesus' healing of a dumb and blind
demoniac. Pictured as perversely engaged in internecine war (see

Fitzmyer, *The Gospel According to Luke, X–XV*, 921), the Pharisees, who call good evil, 'gouge out their own eyes' and so commit the unpardonable folly of 'moral suicide' (*Interpreter's Bible* 7.400). The idea of an unforgivable sin appears also in Hebrews 6:4–8; 10:28–31 (where it seems to be apostasy from the Christian faith) and possibly in 1 John 5:16–17, which refers to a 'sin unto death'.

The early Fathers vary considerably in their interpretations of blasphemy against the Holy Ghost. St Thomas Aquinas (*Summa Theologica*, 2–2a, q.14, a.1) provides a useful summary of readings in his review of the three meanings traditionally assigned to the nature of this sin. The first, with which the body of patristic commentary generally agrees, distinguishes between sin against the Son of man, or Christ in his human nature, and blasphemy against the Son of God, or Christ in his divine nature. As an act of deliberately willed unbelief in the one empowered to forgive, the sin is by its very nature unpardonable. The second meaning, advanced principally by St Augustine, is of final impenitence or despair as a result of contempt, obstinacy, and pride (Augustine, *De correctione donatistarum*, 11.48–50). The sin is unforgivable because it is not repented of. A third interpretation takes blasphemy against the Holy Ghost to mean a considered rejection of the goodness appropriated to that person of the Trinity (cf. Augustine, *Contra litteras Petiliani Donatistae*, 2.62.139–40). Aquinas pictures this sinner as suffering from an incurable illness yet rejecting the very food and medicine necessary for healing. Fundamental to all three interpretations – and here Aquinas follows St Albert the Great – is the notion that 'to sin against the Holy Ghost is to take pleasure in the malice of sin for its own sake.'

Although reference to the unpardonable sin is not prominent in the medieval literary tradition, a remarkable discussion of the subject occurs in *Piers Plowman* (B.17.135–50), where the dreamer is instructed by Charity about the nature of the Trinity. Father, Son, and Holy Spirit are likened to the fist, fingers, and palm of a hand: 'He who blasphemes against the Holy Ghost pricks God as it were in the palm; so whoever sins against the Holy Ghost injures God in the place where he grips and deliberately murders his grace.' Among the specific sins by which the Holy Spirit is blasphemed, says Charity, the most heinous is 'murder of a good man': 'this is the worst – to destroy deliberately... that which Christ bought so dearly' (Goodridge trans.).

Literary interest in the unpardonable sin increased dramatically in the Reformation period. The reprobate who has sinned against the Holy Spirit is a frequent figure in Puritan literature. Often implied in Renaissance drama (notably Marlowe's *Doctor Faustus*), the question of the blasphemy against the Holy Ghost is addressed directly and at length in John Bunyan's *Grace Abounding to the Chief of Sinners,* where the autobiographer's tormented cogitations regarding the nature of the mysterious offence and his guilt or innocence come to rest in his faith. In *The Pilgrim's Progress,* Christian encounters, in Interpreter's House, a Man of Despair locked in an iron cage – past hope of repentance because of wilful blasphemy against the Holy Ghost: 'I have grieved the Spirit, and he is gone...; I have provoked God to anger, and he has left me; I have so hardened my heart, that I *cannot* repent.'

In the latter part of the 18th century, both Christopher Smart and William Cowper explicitly refer to the sin against the Holy Ghost. In the eyes of the former, it is 'INGRATITUDE' (*Jubilate Agno*, B.2.306). For Cowper, the nature of the blasphemy eludes definition: tortured by a sense of indefinable guilt, he sees in Milton's Satan a reflection of himself (J. Quinlan, *William Cowper: A Critical Life*, 1953; rpt. 1970, 181), and his final poem, 'The Castaway', ends on a note of despair. Ann Radcliffe's *The Mysteries of Udolpho* seems specific in taking the unpardonable sin to mean 'the habit of gaming': the unfeeling and unrepentant arch-villain Montoni, kin to the diabolic schemers of Renaissance drama, treats people as pawns, taking pleasure in wrecking the lives of others (2.3). But this pseudo-medieval fiction also appears to consider unforgivable a long and deeply repented premeditated murder (4.15).

Black magic, fratricide, incest, matricide, and malicious cunning in general are some of the unpardonable sins in Matthew Gregory Lewis' *The Monk,* where, in an ending fraught with allusions to Prometheus and Marlowe's Faustus, the proud and luxurious Ambrosio dies defying the heavens.

For all his vagaries regarding his incurable disease, Byron more clearly articulates 'the Fatal Man of the Romantics' (see M. Praz, *The*

Romantic Agony, 1933; 1956, 61). Sick with 'some strange perversity of thought', the Byronic solitary confounds 'good and ill' (*Lara*, 1.18.340, 335) and repeats with Milton's Satan that the self-sufficient mind 'would make a hell of heaven' (*Manfred*, 4.1.73). He is bound, out of pride, to slay 'that which he loved' and die 'unpardon'd' (*Manfred*, 2.2.185–86). By contrast, George Borrow's popular tale of a Methodist preacher in Wales who repents, having committed what he believes is 'pechod Ysprydd Glan', deliberately avoids probing into the nature of that sin (*Lavengro*, chapters 74–79).

In 19th-century American literature, Hawthorne provides the fullest gallery of unpardonable sinners. Chillingworth in *The Scarlet Letter*, Dr Giacomo Rappacini in 'Rappacini's Daughter', the title character of 'Ethan Brand' (initially published as 'The Unpardonable Sin'), and Digby in 'The Man of Adamant: An Apologue' are among Hawthorne's characters suffering from a 'separation of the intellect from the heart' (*The American Notebooks of Nathaniel Hawthorne*, ed. R. Stewart, 1932, 106), or 'the self-destruction of the heart' (S. Dwight, 'Hawthorne and the Unpardonable Sin', in *Studies in the Novel* 2, 1970, 455). They sin by treating others merely as objects of aesthetic amusement or scientific inquiry. Chillingworth, for example, sifts Dimmesdale's soul 'for the art's sake' (*The Scarlet Letter*, chapter 10). James E. Miller, Jr, takes Hawthorne's conception of the unpardonable sin to embrace narcissists and Promethean intellectuals in general and reckons Melville's Ahab such a blasphemer ('Hawthorne and Melville: The Unpardonable Sin', *Publications of the Modern Language Association of America* 70, 1955, 91–114). John Greenleaf Whittier's 'The Answer' summarizes the plight of the moral suicide in words which recall Bunyan's 'iron cage':

> What if thine eye refuse to see,
>   Thine ear of Heaven's free welcome fail,
> And thou a willing captive be,
>   Thyself thine own dark jail? (st. 15)

Like Hawthorne's unpardonable sinners, Dr Sloper of Henry James' *Washington Square* uses people as objects for play and experimentation. His creed: knowledge for its own sake, art for art's sake. D.H. Lawrence's reading of the unpardonable sin invites broad comparison with Hawthorne's: the abstracting intellect's want of reverence for the life of the flesh or instinctive consciousness, 'the most essential self in us', constitutes 'sinning against the Holy Ghost' ('God and the Holy Ghost').

Camille R. La Bossière
University of Ottawa

Unprofitable Servant

The parable of the unprofitable servant is found in Matthew 25:14–30, with a variant version in Luke 19:12–27. Before travelling into a far country, a wealthy man distributes his money among his servants. In the Matthean version he gives five talents ('a large sum of money', *Interpreter's Dictionary of the Bible*) to the first, two talents to the second, and one to the third. After his return he finds that by shrewd investment the first two servants have doubled the sums entrusted to them. He praises each of them for his stewardship ('Well done, good and faithful servant') and promises to reward them: 'Enter thou into the joy of thy lord.' The third servant, who has hidden his talent in the earth, is called wicked and slothful and is scolded for not having at least put the money out on interest. His talent is given to the first servant – 'For unto every one that hath shall be given; and he shall have abundance' (v. 29) – and the 'unprofitable servant' is cast 'into outer darkness', where 'there shall be weeping and gnashing of teeth' (v. 30).

The Matthean context suggests that the lord is Christ and the reckoning is the Last Judgment, the emphasis being on the obligation to be active during the time of Christ's absence.

The Fathers interpreted the money as the 'office of the Episcopate'. St Augustine admonished spiritual leaders to 'look after the salvation of all your household with all vigilance' (*Sermones*, 44; cf. his *De doctrina Christiana*, 'Preface', 8). It could also be seen as the teaching of the gospel (e.g., St Jerome, *In Evangelium Matthaei*) or as the faculty to understand the various meanings of scripture (e.g., Origen, *Tractate 33* on the Gospel of Matthew). By analogy the five talents came also to mean the five human senses or 'each person's ability, whether in the way of protection, or in money, or in teaching, or in what thing soever of the kind' (St John Chrysostom, *Homily on Matthew,* 78.3). The enhancement of the talents consequently meant a deeper understanding of the scriptures (Jerome) or the teaching of them by word and deed (St Gregory, *Homily in Matthaeum,* 9), the 'profit' (v. 27) of which was the good works of the hearers.

The burying of the one talent was seen by Gregory as the misappropriation of a heavenly gift for earthly purposes – a dictum which was later applied by Wyclif to corrupt spiritual leaders of his times, who worked for their own 'honour, advantage, and profit' (*In Omnes Novi Testamenti Libros,* 47b). The thought that God receives his own with usury was taken to be a sign of God's incomprehensible grandeur (Augustine, in *Confessions* 1.4, calls him 'never greedy, yet still demanding profit on his loans') and provoked explanations by later exegetes such as St Thomas Aquinas, who stated that God only demands that good of people which he himself has sown in them (*Summa Theologica* 2–2, q. 62.4 ad 3). The hardness of the lord has usually been seen as irrelevant to the central message (see Calvin, *Harmony of the Gospels*).

Calvin opposed what he called a Roman Catholic teaching – that the unequal distribution of gifts is a matter of personal merit. Later exegetes used the parable to teach the acceptance of God's will and of one's station in life (e.g., Samuel Clarke, *Sermons,* 6). The narrative was also used by English churchmen to denounce the Puritan emigrants as unprofitable servants and America as the 'outer darkness' – a thought which Cotton Mather, in *Magnalia Christi Americana* (Introduction, sect. 3), sharply rejects.

The Middle English dialogue *Vices and Virtues* (Early English Text Society old series 89, 17) follows Gregory in likening the talents (*besantes*) to the five bodily senses: God expects humans to put them to use (cf. a similar use in a sermon collected in Early English Text Society old series 209, 39–40). In *Piers Plowman* (C.9.247–59) Hunger paraphrases the parable of the 'wrecche', illustrating to Piers his contention that the Bible reproves idleness. In another place, Imaginatif quotes verses 21 and 23 to prove that God will not always reject unbaptized people but that he rewards those who are true beyond what he promises (C. 15.214).

St Thomas More uses the slothful servant's fear as an example of pusillanimity and concludes that 'all this fear commeth by the devilles dryft, wherin he taketh occasion of the fayntnes of our good & sure trust in God' (*Dialogue of Comfort Against Tribulation,* 2.13). In Shakespeare's *Twelfth Night,* the Clown playfully refers to verse 29 and wishes that 'God give them wisdom that have it: and those that are fools, let them use their talents' (1.5.14–16). The Duke's opening speech in *Measure for Measure* (1.1.29–40) echoes the parable and, indeed, the play's basic dramatic situation resembles that of the parable.

George Herbert's poem 'Redemption' refers to Luke's version of the parable but reverses the part which speaks of Christ's going to heaven and returning to earth (Luke 19:12). He pictures Christ as a 'rich Lord' who has left heaven to go 'About some land, which he had dearly bought / Long since on earth, to take possession'. Milton's famous 'Sonnet 19' sees the exercise of the poet's 'one Talent which is death to hide' as impeded by his blindness. But he arrives at the assurance that the will to serve his Maker may be enough: 'They also serve who only stand and waite.' John Bunyan uses the parable to account for his call to the ministry (*Grace Abounding,* sect. 270), and Dryden sees it fulfilled in the charitable life of the Countess of Abingdon: 'Of her five talents, other five she made; / Heav'n, that had largely giv'n, was largely paid' ('Eleonora', 24–25; for further laudatory uses see Samuel Johnson's 'On the Death of Dr Robert Levet' and Robert Southey's 'A Vision of Judgment', 7).

Fielding twice alludes to the parable in *Joseph Andrews* (1.3 and 2.8), suggesting that one should not 'lament his Condition in this World' but rather endeavour 'to improve his Talent, which was all required of him'. Swift's sermon 'On Mutual Subjection' stresses that 'No Man is without his Talent' and ironically observes that worldly kings 'have often most abominable Ministers and Stewards, and those generally the vilest, to whom they entrust the most Talents'. Cowper considers the question of whether life is 'an intrusted talent, or a toy' to be one of the marks distinguishing humans from animals ('Retirement', 650). In 'Table Talk' (546) he warns against the preoccupation with 'subjects mean and low,' since 'Neglected talents rust into decay' (cf. his allusion to the parable in 'The Task', 2.725, and his ironic reference in 'Conversation', 425).

The Romantic theory of art is evidenced in Blake's *Jerusalem* (pl. 77), where the poet equates the talent 'which it is a curse to hide' with 'Mental Studies and Performances'; elsewhere the talent represents his artistic gifts ('Letter to Thomas Butts', 16 August 1803). Shelley's allusion to Matthew 25:24 in 'Song: To the Men of England' is to alert the poor labourers of England to their unjust social situation: 'The seed ye sow, another reaps;... Sow seed, – but let no tyrant reap;...' (for other social applications of the parable cf. Ruskin, 'A Joy For Ever', 2.115–20; *Fors Clavigera*, 5.53.8 and 6.68.2, where he clearly distinguishes between God and the image of the 'hard man' in v. 24).

When Carlyle's narrator in *Sartor Resartus* (2.7) establishes a solidarity of sinners by calling all people unprofitable servants, he does so in order to exculpate Professor Teufelsdröckh from being a wicked infidel. In Charlotte Brontë's *Shirley* (chapter 23), Rose Yorke has a discussion with Caroline Helstone about whether change is necessary to happiness. She insists, 'Better to try all things and find all empty than to try nothing and leave your life a blank. To do this is to commit the sin of him who buried his talent in a napkin – despicable sluggard!'

Dickens refers to the parable in *David Copperfield,* chapter 9, where David calls his nurse Peggotty 'that good and faithful servant... unto whom my childish heart is certain that the Lord will one day say: "Well done."' In similar fashion Abel Magwitch, the escaped convict in *Great Expectations,* thanks his protégé 'Pip' for helping him to leave England: 'Faithful dear boy, well done. Thankye, thankye!' (chapter 54). Further allusions can be found in Joyce's *Ulysses* (Vintage, 1961, 421) and Beckett's *Waiting for Godot* (Faber, 33).

In early American literature Michael Wigglesworth's *The Day of Doom* (st. 60) makes use of the parable's eschatological implications. Another Puritan divine, Edward Taylor, made verse 21 the motto of three of his *Preparatory Meditations* (1.47–49), in which he promises God to use and to improve his poetic and musical gifts.

In his essay 'Spiritual Laws' R.W. Emerson (who also alludes to the parable in 'Prudence' and 'Address to Kossuth') uses 'gnashing of the teeth' as a synonym for self-inflicted intellectual and moral complications in a person's life (for a similarly hyperbolical use of this expression, cf. Stephen Crane's poem 'I weep and I gnash', in *War is Kind*, 97).

Melville's narrator in *Pierre* scorns the 'downright matter-of-fact' world which does not recognize the spiritual meaning of verse 29 but follows the passage in a rather materialistic manner by 'giving unto him who already hath more than enough, still more of the superfluous article, and taking away from him who hath nothing at all, even that which he hath...'. In his usual ambiguous way he goes on to suggest that if God really meant this, 'then is the truest book in the world a lie' (18.2). When Elmer Gantry, Sinclair Lewis' infamous evangelist, alludes to the parable in one of his sermons, it is to convince businessmen of the 'cash value of Christianity' (*Elmer Gantry*, 11.6). In Faulkner's *As I Lay Dying*, on the other hand, Anse Bundren reverses verse 29, claiming that in heaven God will create equality among people by giving to them who have not and taking from them who have.

Harry, the dying protagonist of Hemingway's 'The Snows of Kilimanjaro', accuses himself of destroying his writing talent 'by not using it... by laziness, by sloth, and by snobbery...'. Randall Jarrell says of the American conquerors of the Pacific islands that they, who 'hid their single talent in Chicago, / Des Moines, Cheyenne, are buried with it here', apparently equating 'talent' with life in general ('The Dead in Melanesia').

The question of God-given talents has an important place at the beginning of John Updike's *Rabbit, Run*. There, in a children's television programme, the way to happiness is described as learning to understand one's talents, something which is quite out of keeping with the small-town world in which 'Rabbit' Angstrom lives. The parable figures even more largely in Updike's *The Centaur*. There George Caldwell, the frustrated science teacher, believes that he has no talents, but as the man with two talents, who 'didn't get sore at the man with five', he comforts himself by saying, 'Some have it and some don't. But everybody has something, even if it's just being alive' (chapter 4). According to his family's sardonic comment, his one talent is 'to think up some new way of getting sympathy' (chapter 8).

Manfred Siebald
Johannes Gutenberg Universität, Mainz, Germany

Wheat and Tares

Jesus' parable of the wheat and the tares (Matthew 13:24–30) concerns a man who sows wheat in his field. When all are asleep, his enemy sows tares (*lolium temulentum*, 'noxious weeds'), which grow up among the wheat. When the proprietor's servants recognize this and want to pull out the tares, he determines to let both grow together until the harvest, when his reapers will gather and burn the tares and save the wheat. Jesus later explains the parable to his disciples (Matthew 13:36–43), identifying the field as the world, the good seed as the children of the kingdom, and the tares as the children of the wicked one. The enemy is the devil, the harvest is the end of the world, and the reapers are the angels. The explanation ends in a description of Christ's judgment, which will separate the righteous from the wicked, among whom 'there shall be wailing and gnashing of teeth' (v. 42).

Christ's explanation made the allegorical implications of the parable so clear that the Fathers added little. For Origen (*In Matthaeum*, 10.2) the tares signify 'evil words' and 'bad opinions', and for Bede the sleeping men (v. 25) are the teachers of the Church (*In Matthaei Evangelium Expositio*; cf. also Latimer, Sermon 42). A notable variation occurs in the pseudo-Clementine literature of the 3rd–4th century, where the 'enemy' is St Paul, who supposedly sowed the tares of antinomianism among the good seed of the gospel (*Letter of Peter to James*, 2; cf. *Clementine Recognitions*, 1.70–71).

The parable has been frequently quoted – usually by the advocates of moderation – in controversies over broad or narrow concepts of Church. Among these are the conflict between St Callistus and St Hippolytus (Hippolytus, *Philosophoumena*, 9.12), the Donatist schism (St Augustine, *Sermons on New Testament Lessons*, 38.21), the Protestant Reformation (Luther, *Weimarer Ausgabe* 52.835–36), and the controversy over the admission to the Lord's Supper in Puritan America (Jonathan Edwards, *Humble Inquiry*, 3.6).

Many exegetes have seen the parable as warning against the use of violence against even the wicked or heretics within the visible church. They offer three main arguments: (a) the distinction between wheat and tares is difficult because of the possible coexistence of both within the human judge himself (Augustine, *Sermons on New Testament Lessons*, 23.4; Thielicke, *Das Bilderbuch Gottes*, 88–89; Hunter, *The Parables Then and Now*, 48); (b) the wicked should not be denied the chance to repent, 'for it is possible for them even to become wheat' (St John Chrysostom, *Homily on Matthew*, 46; cf. also Luther, *Weimarer Ausgabe* 38.560–61; St Thomas More, *Confutation of Tyndale's Answer*, 8.2; Thielicke, *Das Bilderbuch Gottes*, 89–93); (c) to destroy heresies does not necessarily imply 'rooting up' (Chrysostom, *Homily on Matthew*; Calvin, *Harmony of the Gospels*).

In his defence of unlicensed printing in the final section of *Areopagitica*, Milton uses the parable to argue that within the Church it is not possible 'to sever the wheat from the tares...; that must be the angels' ministry at the end of mortal things'. As a consequence he suggests 'that many be tolerated, rather then [sic] all compell'd'. Sir Thomas Browne speaks of his view of the soul being 'not wrung from speculations and subtilties, but from common sense and observation; not pickt from the leaves of any author, but bred amongst the weeds and tares of mine own brain' (*Religio Medici*, 1.36) – an interesting use of the parable to defend private judgment. Jonathan Swift accuses the 'Dissenting Teachers' of his day of sowing tares among the wheat and of being more successful financially than 'Men of a liberal Education' (*Examiner*, 42; cf. also 'Some Remarks upon a Pamphlet').

Blake's allusion ('My crop of corn is but a field of tares') in *An Island in the Moon* suggests that the field is life and the harvest is death. In Shelley's 'The Mask of Anarchy', people are summoned

> From the haunts of daily life
> Where there is waged the daily strife
> With common wants and common cares
> Which sows the human heart with tares – (283–86).

A similar application of the parable is found in Byron's *Childe Harold* (4.119–20), and in *Don Juan* (13.25) the poet guards himself against 'censorious' men who 'sow an author's wheat with tares', that is, 'Reaping allusions private and inglorious, / Where none were dreamt of...' (cf. John Donne, 'To Mr Rowland Woodward', 5–6; John Ruskin, *Fors Clavigera*, 8.88.6).

In *The Stones of Venice* (3.4.2.94) Ruskin interprets the

Reformation (which he calls a reanimation) in the light of this parable, concluding that for the Reformers 'there was no hope of ever ridding the wheat itself from the tares'. George Eliot entitled the fifth book of *The Mill on the Floss* 'Wheat and Tares', which hints at the experiences endangering Maggie Tulliver's religious resolutions.

Thomas Hardy makes figurative use of the parable in *The Dynasts* (1.2.5), where the 'Phantoms of Rumour' are suspected of sowing tares – false tidings – to coax the population into a fancied safety. Hardy's poem 'On the Portrait of a Woman about to Be Hanged' arrives at the question of theodicy: Why has the condemned murderer's Causer 'Sowed a tare / In a field so fair'? – implicitly equating the 'enemy' with God himself.

Manfred Siebald
Johannes Gutenberg Universität, Mainz, Germany

Whited Sepulchre

A metaphoric designation for the hypocrite, *whited sepulchre* originates from the sixth of the seven woes pronounced by Christ in Matthew 23:27–28: 'Woe unto you, scribes and Pharisees, hypocrites! for ye are like unto whited sepulchres, which indeed appear beautiful outward, but are within full of dead men's bones, and of all uncleanness. Even so ye also outwardly appear righteous unto men, but ye are full of hypocrisy and iniquity.' (Cf. St Paul's denunciation of Ananias as a 'whited wall' in Acts 23:3.) The actual image comes from the ancient Jewish practice of whitewashing the outside of tombs before the feast of Passover to make them more visible and thus to help prevent Jews from becoming ritually unclean by accidentally touching them.

Hypocrites here transliterates Greek *hypokritai* (sing. *hypokrites*), which, from the 2nd century forward, signifies actors or role players. As St Augustine, following Origen's lead, comments, the kind of dissembling which is called hypocrisy is a pretence of sanctity by those who have no genuine desire for the reality they mimic. St Isidore of Seville reckons the hypocrite a wearer of masks and creator of illusions, like the stage actors of antiquity. The New Testament meaning of *hypocritical* may be closer to 'hypercritical' in the sense of 'hair-splitting legal scrupulosity', which brings the Law into desuetude.

The denunciation of hypocrisy is a standard feature in the literature of moral reform, especially of protestation against ecclesiastical corruption; in such literature the 'whited sepulchre' image occurs frequently. In *Piers Plowman* (B.15.113), Langland's 'Prologue to Do Better' combines the whited wall from Acts 23:3 with a dunghill shrouded with snow, to picture the teachers and churchmen who falsify true learning and the laws of God: they are dissemblers, 'whitewashed with fair words and surplices of linen'. In Shakespeare's *Merchant of Venice,* a play concerned very much about hypocrisy, a golden casket is discovered to be full of dead men's bones: 'gilded [like 'whited'] tombs, do worms infold' (2.7.69). Milton, in *Tetrachordon,* reckons of a hypocrite that 'the whole neighbourhood / Sees his foule inside through his whited skin' (1.16.40). In Blake, the call for reform is apocalyptic: 'Wo Wo Wo to you Hypocrites!' he warns 'the Modern Church' or those who, 'having no Passions of their own because No Intellect, Have spent their lives in Curbing & Governing other People's' (*A Vision of the Last Judgment*).

Though the phrase 'whited sepulchre' has currency in the literature of 19th-century Britain – for example, Walter Scott, *Quentin Durward* (chapter 28); Charles Kingsley, *Alton Locke* (chapter 4); Hall Caine, *Manxman* (428) – the figure has by this time considerably diminished in its power to shape a moral critique. Not so in America. In the 'Appendix' to his *Narrative of an American Slave,* Frederick Douglass likens 'the Christianity of America' to the double-dealing of the Pharisees and scribes, citing Matthew 23:4–28 in its entirety. Hawthorne's *The Scarlet Letter* is ironic in its probing and articulation of the duplicity inherent in hypocrisy. In chapter 10, after evoking Christian's meeting with Hypocrisy and Formalism in *The Pilgrim's Progress,* the author likens Chillingworth to 'a sexton digging into a grave' to retrieve a precious gem: the man of law and learning will discover if Dimmesdale, 'looking pure as new-fallen snow', has an interior to match. In the second part of Melville's *The Paradise of Bachelors and the Tartarus of Maids,* the 'large whitewashed building' of 'a paper-mill' is likened to 'some great whited sepulchre'. In Eugene O'Neill's *Mourning Becomes Electra,* Christine, decking her house with flowers, comments, 'I felt our tomb needed a little brightening. Each time I come back after being away it appears more like a sepulchre! The "whited" one of the Bible – pagan temple front stuck like a mask on Puritan gray ugliness!'

With Conrad, the whited sepulchre returns to British literature with renewed force. Marlow of *Heart of Darkness* recalls a European capital which always makes him 'think of a whited sepulchre' (pt. 1); however, as the lie to the intended and the pervasive gloom of the final pages insinuate, neither Conrad's narrator nor London is spared participation in hypocrisy. In *Chance* (1.2), the moralist and social reformer Mrs Fyne is likened to the Pharisees, which comparison, as Purdy suggests (85–88), applies to Marlow as well. The final chapter of *Victory* makes frequent reference to Matthew 23 (see Purdy, 84–85), for example, in the description of the dead outlaw Jones as 'a heap of bones in a blue silk bag'. D.H. Lawrence's 'How Beastly the Bourgeois Is' follows in the tradition of Blake, though on a more domestic prophetic plane: 'the fresh clean Englishman, outside' is 'all wormy inside'.

Camille R. La Bossière
University of Ottawa

Whosoever Will Save His Life

On a variety of occasions Jesus said to his disciples in some fashion what is reported in Matthew 16:24–25: 'If any man will come after me, let him deny himself, and take up his cross, and follow me. For whosoever will save his life shall lose it: and whosoever will lose his life for my sake shall find it' (cf. Mark 8:35; Luke 9:24; 17:33; John 12:24–26). This type of statement, according to John Wyclif (*De Veritate Sacrae Scripturae*), illustrates that in the intrinsic logic of the Bible, the Aristotelian logic of non-contradiction is sometimes confuted: death *may* be life. The principle as well as the phrase is variously echoed in literature, but Thoreau's *Civil Disobedience* offers a classic allusion. Opposing Paley's 'Duty of Submission to Civil Government' Thoreau writes: 'If I have unjustly wrested a plank from a drowning man, I must restore it to him though I drown myself. This, according to Paley, would be inconvenient. But he that would save his life, in such a case, shall lose it. America must cease to hold slaves, and to make war on Mexico, though it cost them their existence as a people.'

David L. Jeffrey
University of Ottawa

Widow's Mite

Jesus, observing wealthy Jews ostentatiously casting money into the Temple treasury box, noticed 'a certain poor widow' who threw in 'two mites' (Mark 12:42; Luke 21:2). Jesus told his disciples that 'this poor widow hath cast more in, than all they which have cast into the treasury: For all they did cast in of their abundance; but she of her want did cast in all that she had, even all her living' (Mark 12:43–44; cf. Luke 21:3–4).

The Fathers treat the passage as indicative of the 'mathematics of the kingdom', in which material quantity and spiritual quality are regularly distinguished: 'little' can be all; 'much' can be inadequate. St John Chrysostom (*Homily* 52, on the Gospel of Matthew) mentions the widow's mite in the context of his discussion of almsgiving:

> For though thou be exceedingly poor, and of them that beg, if thou cast in two mites, thou hast effected all; though thou give but a barley cake, having only this, thou art arrived at the end of the art.

Allusions to 'the widow's mite', frequent in English literature, begin as direct references to the biblical widow singled out by Christ. Later references branch out into a broader sense identified by the *Oxford English Dictionary*: 'with allusion to Mark 12:43, one's mite is often used for the small sum which is all that one can afford to give to some charitable or public object.' The phrase has tended to become even more figurative over time, so that it can now be 'applied to an immaterial contribution (insignificant in amount, but the best one can do) to some object or cause'.

The earliest allusions to the widow's mite are the most direct, referring specifically to the biblical woman. She is mentioned in *The Ayenbite of Inwyt* (12.42–43), Langland's *Piers Plowman* (13.196), and

Goodwine's dedication to *Blanchardine*. St Thomas More in his *Confutation* stresses the biblical background of the phrase:

> Christ blamed not those that offered into the treasury of the temple, nor said that they offered too much; but rather, by praising of the poor widow that offered somewhat of her poverty, rebuked the rich folk for offering too little, albeit that, as the gospel saith, many offered much. (7.674 B)

Later allusions to the verse in Mark suggest the broader sense of 'mite' as the pittance which is all a donor can afford to contribute to a social cause. Dryden writes in 1687, 'Are you defrauded, when he feeds the poor? Our mite decreases nothing of your store' (*The Hind and the Panther*, 3.113). Swift asks a similar question about public charity: 'Did I e'er my Mite withhold? / From the Impotent and Old?' ('Epistle to a Lady', 71–72).

As a result of a kind of metaphoric inflation, the biblical mite tends to become ever less substantive in English literary allusion – as its use expands it tends to devalue. Swift by 1709 pays his mite not in currency but in counsel: 'I hope I may be allowed among so many far more learned men to offer my mite' (*Critical Essays*, 2.1.140). And Berkeley offers in 1747 to 'contribute my mite of advice' ('Tar-water in Plague', 3.479). This non-monetary use of the term made its way to America as well, where Benjamin Franklin says in his 1784 *Autobiography* that his 'mite for such purpose was never refused' (103).

References to 'the widow's mite' proliferate in the 19th century. Byron seems particularly enamoured of widows' mites. In *Don Juan*, possessing 'no great plenty', he gives up for love all that he had – his heart: "T was the boys' "mite", and, like the "widow's", may / Perhaps be weigh'd hereafter, if not now' (6.41). 'Let each,' he admonishes, 'give his mite!' ('The Irish Avatar', 173). Jane Austen ('very glad that she had contributed her mite') alludes twice to the widow's mite in *Mansfield Park*. Herman Melville refers to the 'widow's last mite' in *Moby Dick*.

In the 20th century, references are often parodic. George Bernard Shaw alludes to the phrase ironically in *Major Barbara*: 'The odd twopence, Barbara? The millionaire's mite, eh?' (2.297). In Joyce's *Ulysses*, Bloom ponders 'That widow on Monday was it outside

Cramer's that looked at me. Buried the poor husband but progressing favourably on the premium. Her widow's mite.' Joyce's allusion to the biblical phrase in *Finnegans Wake* is twisted by punning: 'which I'm sorry, my precious, is allathome I with grief can call my own but all the same, listen, Jaunick, accept this witwee's mite.'

Steven C. Walker
Brigham Young University

Wise and Foolish Builders

In Matthew 7:24–27, as he ends his Sermon on the Mount, Jesus compares those who hear his words and do them to a wise man who builds his house upon a rock, where rain, floods, and winds cannot shake it. On the other hand, those who hear Jesus' words without acting upon them are compared to a man building on sand. His house falls down from the force of the elements. A parallel in Luke 6:47–49 stresses the building process ('digged deep and laid the foundation upon a rock') and mentions only one of the elements ('flood' or 'stream').

Along with other 'rock' metaphors in the New Testament, the rock of verses 24 and 25 has often been identified allegorically with Christ (because of 1 Corinthians 10:4; cf. St Augustine, *De sermone Domini in Monte*, 2.25.87; Bede, *In Matthaei Evangelium Expositio*; St Thomas Aquinas, *Expositio in Evangelium S. Matthaei*; Luther, *Weimarer Ausgabe* 32.532–35; Richard Hooker, Sermon 6), with the Church (because of Matthew 16:18; cf. Augustine, *In Joannis Evangelium Tractatus* 124.7.14; Jonathan Edwards, *Humble Inquiry*, 2.6), and with the steadfastness of doctrine (St John Chrysostom, *Homily on Matthew*, 24.3; Hooker, Sermon 6).

If Christ is considered the builder, he can be said to build the Church upon himself, according to St Thomas. But the house of the parable was also taken by some (e.g., Chrysostom) to be the soul, or the two houses were seen as being Jerusalem and Babylon (e.g., Haymo, *Expositio in Apocalypsin*, *Patrologia Latina*, 117.1139).

Rain, floods, and winds were interpreted by various writers as 'things present', such as temptations, superstitions, rumours, carnal lusts, the devil, Antichrist, and evil spirits. Occasionally they were taken to represent the Last Judgment (e.g., Bede; Hooker; Josef Schmid, *Das Evangelium nach Matthäus*, 153).

The common interpretation of the early Church that 'without works nothing is sufficient' did not remain undisputed. Rejecting any justification by works, some Reformation exegetes warned against acting from the wrong motives. Calvin concludes from the text that 'genuine piety can be distinguished from imitated piety only when put to the test' (*Harmony of the Gospels*), and Luther accuses the Catholic clergy and the monks of building 'on the shifting sand of their own foolish conceitedness' and 'their own holiness'. Modern exegetes again put the emphasis on the 'doing' of Christ's words and read the parable as a 'call to Christian action' (Hunter, *The Parables Then and Now*, 86).

In English literature, Spenser's *The Faerie Queene* (1.4.5.5) offers an early reference: Lucifera's House of Pride is built 'on a sandie hill'. George Herbert's poem 'Giddinesse' complains of man's fickleness by alluding to the parable:

> He builds a house, which quickly down must go,
> > As if a whirlwinde blew
> And crusht the building: and it's partly true,
> > His minde is so.

Charles Dickens in *David Copperfield* furnishes an example of the secularization of the parable. The protagonist says, when talking about his new wife, Agnes, that his love of her is founded on a rock (chapter 62; a similar allusion is found in chapter 45, 'Annie and the Doctor'). Christina Rossetti's poem 'A Testimony' uses the second builder as an illustration of the vanity she discovers everywhere (260).

In black poet Countee Cullen's 'Lines to my Father', the Methodist minister is depicted as one whose dreams have come true because they were built on rock. Finally, in James Baldwin's *Go Tell It on the Mountain* (77), a flashback depicts Florence's life on a Southern plantation. She and her fellow slaves know that the 'house of pride' where the white folks live will come down, because it has not 'so sure a foundation' as Florence's. The reference to the Word of God provides both comfort and hope to the slaves.

Manfred Siebald
Johannes Gutenberg Universität, Mainz, Germany

Wise and Foolish Virgins

One of several parables on preparedness in Matthew 24 and 25, the parable (Matthew 25:1–13) tells of ten bridesmaids who are to meet the bridegroom and accompany him to the wedding. At midnight, when the bridegroom arrives late, five of them turn out to be short of oil for their lamps. Since the others do not have oil to spare, the foolish ones have to go to buy oil – only to find on their return that, being late, they are not admitted to the bridegroom's house. He answers them, 'I do not know you' (v. 12). The parable closes with a call for watchfulness which is a repetition of Matthew 24:42.

In classical Christian tradition the parable is interpreted allegorically, and most exegetes have agreed on the basic points of comparison. Following verse 13, they take the bridegroom to be Christ (Origen's allegorical interpretation draws a further parallel to the bridegroom in Canticles, Song of Songs, 3.11) and the feast to be the Second Coming. The virgins are usually seen as representing the whole Church, the number five being derived from the five human senses, and virginity signifying abstention from evil (St Augustine, Sermones, 43.2) or from possessions (St John Chrysostom, Homily on Matthew, 78.2). The bridegroom's tarrying leads 'His disciples away from the expectation that His kingdom was quite immediately to appear,' according to Chrysostom; the virgins' sleep, according to Augustine, means death. For most Fathers, the oil which the foolish maids lack represents almsgiving and good works (e.g., St Jerome, Epistle 125; Bede, In Matthaei Evangelium Expositio). Consequently, according to Chrysostom, the merchants to whom the foolish ones are sent are the poor. Since their service is of no avail, however, Augustine believes them to be the worldly flatterers.

This emphasis on good works was, of course, contradicted by the Reformers and subsequent Protestant exegetes. Wyclif, who interprets the virgins as those with a calling to the contemplative life, still clings to the traditional reading but stresses the possibility of having wrong motives in doing good works (In Omnes Novi Testamenti Libros). For St Thomas More the lamps mean faith, and the oil, goodness (Confutation, 9.824). For Luther the virgins' lamps signify charity, and the oil represents faith (Sermon of 21 October 1522).

Calvin (in his commentary on Matthew) holds that the virgins' being directed to the merchants is not a command but a reproach, since the gifts of grace cannot be purchased but only accepted by faith. Puritans, both in England and America, used the parable for exposing hypocrisy. Bunyan considers the foolish maids 'visible saints', who are yet cast away on account of their 'secret sins' (*The Holy City*, 4.5), and Thomas Shepard, in his lengthy treatise on the parable, calls them 'gospel hypocrites' (*Parable of the Ten Virgins*, 1.14.1; cf. also Jonathan Edwards, *Humble Inquiry*, 2.2).

Modern commentaries have dealt with the question of whether or not the parable is an allegory proclaiming Jesus' Parousia (e.g., Michaelis, *Gleichnisse*, 92–94; Jeremias, *The Parables of Jesus*, 51–53). Linnemann echoes Chrysostom in asserting that it teaches how foolish it is for the Church not to expect a long postponement of the Second Coming (*Gleichnisse Jesu*, 125–27), and for Christian socialist Leonhard Ragaz the parable warns against several wrong kinds of waiting: against the attitudes of liberalism, servilism, and Christian fatalism (*Gleichnisse Jesu*, 189–98).

The parable provides the dominant motif for the 12th-century Latin–French play *Sponsus* (in effect a Last Judgment play); a German 'Zehnjungfrauenspiel' followed in the 14th century. Both of them modify the parable by suggesting that only the foolish virgins have fallen asleep. Dan Michel's *Ayenbite of Inwyt* (Early English Text Society, 1866, 189, 218, 232), however, follows the traditional interpretation faithfully. Langland, in *Piers Plowman*, directs the Vulgate version of verse 12 (*Amen dico vobis, nescio vos*) against wrongdoing clergy, the king, and the lawyers (B.5.56; cf. also B.9.65). John Donne creates a bold metaphor when he makes the blood of the martyrs of the Christian Church 'Oyle to th' Apostles Lamps, dew to their seed' (*The Second Anniversary*, 352).

The girl addressed in Milton's ninth sonnet is credited with an exemplary way of living and is hailed as one of the parable's virgins, who fills her 'odorous Lamp with deeds of light'. Milton takes the identification so far as to predict,

> Therefore be sure
> Thou, when the Bridegroom with his feastful friends

Passes to bliss at the mid hour of night,
Has gain'd thy entrance, Virgin wise and pure.

In similar fashion, Marvell's 'Upon Appleton House' (62) compares the Cistercian nuns to the wise virgins, who trim their 'chast Lamps' hourly, 'Lest the great Bridegroom find them dim'; and Henry Vaughan ('The Dawning') and Michael Wigglesworth (*The Day of Doom*) open their poems, respectively, on the Second Coming and the Judgment, by evoking the parable's nocturnal atmosphere.

The scientific mind of Sir Thomas Browne connects the number of the wise and foolish virgins with Antiquity's (especially Plutarch's) belief that five was the 'Conjugall or wedding number', consisting of 'two and three, the first parity and imparity, the active and passive digits, the materiall and formall principles in generative Societies' (*Garden of Cyrus,* chapter 5). A passage in William Cowper's poem 'Retirement' skilfully exploits the double meaning of 'midnight oil'. The poet favours the minds occupied with the Last Judgment over those 'that give the midnight oil to learned cares or philosophic toil' (661–62). William Blake, on the other hand, says in a letter (no. 21) that those 'who are fond of Literature & Humane & polite accomplishments' are they that 'have their lamps burning'. (He also alludes to the parable in *The Four Zoas,* 8.541.)

John Ruskin makes a humorous allusion to the virgins' oil in *Fors Clavigera,* 4.45.19. Elsewhere he puts the parable in a social context by turning it against those who distribute only their 'inestimable wisdom' to the poor, but not their 'estimable rubies'. The ironical justification given for the latter is verse 9. Melville's Wellingborough Redburn laments the fate of small ships which are run down by larger ones because of 'their own remissness in keeping a good look-out by day, and not having their lamps trimmed, like the wise virgins, by night' (*Redburn,* chapter 20). Melville refers to the parable again in chapter 81 of *Moby Dick,* 'The *Pequod* Meets the Virgin'. The German whaler *Jungfrau* (*Virgin*), which has not yet captured one whale, has run out of lamp oil. The fact that the captain has to borrow oil from Ahab indicates an inexperience borne out by the *Jungfrau's* defeat in the race after a sperm whale.

Harriet Beecher Stowe's Uncle Tom, in his simple mysticism,

associates Eva St Clare's impending death with the midnight hour of the parable (*Uncle Tom's Cabin,* chapter 26). The theme of belatedness is dealt with in Tennyson's *Idylls of the King* ('Guinevere') when a young girl in a convent sings 'Too late, too late! ye cannot enter now. / No light had we: for that we do repent' – verses which illustrate Queen Guinevere's fate.

The renderings of the parable by Christina Rossetti are rather straightforward ('Advent Sunday', 'Easter Tuesday', 'I know you not'), but Thomas Hardy only lends some biblical overtones to his depiction of the thoughts of an English country bride by entitling his poem 'The Tarrying Bridegroom'.

In *Ulysses* James Joyce makes two references to the wise virgins which serve as ironic foils to an environment of prostitution. Faulkner follows the same line when, in *Requiem for a Nun* (2.1), he has Temple Drake call herself 'the foolish virgin', because she stays in a brothel voluntarily.

The title of Eugene O'Neill's play *The Iceman Cometh* is obviously modelled after verse 6, and there are a number of parallels between the drama and the parable. The main difference, however, is to be found in the character of Hickey, the 'Iceman of Death'. With O'Neill, eschatology is narrowed down to the imminence of death for everybody.

Manfred Siebald
Johannes Gutenberg Universität, Mainz, Germany

Wise as Serpents

Commissioning his disciples for their difficult and dangerous task of announcing the kingdom, Jesus warned them: 'Behold, I send you forth as sheep in the midst of wolves: be ye therefore wise as serpents, and harmless as doves' (Matthew 10:16). In his sermon on the text, St Augustine describes it as indicating 'how our Lord Jesus Christ strengthened his martyrs by his teaching'. Noting how apparently absurd it is to send a few sheep in among many wolves, he then reflects on the advice of Jesus, 'who has promised the crown, but first appointed the combat'. Whoever really understands Jesus' words and holds to them, he adds, 'may die secure in the knowledge that he will not really die' (*Sermo*, 44.1–2). He then considers the oxymoron, offering exegetical reflections which incorporate contemporary animal lore:

> Now if the simplicity of doves be enjoined us, what has the wisdom of the serpent to do with that? What I love in the dove is that she is without gall; what I fear in the serpent is his poison. But do not fear the serpent altogether for he has… something for you to imitate. For when the serpent is weighed down with age and feeling the burden of his many years he contracts and forces himself into a hole, and casts off his old coat of skin that he may spring forth into new life… And the Apostle Paul says to you also, 'Put ye off the old man with his deeds, and put ye on the new man' [Colossians 3:9; Ephesians 4:22–24]. So you do have something in the serpent to imitate. Die not for the 'old man', but for the truth. Whoever dies for any temporal good dies for the 'old man'.

Augustine observes, further, how the adder strives to protect its head when attacked; so also should the Christian, whose head and life is Christ (44.3). The simplicity of the dove is then to be imitated without the caution occasioned by the serpent's poison:

> Mark how the doves rejoice in society; they fly and feed together always; they do not love to be alone, they delight in communion, they preserve affection; their cooings are the plaintive cries of love; with kissings they beget their young. Even when doves dispute about their nesting places, it is a peaceful sort of strife – how different from the strife of wolves! Do they separate because of contention? No, still they fly and feed together, and any strife is very peaceful. (44.4)

Calvin follows Augustine's commentary on the first half of the verse but reduces the elaborate exposition on the second half, reading it rather as a pragmatic warning for Christians in a hostile world: 'Briefly, discretion is to be so tempered with caution, that they are not to be excessively timid, nor yet over slow in their work.' Calvin says the 'double simile' serves to condemn too much 'prudence of the flesh' on the part of those who 'do not want to take any risks, and so... renounce the call of Christ' (*Harmony of the Gospels,* on Matthew 10:16).

The phrase gained wide currency in English literature of the 19th century. Melville employs it in its Calvinist sense of prudential wisdom when speaking of Billy Budd: 'With little or no sharpness of faculty, or any trace of the wisdom of the serpent, nor yet quite of a dove, he possessed that kind and degree of intelligence which goes along with the unconventional rectitude of a sound human creature' (chapter 2). The prudential theme is engrafted into discussions of ethical pragmatism in numerous 19th-century texts. Ruskin speaks in *Modern Painters* of the character which he imagines ought to pertain to a gentleman, saying that there is a 'difference between honourable and base lying... "Be ye wise as serpents, harmless as doves" is the ultimate expression of this principle.' Once so construed, the phrase readily admits of parody and inversion, often by or in reference to those less circumspect than Ruskin's ideal. Such a one is Aunt Althea Pontifex in Butler's *The Way of All Flesh,* one of whose 'wicked sayings about Dr Skinner' is that 'he had the harmlessness of the serpent and the wisdom of the dove' (chapter 28). In Dorothy Sayers' *Unnatural Death* it is said of Dr Edward Carr that he is 'conscientious but a little lackin' in worldly wisdom – not serpentine at all, as the Bible advises, but far otherwise' (chapter 4). The backhanded compliment of the narrator hidden in this remark is missing in Somerset Maugham's *Then and Now,* where a similar character is described: 'He is goodness itself, but it cannot be denied that he is a little simple. He does not combine the innocence of the dove with the craftiness of the serpent' (chapter 18). Aldous Huxley seems to have captured well the development of Jesus' injunction as a proverb of secular wisdom:

> Men of good will have always had to combine the virtues of the serpent with those of the dove. This serpentine wisdom is more than ever necessary to-day, when the official resistance to men of good will is greater and better organized than at any previous period. (*Ends and Means,* chapter 10)

David L. Jeffrey
University of Ottawa

Wolves in Sheep's Clothing

In his Sermon on the Mount, after Jesus has distinguished between the narrow way leading to life and the broad way leading to destruction, he warns his hearers to 'beware of false prophets, which come to you in sheep's clothing, but inwardly they are ravening wolves' (Matthew 7:15). Early commentaries readily associated these 'wolves' with heresy, hypocrisy, and misuses of priestly office (e.g., St Augustine, *Sermo*, 137.12; *De sermone Domini in Monte*, 2.24.80; cf. St Ambrose, *De Spiritu Sancto*, 2.10.108–09; St Jerome, *Epistle* 22.38; 147.11).

English literature likewise reserves the appellation almost exclusively for false or corrupted members of the clergy. Chaucer provides vivid portraits of such characters in his Friar, Summoner, and Pardoner, all of whom are 'false prophets' in this sense; Langland quotes Jesus' words to denounce hypocrisy – 'a braunche of pruyde' for which he says the clergy are notorious (*Piers Plowman*, C.17.268–70). In Shakespeare's *1 Henry VI* Gloucester is angered by the Bishop of Winchester's betrayals, concluding that Winchester is less an ally than a 'wolf in sheep's array' (1.3.55). Thoreau, arguing that some members of the clergy played a deceptively ambiguous role in the slavery issue, uses the words of Jesus to condemn them in 'A Plea for Captain John Brown'. The 'wolf in sheep's clothing, a bloodthirsty hypocrite, wearing the garb of innocence' in Thackeray's *The Newcomes*, is one among the 'farrago of old fables' with which the novel begins, setting the theme which the author's stage 'critics' deride. In Samuel Butler's *The Way of All Flesh* Ernest's considered opinion of the clergy of the Church of England is that most of them fall into this category; the narrator says 'now that he had seen them more closely, he knows better the nature of these wolves in sheep's clothing, who are thirsting for the blood of their victim'.

David L. Jeffrey
University of Ottawa

Characters and Events

Crucifixion *see* Passion of Christ

Eucharist *see* Last Supper (Eucharist)

Jesus Christ

The name Jesus comes from the Greek *Iesous*, the adaptation of the Hebrew name *Yehoshua* (Aramaic *Yeshua*) the name of the great hero of the conquest of Canaan, familiar to Old Testament readers as Joshua. The term Christ is adapted from the Greek *Christos*, which translates the Hebrew *mashiah* (from which the term *Messiah* is derived), meaning 'anointed'. Christ is thus originally not a name but a title reflecting the early Christian conviction that Jesus is the Messiah, the 'anointed one', who fulfils the hope for a God-sent saviour.

The four gospels of the New Testament are our major source of information about Jesus of Nazareth and the primary basis for the picture of him which is accepted by traditional Christianity. Commonly dated by scholars between AD65 and 95, they are also recognized as embodying the Jesus tradition of much earlier years. With the rise of modern historicism, especially in the 19th century, many strove to construct a somewhat detailed, chronologically arranged life of Jesus from the gospels. Albert Schweitzer's classic *The Quest of the Historical Jesus* traces the failure of this enterprise, and New Testament scholars today recognize that the gospels (like all ancient biographical literature) were not written to provide a chronological or developmental account of their subject but were intended as collections of Jesus tradition and interpretations of him for the religious needs of 1st-century churches. Nevertheless, nearly all New Testament scholars today are persuaded that, although a detailed life of Jesus cannot be written, the gospels do provide a basis for a more modest historical description of Jesus' ministry and message which accords with the standards of modern historical criticism. The traditional picture of Jesus was formed by a harmonistic reading of the gospels, the following elements of which are most important for the literary tradition. Jesus was miraculously conceived in Mary without a human father, born in Bethlehem of Judah in the time of Herod the Great (37–4BC; see Matthew 1–2; Luke 1–2), and grew up in Nazareth of Galilee. In his young adult years he was baptized by John the Baptist, his cousin (who preached a message of radical religious reform among the Jews), on which occasion he was acclaimed by God as his 'beloved Son' (e.g., Mark 1:1–11).

Shortly after his baptism and a period of testing in the wilderness, Jesus began his own ministry. His message focused upon the approach of the kingdom of God (e.g., Mark 1:14–15) and was often conveyed by means of parables (Matthew 13; Mark 4). He collected disciples and with them travelled about, preaching his message, which was accompanied by healings, exorcisms, and other miraculous works (Mark 1:34, 39). He clashed with Jewish scribes over matters of religious practice, such as Sabbath observance and his fellowship with 'sinners' (e.g., Mark 2:1 – 3:6), and defended his positions with assertions of special, divinely authorized authority. Jesus' ministry began in Galilee and eventually took him to the holy city, Jerusalem, where his conflict with Jewish religious authorities intensified over such matters as his condemnation of the priestly leadership and claims to direct authority from God (e.g., Mark 11:15 – 12:44). As a result, these leaders sought to do away with him. With help from Judas Iscariot, a disciple of Jesus who betrayed him, the Jewish authorities arrested Jesus during Passover celebrations (Mark 14:26–50). After a hearing by the high priest (e.g., Mark 14:53–65), Jesus was condemned for blasphemy, taken to the Roman governor, Pontius Pilate, and accused of making himself King of the Jews, which constituted rebellion against Caesar (e.g., Mark 15:1–26). Jesus was executed by the Romans, with the full encouragement of the Jewish leaders, and was forsaken by his disciples, including Simon Peter, who publicly denied being Jesus' disciple (e.g., Mark 14:50, 66–72).

On the third day after his execution, however, Jesus was seen by his disciples alive and glorified, having been raised from death by God (e.g., Matthew 28:1–10, 16–20; John 20:19–29). He restored the disciples who had forsaken him and charged them to preach the gospel message to all nations.

The gospels present Jesus as the true Messiah of Israel (e.g., John 1:40–41, 45, 49), the fulfilment of all God's promises of salvation. He is also called 'the Son of God' (e.g., Matthew 27:45) and is acknowledged as such by God himself (e.g., Mark 1:11; 9:7). According to the gospels, Jesus foresaw his rejection and execution (e.g., Mark 10:33–34), viewed his death as redemptive (Mark 10:45; 14:22–25), and endured his bitter fate as the will of God (Mark 14:32–36; John 12:27). Jesus was therefore not a victim, and his suffering and death were his greatest acts of love for his own (e.g., John 15:13).

Even in ancient times readers of the gospels noticed that the four books varied in their emphases, arrangement, and style. Thus, Matthew was seen as the gospel of the royal Messiah of Israel, Mark as the gospel of the obedient Son of God, Luke as the gospel of the ideal Son of man and noble martyr, and John as the gospel of the divine Son of heavenly origin. The picture of Jesus in John's Gospel is particularly distinctive. Jesus here speaks of himself much more explicitly as the divine Son who knows himself to have been preexistent with God (e.g., 5:19–25; 6:51; 8:23, 56–58; 9:39), and he demonstrates a kind of divine insight into things (1:47–48; 2:24–25; 13:1, 3). John's Gospel was sometimes called 'the spiritual gospel', because Christians recognized in it the much more overt emphasis upon Jesus as the redeemer of heavenly origin.

Other noteworthy presentations of Christ in the New Testament include Hebrews' theme of Jesus as the new high priest who replaces and supersedes the Old Testament priesthood and its sacrificial system and Revelation's theophanic imagery in 1:12–20, its triumphant Lamb who executes the divine book of redemption in 5:1–14, and its heavenly warrior of final judgment in 19:11–16.

The development of the Christian doctrines of the Trinity and the 'two natures' of Christ (divine and human) took several centuries, but already in the New Testament the essential steps are taken. Here Jesus is presented as genuinely human (e.g., Hebrews 2:14–18) – the reality of his death is powerfully insisted upon – but he is also understood to be of heavenly origin (e.g., John 1:1–18) and worthy of worship (e.g., Philippians 2:9–11). All things were created through the preexistent Christ (e.g., Colossians 1:15–20), and in Jesus of Nazareth, now glorified at God's 'right hand', God was (and is) genuinely manifested (e.g., Colossians 2:9). In Paul's words, 'God was in Christ reconciling the world' (2 Corinthians 5:19). Christ is now the divinely appointed saviour of all (e.g., Acts 4:10–12), and through him the entire plan of redemption is to be executed to rescue humankind from the effects of Adam's Fall (e.g., 1 Corinthians 15:20–28).

This dual affirmation of Jesus as genuinely human and yet also truly divine continues on and is sharpened by such early Christian theologians as St Ignatius of Antioch (1st and early 2nd century). The logical difficulties involved in such a view of Christ are illustrated by the various heresies of the early centuries, which can be seen as attempts to simplify matters by minimizing either the human or the divine in Jesus. The development of the doctrine of Christ is marked by two events of special importance. The Council of Nicaea in AD325 stated the full divinity of Christ against attempts (e.g., those of the Arians) to define Christ as a lesser divinity. The Council of Chalcedon in AD451 produced a statement which emphasized both Christ's human and divine natures over against various interpretations which were viewed as failing to do justice to the unique union of divine and human in Jesus. These two early Christian councils attempted to state as precisely as possible the traditional Christian belief that Jesus is the unique incarnation of God; the position statements they arrived at have endured as major touchstones of orthodox Christian doctrine to the present time.

A quite different type of Christian thought on the subject of Jesus is to be found in the tradition of literary apocrypha. The silence of the gospels on so much of the life and activities of Jesus and his family soon led to pious curiosity, which gradually produced a corpus of largely imaginative stories. Among the earliest examples of these are the pseudepigraphal Protevangelium of James, whose author indicates, for example, that it was Mary who wove the veil of the Temple which was rent in twain at her son's death; the Infancy Gospel of Thomas, in which the boy Jesus claims to possess an occult knowledge of the meaning underlying the letters of the Greek alphabet; and the Acts of Pilate, with its touching picture of the Roman standards of the imperial ensigns bowing to Jesus against the wishes of the pagans who hold them.

Among the early poetical lives of Jesus were the *Historiae*

Evangelicae Libri Quattuor, written about AD300 by the Spanish priest Juvencus, and the anonymous Old Saxon alliterative epic *Heliand*, that is, *Saviour*, of about 825–840, which presented Jesus to contemporary Low Germans in the guise of a prototypical warrior leader, the 'might-wielding Christ'. These verse accounts were followed later in the Middle Ages by several prose lives in Latin, including the *Meditationes Vitae Christi*, sometimes attributed to St Bonaventure and translated with adaptations into English by Nicholas Love under the title *Mirrour of the Blessed Lyf of Jesu Christ*; Simon Fidati's *De Gestis Domini Salvatoris*; and Ludolph of Saxony's *Vita Jesu Christi*. In 1602 the Jesuit Hieronymus Xavier completed a life of Jesus in Portuguese, which was subsequently translated into Persian and Latin: it depicts a somewhat triumphalist religious leader, many of whose achievements depend only on the authority of the Apocrypha of the 1st and 2nd centuries. In 1649 Jeremy Taylor published what may have been the first original life of Christ to be written in English, *The Great Exemplar*. A classic of English devotional literature, it was followed by Abraham Woodhead's *Historical Narrative of Our Lord* (1685), Edmund Law's *Discourse on the Character of Christ* (1749), George Benson's *History of the Life of Jesus Christ* (1764), and John Fleetwood's *Life of Our Lord* (1767).

The earliest example of a biographer of Jesus writing for strictly secular motives was Karl Friedrich Bahrdt, who in several publications written towards the end of the 18th century maintained that Jesus was a Hellenistically trained member of the Essenes. This conception of Jesus was further developed by Karl Heinrich Venturini in his *Natürliche Geschichte des grossen Propheten von Nazareth* (1800–1802). Perhaps the most popular of the 19th-century lives of Jesus was Ernest Renan's *Vie de Jésus* (1863), which is in some respects a historical novel rather than a work of scriptural scholarship. Religiously more orthodox was the life of Christ written by Henri Didon and published in 1890, which was also widely read. Many lives of Jesus were written in English during the Victorian period, including the anonymously published *Ecce Homo* (1865), actually the work of John Seeley, William Hanna's *The Life of Our Lord upon Earth* (1869), F.W. Farrar's *The Life of Christ* (1874), and J. Cunningham Geikie's *Life and Words of Christ* (1877).

Among the examples of what can properly be termed modern apocrypha, two of the best known are Robert Graves' *King Jesus* (1946) and Nikos Kazantzakis' *The Last Temptation of Christ* (1953). Both involve a considerable degree of learned fiction: the Jesus of Graves is presented as the child of a secret wedding between the second Antipater and Mary before she was betrothed to Joseph; the Jesus of Kazantzakis is faced with a final temptation before his death: a vision of life in which he enjoys romantic love, marriage, children, and longevity. Such examples of imaginative Christological fiction should be distinguished from the academic lives of Jesus which have appeared in the last century or so, for example, those of Alfred Edersheim, Joseph Klausner, and Everett Harrison, and the more popular biographies of recent years, for example, Giovanni Papini's *Story of Christ* (1921), John Erskine's *The Human Life of Jesus* (1945), Frank Slaughter's *The Crown and the Cross* (1959), and Robert Payne's *The Shepherd* (1959).

In a general sense the person and doctrines of Jesus Christ underlie most English religious literature (e.g., hymnody, meditative poetry and prose, and sermons) of both Christian and non-Christian writers. In the Old English period some of the best pieces of Jesus literature are poems, including *Christ and Satan* (anonymous, c. 790–830), *Christ* (in three parts, the second definitely by Cynewulf, 9th century), and *The Dream of the Rood* (anonymous, early 9th century). An East Midland poem in dialogue, *The Harrowing of Hell*, constitutes a precursor to the later miracle plays, in several of which Jesus has a central role. The life of Christ – especially his incarnation and passion – is the principal subject of many medieval lyrics, as well as of devotional verse in the Renaissance and 17th century (e.g., John Donne, 'La Corona'). In 1610 Giles Fletcher the Younger published *Christ's Victorie, and Triumph in Heaven, on Earth, over, and after Death*, an important anticipation of Milton's *Paradise Regained*.

John Milton (1608–74) is perhaps the most important English contributor to the literature about Jesus Christ. In *Paradise Lost* (published 1667) Milton assigns a significant part of the process of creation to God the Son. God the Father in effect withdraws, and the Word, God the Son, shapes the universe from the unformed matter which had originated with the Father. Underlying this Christian interpretation of the Genesis creation account is the Johannine conception of Jesus as the Logos, who existed from all eternity. Jesus as saviour and redeemer is the hero of *Paradise Regained* (published 1671). Milton concentrates on the gospel accounts of Jesus' baptism, the proclamation that he is the Son of God, and his heroic overcoming of the temptations of Satan. The first significant 18th-century contributor to the literature of Jesus was Sir Richard Steele, who proposed in his literary manual of ethics entitled *The Christian Hero* (1701) that the best preceptor of conscience was Christ rather than any of the classical philosophers. Alexander Pope's *Messiah* (1712), a sacred eclogue on the messianic prophecies of Isaiah, is a noteworthy presentation of Old Testament prophetic expectations, understood as having their fulfilment in Christ.

It was not until the 19th century that Jesus and Jesus-like heroes became incorporated in the novel. This development was partly an offshoot of Christian socialism. Its first two exemplars were Elizabeth Linton's *The True History of Joshua Davidson* (1872) and Elizabeth Phelps' *A Singular Life* (1895). Both present a socialistic hero. Linton's Joshua Davidson, the son of a carpenter in a small Cornish village, comes to London and there meets Félix Pyat, clearly meant to represent Karl Marx. A prostitute whom Joshua helps, Mary Prinsep, is the counterpart of Mary Magdalene. Joshua is eventually trampled to death by a London crowd when he vainly attempts to convince them that Christ and his apostles were communists. The implication of this rather awkwardly written novel is that, if Jesus were alive today, he would be an egalitarian working man with a provincial accent and a home in the slums of London who would vituperate against capitalists, landlords, Sabbatarians, bishops, and residents of the West End.

Less extreme in her views, the American author Elizabeth Phelps proposes as her Jesus hero in *A Singular Life* a young clergyman, Emanuel Bayard, whose late father, Joseph, a clergyman and carpenter, had married his wife, Mary, in the New England village of Bethlehem. Emanuel's theology is not impeccably orthodox, so his application for the pastorate of the wealthy church of Windover is turned down by the congregation. Instead, he remains to minister to the poor fisherfolk of the town. He practises Christian socialism for the rest of his brief life, advocates teetotalism, and causes a scandal by befriending a local prostitute named Lena. By the age of thirty-three, having alienated the town fathers and the local liquor interests beyond reconciliation, he dies as the result of being struck by a stone hurled at him by a grog-shop owner nicknamed Judas. Both of these novels are characterized by rigorous attention to the chronological sequence in the gospels, by their undisguised moral earnestness, and by their obvious highlighting of the biblical parallels.

Writers of this genre in the 20th century have been generally more sophisticated. John Steinbeck's *The Grapes of Wrath* (1939) recounts the Exodus-like wanderings of the poverty-stricken Joad family, who leave the Oklahoma dust bowl with a horde of others like them and set out for California in an old, dilapidated car. Set against this Old Testament pattern is a secondary motif derived from the New Testament, involving a leader with the same initials as Jesus Christ – Jim Casy – and his twelve fellow migrants, the Joad family. Casy is a former preacher who gradually moves from being an orthodox revivalist Christian to being a believer in the essential sanctity of man. While his religious thinking is slowly changing, Casy goes to prison to protect Tom Joad. Shortly after his release, he is killed by one of a group of anti-union men who hate his intentions. His attitude towards his attackers is epitomized in the words 'You don't know what you're a-doin,' words which echo Jesus' appeal on the cross, 'Forgive them, Father, they know not what they do.'

Graham Greene's *The Power and the Glory* (1940) has as its hero a nameless whisky priest. Shifty and alcoholic, he lives in the virtually Marxist state of Tabasco in Mexico. His antagonist, the police lieutenant, is a fanatical atheist; he has all the fervour about his beliefs which the priest should have but lacks. The priest is ultimately executed by the state; he gives up his life for the sake of the criminal James Calver, a bank robber and murderer whose name suggests Calvary. Peter's denial of Jesus is symbolized by Padre José, who refuses to hear the whisky priest's confession, and Judas is represented by the mestizo, who in effect causes the hero's arrest.

The Jesus hero of Harold Kampf's *When He Shall Appear* (1953) is Janek Lazar, a Russian Jew living in London, who practises faith healing, gains disciples, and preaches a religion of simplicity. He is convinced that Christianity has become too dogmatic and has ceased to be a way of life. The clergy of all denominations unite against him, and he is subsequently arrested on a Thursday in the gardens of Leicester Square. Though the judge dismisses the charges, the clergy plot to have him banished. They are eventually successful, and Lazar is deported to Russia.

The Christ motif appears in a number of William Faulkner's works but nowhere more directly than in *A Fable* (1954). The Jesus figure here is the corporal, whose name, Stephan, is mentioned only once, after his death. Born at Christmas in a Middle Eastern stable, he associates himself with twelve men of his squadron and is executed at the age of thirty-three. Parallels with the gospel accounts are ubiquitous: they include a Judas figure, Polchek, who commits suicide by hanging himself, and two women who claim the corporal's body after his death, Marthe and Marya.

Gore Vidal's novel *Messiah* (1954; somewhat revised in later editions) is to a considerable degree a parodic reflection on the spread of 1st-century Christianity. The central character, John Cave, is a mortician from the state of Washington who comes south to California at the age of thirty and preaches that life on this earth is not worth living and that it is good to die. Suicide thus becomes a supremely virtuous act, provided that this 'better way' is chosen for the proper reasons. Cave quickly develops a huge following, and millions express their belief in Cavesword or Cavesway, the new religion, created largely by publicity agents, which soon displaces Christianity. Cave himself writes nothing, but his brilliant follower, Paul Himmell, publicizes Cave's oral teachings. Three years after Cave's arrival in California Himmell arranges to have him murdered and cremated and his ashes spread over the United States from a jet plane. Subsequently a special Congressional hearing proclaims Cavesword as the national religion.

John Barth's *Giles Goat-Boy or, The Revised New Syllabus* (1966) is also a parodic novel. The long and complicated plot evolves in a hypothetical university world controlled by the heartless computer WESCAC. The Shepherd Emeritus, Enos Enoch, is analogous to Jesus, and George Giles, by imitating him, constitutes a secondary Jesus figure, whose mission in life is to redeem the university. The

Virgin Mary, John the Baptist, Pontius Pilate, Mary Magdalene, and other biblical figures are represented by roughly comparable characters. This protracted and irreverent work constitutes in effect an undisguised literary caricature of Jesus and his followers.

An entirely different category of Jesus literature is devoted to stories of imaginary appearances of Jesus in modern times: early examples include an interpolated episode in Archibald McCowan's novel *Christ, the Socialist* (1894), William Stead's *If Christ Came to Chicago* (1894), and Edward Everett Hale's response to Stead, *If Christ Came to Boston* (1895). Jerome K. Jerome's play *The Passing of the Third Floor Back* (1907) presents a Jesus who lives in a London boardinghouse and works miracles for the benefit of his fellow lodgers. Perhaps the most meritorious contribution of this kind is Upton Sinclair's novel *They Call Me Carpenter* (1922), in which the narrator, having fallen unconscious in a church in Western City, dreams that Jesus steps down from a stained-glass window and enters public life under the name of Mr Carpenter. He supports a strike by the local tailors' union and is befriended by a film star named Mary Magna. Later he is betrayed by an agent of the American Legion posing as one of his disciples and is ordered to appear in the court of Judge Ponty. Before the trial takes place, the narrator's dream comes to an end.

A few inspirational novels in English present heroes who deliberately attempt to pattern their lives on what they believe Jesus would have done had he been in their place. The two best-known examples of this genre are Mary Augusta Ward's *Robert Elsmere* (1888), the tale of an English vicar who leaves his parish to form a 'New Brotherhood' of working men in the slums of London, and Charles Sheldon's *In His Steps, or What Would Jesus Do?* (1896), which tells of an American Congregationalist minister's campaign to persuade his followers not to do anything without first asking themselves 'What would Jesus do?' Glenn Clark's sequel to this novel, entitled *What Would Jesus Do?* (1950), incorporates a similar moral ideal for readers living in the post-World War II era.

Jesus has also been the subject of a number of 20th-century radio plays, films, and television series. These generally make no pretence to literary worth, but among the exceptions are Dorothy

Sayers' *The Man Born to Be King* (1943) for radio and Anthony Burgess' *Jesus of Nazareth* (1977) for television.

David Greenwood (deceased)
University of Maryland
Larry W. Hurtado
University of Manitoba

John the Baptist

The appearance of John the Baptist in the wilderness signals 'the beginning of the gospel' (Mark 1:1, 4; Acts 1:22; 10:37). Luke is unique in furnishing an account of John's birth which parallels that of Jesus (Luke 1, 2). John was of priestly descent, son of the aged Zacharias and Elisabeth (Luke 1:5–7). When the angel Gabriel's annunciation was questioned by Zacharias, he was afflicted with dumbness (Luke 1:8–23), which did not depart until after the birth of John, an event which Zacharias was inspired to hail in the words of the Benedictus (Luke 1:57–79). Mary's visit to her cousin Elisabeth ties the two stories together (Luke 1:39–56). A single verse alludes to John's infancy and youth (Luke 1:80).

In the synoptic gospels John is an ascetic figure whose dress recalls the ancient prophets (Matthew 3:4; Mark 1:6). He preaches the coming judgment (Matthew 3:7–10, 12; Luke 3:7–9, 17) and summons the people to a 'baptism of repentance for the remission of sins' (Mark 1:4), hence his title 'the Baptist'. A short summary of John's ethical teaching is peculiar to Luke (3:10–14). John proclaims the coming one, mightier than he, the agent of God's judgment who will baptize 'with the Holy Ghost and with fire' (Matthew 3:11, 12; Luke 3:15–18; Mark 1:7, 8 omits 'with fire').

Jesus is baptized by John in the Jordan. Mark simply states this as a fact (1:9); Luke glosses over it (3:21); in Matthew Jesus assures John that 'it becometh us to fulfil all righteousness' (Matthew 3:13–15); the fourth gospel has John refer to the incident indirectly (John 1:32, 33).

The New Testament presents John as the forerunner of Jesus and identifies Jesus with the coming one prophesied by John, although in the synoptics and especially in Mark this is implied rather than stated. Matthew and Luke depict John near the end of his life as unsure of Jesus' identity and sending disciples to ask, 'Art thou he that should come, or do we look for another?' (Matthew 11:2–6; Luke 7:18–23). Several sayings indicate Jesus' high opinion of John (Matthew 11:7–19; 21:23–27, 32; Mark 11:27–33; Luke 7:24–35; 16:16; 20:1–8; cf. John 5:35).

Only the fourth gospel mentions a period when Jesus' and John's ministries overlap (John 3:23, 24). John's arrest by Herod Antipas, his imprisonment and death are narrated in Mark 6:17–29 (cf. Matthew 14:3–12). John attracted a circle of disciples (Matthew 11:2; Luke 7:18; John 3:25; 4:1) who practised prayer (Luke 11:1) and fasting (Matthew 9:14; Mark 2:18; Luke 5:33). The fourth gospel stresses the transfer of allegiance of such disciples from John to Jesus (John 1:35–40), but Acts 19:1–7 suggests the continuance of a 'Baptist' sect after John's death.

For writers in the Middle Ages as for the Fathers of the Church, John the Baptist is the model ascetic whose words and example rebuke the worldly. His life of temperance provides a standard by which Dante's repentant gluttons can measure their sin (*Purgatorio*, 22.151–54), and his desert hermitage is not the place for the self-indulgent False-Seeming in the *Romance of the Rose* (6998–7000). The denunciation of the varieties of 'luxury' which opens *The Pardoner's Tale* recalls the execution of the 'ful giltelees' Baptist John at the command of a drunken Herod (6.488–91). John Gower in *Vox Clamantis* appropriates the Baptist's voice to denounce the materialism of his time and call people to repentance. In *Piers Plowman*, John is imagined with the other souls in Limbo, where he is reported as announcing that the time of their release and the kingdom of Christ are near at hand (B.16.82, 249–52). Late medieval and early Renaissance drama contrasts the virtue of John with the vices of Herod, Herodias, and Salome, the wantons instrumental in his beheading.

John's ministry and his poverty are a standing rebuke to worldly prelates for Milton. John is also 'the great Proclaimer' of the Son of God's coming and a hero of the Spirit whose baptizing and anointing of the previously unknown son of Joseph launches the action of *Paradise Regained* (1.18–38). By contrast, the role of Blake's John is largely limited to that of the polemicist arguing in 'All Religions Are One' that 'the true Man is the source [of all Religions], he being the Poetic Genius'. The scripture which heads the seven Blakean theses set out here – 'The Voice of one crying out in the Wilderness' – more than suggests their author's adoption of the Proclaimer's *persona*. In 'Nehemias Americanus', Cotton Mather's tribute to John Winthrop in *Magnalia Christi Americana*, the recollection of the early Massachusetts governor brings the Baptist to mind: as humble as he was firm, he wore rude clothing and ate plain fare.

As exemplary ascetic and heroic proclaimer of the heavenly kingdom, the figure of John in Dryden's *MacFlecknoe* provides an inverted image of the fools targeted by the mock-epic writer. The bloated and licentious prince of unreason Flecknoe defers to the 'thoughtless majesty' of his successor: 'I... / Was sent before but to prepare thy way' (26, 32). Flecknoe is an anti-Baptist, and the one he announces an anti-Christ who will 'reign, and wage immortal war with wit' (12). Allusion to the Baptist and his ministry serves a similar purpose in Pope's *Dunciad,* where the Goddess of Folly anoints with 'the sacred Opium' a new monarch in the empire of Dulness: 'All hail! and hail again! / My son! the promised land expects thy reign' (1.288, 291–92). When addressed typologically in Pope's earlier 'Messiah: A Sacred Eclogue', the theme of John's proclaiming and baptizing of Christ is given neo-classical dress: 'Hark! a glad voice the lonely desert cheers' (29). In poems such as Thomas Parnell's *The Hermit* and James Beattie's *The Minstrel,* the figure of John as the fearless critic of vice is displaced by the shepherd-swain living frugally in a mossy seat far from the noise and corruption of urban existence. Sterne's robustly unsentimental *Tristram Shandy* names John once: 'May... the praecursor, and... the Baptist', Dr Slop reads from his interminable litany of curses (3.11).

Carlyle, in a manner which invites comparison with Blake, assumes the dual role of Baptist and Jeremiah to his age. The 'wild Seer' of *Sartor Resartus* is pictured not altogether seriously as 'shaggy, unkempt, like a Baptist living on locusts and wild honey'. Teufelsdröckh's power of insight allows him to penetrate the most profound mysteries in 'the Life of Man', and so qualifies him to serve as teacher of the true way (1.4). That volcanic seer partially anticipates his author, who comes with increasing earnestness to clamour against and lament the evils of Mammonism in his self-proclaimed role as latter-day prophet. The narrator of Melville's *The Piazza* makes plain his estimate of the biblical prophet's efficacy as teacher: the sight of 'Jacks-in-the-pulpit' brings to mind 'their Baptist namesake', who 'preached but to the wilderness'. Longfellow's 'Vox Clamantis' dramatizes the impact of John's preaching repentance upon the Priest, Scribes, and Pharisees who suspect him of making himself a Messiah.

With the growth of a literature of sensuality in the second half of the 19th century, Edward FitzGerald's *Rubáiyát of Omar Khayyám* renounces the gospel of 'Repentance' proclaimed by 'foolish Prophets' (stanzas 7, 26), and the agents and circumstances of John's execution come to draw close attention. The picturing of the Baptist's severed head and Salome's white breasts creates a sensation in *Fra Lippo Lippi*, Browning's ironic treatment of carnality in religious art and, implicitly, of Victorian prudery, while Wilde's *Salomé* dramatizes something of the complex dynamics of love and hatred, sex and death, the flesh and the spirit.

References to John are frequent in Conrad – for example, in *Heart of Darkness* (pt. 2), *Nostromo* (1.3), and *The Secret Agent* (3.13). Purdy has argued that 'the ferocious gospel figure' provides Conrad and his reader with 'a model of perfect fidelity' against which to measure shams (92). It is likely as well that the association of John with false prophets and treacherous leaders, as in the 'Gian' Battista Fidanza' of *Nostromo* (3.11), does not leave the Conradian biblical figure untouched. T.S. Eliot's dramatic monologue 'The Love Song of J. Alfred Prufrock' also sets a modern John against the biblical character and in a tone which suggests impotent nostalgia: 'But though I have wept and fasted, wept and prayed, / Though I have seen my head (grown slightly bald) brought in upon a platter, / I am no prophet...' (81–83). A 'plump and pink' minister is imagined falling into a swoon at the sight and sound of the Baptist in Margaret Laurence's *The Stone Angel* (chapter 1), and in Updike's *Rabbit, Run,* the Episcopal minister, Eccles, appears to Harry Angstrom as John the Baptist reminding him of repentance. The most complete John the Baptist figure in modern literature, however, is probably Jean-Baptiste Clamence, the narrator in Albert Camus' *The Fall,* who discourses at length on 'my career as a false prophet crying in the wilderness and refusing to come forth'.

Camille R. La Bossière
University of Ottawa
Charles H.H. Scobie
Mount Allison University

Last Supper (Eucharist)

The apostle Paul gives the earliest written citation of the tradition of the last meal held by Jesus with his disciples before his betrayal and death (1 Corinthians 11:23–26), and all four gospels describe the event. While a Passover meal is indicated in the synoptics, John places the meal before the official Passover and replaces the account of the significant eucharistic features of the meal with the story of how Jesus washed the disciples' feet after it; the differences may be due to the use of different calendars and a desire to place the eucharistic teaching of Jesus in a broader context (John 6:51–58). Within the context of the Passover meal Jesus gave new significance to the bread and cup as symbols of his body and blood. Drawing on language from Exodus 24, Isaiah 53, and Jeremiah 33, he spoke of giving himself in sacrifice on behalf of all people in order to inaugurate the New Covenant through which sins are forgiven. The token meal was to be celebrated as a foretaste of the messianic banquet. In obedience to the Lord's intention the early Church adopted the pattern of the meal for its own regular 'Lord's Supper' at which it proclaimed the Lord's death, enjoyed fellowship with him, and looked forward to his future coming.

The accounts of the meal, although clearly based on actual reports of the event, are liturgically shaped in that they present those features of the Supper which became significant for the pattern of the Church's meal. The precise wording of the accounts differs, suggesting two lines of transmission (Lucan/Pauline and Marcan). The Passover setting emphasized in Mark's narrative provides the atmosphere for the meal with its remembrance of God's act of redemption under the Old Covenant and its eager anticipation of his future, final act of redemption. The disciples, reflecting anew on the significance for their people of the exodus from Egypt, would have interpreted Jesus' words 'This do in remembrance of me' in light of the Passover, and recalled how he had previously spoken of the 'exodus' which he, as one 'greater than Moses', would accomplish for all humankind through his death.

The meal table expresses the motifs of table fellowship with Jesus (seen in the post-resurrection context in the Emmaus story) and also of spiritual nourishment for those who partake of the elements. Notably, it is the cup rather than the wine which is specifically mentioned: attention should be directed to Old Testament cup imagery rather than simply to vine and wine imagery (e.g., Psalms 16:5; 23:5; 116:13; cf. Jeremiah 16:7). Above all, the contrast between the Old and New Covenants is decisive for interpreting the Supper. The narratives show an increasing interest (from Mark via Luke to John) in the teaching given by Jesus at the meal, suggesting the principle that Word and Sacrament belong together. Finally, the Supper demonstrates how Jesus turned the fate which he suffered as a result of opposition to his message of the kingdom of God into the means of reconciliation and salvation for others through his vicarious, sacrificial death, and how he called his disciples, who shared in the Supper, to be ready to tread the same path of suffering and service.

The Greek term *eucharistia,* which appeared in the 1st century in connection with the Lord's Supper, and which has predominated since, derives from the word for 'gratefulness', reflecting the thanksgiving of Jesus at the Last Supper (Matthew 26:27; Mark 14:23; Luke 22:19; 1 Corinthians 11:24) and signifying not only an attitude of thankfulness but also its outward evidence. The concept traces to the Hebrew equivalent of 'blessing' the Lord, a form of praise which, as in the Psalms, specifically recounts God's generosity and mercy. It is the action of thanksgiving which actualizes, in this sense, God's gift of grace, allowing it to be real and present to the recipient.

For the early Church the Eucharist was the central point of life and worship. St Justin Martyr, St Ignatius, and St Irenaeus likened it to the feeding of the five thousand (John 6). Artistic representations of the Eucharist in early 2nd-century catacomb art show a basket of bread containing a cup of wine resting upon a fish (W. Lowrie, *Art in the Early Church*, 1947, pl. 13b, c, 15). For Ignatius it was 'the elixir of immortality, the antidote that we should not die but live in Christ Jesus for ever' (*Ephesians* 20:2); for Justin, 'The food which is blessed by the prayer of his Word, and by which our blood and flesh by transmutation are nourished... the flesh and blood of that Jesus which was made flesh' (*Apology* 1.66–67; cf. St Augustine, *Sermo*, 57.7, 'On the Lord's Prayer'). Such language, when reported to hostile Roman authorities, was enough to arouse the convenient charge of cannibalism (e.g., Pliny the Younger).

It was customary in the life of the early Church to recite or sing the prologue to John's Gospel (1:1–14) as the last element in the service; that is, the transmutation was understood in a spiritual sense, such as later is reflected in Augustine's phrase, 'Believe and thou hast eaten' (cf. Hugh of St Victor, *De Sacramentis*, 2.8.5); for Augustine the incarnational union of Christ with human flesh continues in every generation as the Church continues to celebrate the Eucharist (*Sermo*, 131, on John 6:53; cf. *Sermo*, 112.4–5). The vigour of this idea can still be felt (c. 1100) in St Anselm of Canterbury's eucharistic hymn 'To Our Lord in the Sacrament', which begins, 'Hail! Christ's pure body – born of the Holy Virgin – / Living flesh, and true Man, and perfect Godhead!'

From the 3rd century, careful attention was paid to Christ's words in the institution. Accordingly, Tertullian and St Cyprian identify the bread and wine with the body and blood of Christ, Cyprian developing the idea of the Eucharist as a sacrifice. Tertullian, however, also calls the bread a *figura* of the body, and Origen elaborates an extensive allegory of the Lord's Supper. St Ambrose (*De mysteriis*, 9.50–55), along with Fathers of the Greek church such as St John Chrysostom and St Cyril of Jerusalem, alludes to a transformation of the elements themselves on an analogy with the transformation of water into wine at the marriage feast in Cana and the transformation of Moses' rod into a serpent (Exodus 4). These ideas are foundational to the doctrine of transubstantiation, although the doctrine was not fully developed until the 12th century nor systematically defined until the analysis of St Thomas Aquinas in the 13th century and the declaration of the doctrine in the decrees of the Fourth Lateran Council (1215). Much of the difficulty and controversy surrounding the doctrine may relate, ironically, to semantic difficulties: *substantia* meant 'spiritual' substance to writers of the 12th century – that is, they understood it in the sense in which it is used in the Creed, where Christ is said to be 'one substance with the Father' before his incarnation; from the 16th century, popular usage began to apply the term largely to material substance (our modern usage), which character it bears almost exclusively from the empiricists (e.g., John Locke) onward.

It is the Anglican tradition which chiefly characterizes poetry on the Eucharist in the 17th century. Among the finest of these meditative poems are Henry Vaughan's 'The Feast' from the second part of his *Silex Scintillans,* which contains the stanza:

> Spring up, O wine,
> And springing shine
>   With some glad message from his heart,
> Who did, when slain,
> These means ordain
>   For me to have in him a part.

These lines reflect both the Anglican liturgical practice of receiving the two elements and the strengthened meditative emphasis on direct relationship between the participant and Christ in his sacrifice. John Donne, who left the Catholic Church to become an Anglican divine, wrote a number of powerful poems relating to Christ's sacrifice (e.g., 'Good Friday, 1613') but has little to say about the Eucharist directly (cf. 'The Crosse'). For George Herbert, another priest-poet of the Anglican Church, a deep devotion to the Eucharist is coupled with a fideist's scepticism concerning the possibility of adequately describing or even intellectually apprehending the mystery of Christ's presence in the sacrament. Accordingly, he follows in his poems the advice he gives to theologically uncertain country parsons in *A Priest to the Temple,* saying of the faithful parson that 'Neither finds he any issue in this, but to throw himself down at the throne of grace, saying, Lord, thou knowest what thou didst, when thou appointedst to be done thus; therefore doe thou fulfill what thou didst appoint; for thou art not only the feast, but the way to it' (chapter 22). The apparent dichotomy between the appearance of bread and the reality of the flesh of Christ offered in sacrifice is, in the brilliant dialectic of his second poem on 'H. Communion', resolved in rerooting and expanding the reader's sense of substance:

> I could beleeue an Impanation
> At the rate of an incarnation,
>   If thou hadst dyde for Bread... (25–27ff.)

Here, as in his first poem on 'H. Communion',

> Onely thy grace, which with these elements comes,
>   Knoweth the ready way,
>   And hath the privie key,
> Op'ning the soul's most subtile rooms. (19–22)

As in 'An Offering' and 'The Banquet', an attitude of thankfulness is the best preparation for the sacrament in which, as he says in 'The Elixir' (echoing Irenaeus), 'all may of thee partake'. Herbert then compares the sacrament to the philosopher's stone:

> This is the famous stone
> That turneth all to gold:
> For that which God doth touch and own
> Cannot for lesse be told.
> (Cf. Chaucer, *The Canon's Yeoman's Tale*, 8.1428–71)

Herbert's sentiments accord with the general line of theological argument reflected by Jeremy Taylor a generation later in his *The Real Presence and Spirituall of Christ in the Blessed Sacrament* (1654) and also *The Worthy Communicant* (1660), in which the lyrical Bishop argues that there is danger on all sides in trying to reduce *mysterium*, like metaphor, to material analytics. From a Puritan perspective the danger was primarily that of making religion mystical; the American Calvinist Edward Taylor's celebrated verse in *Preparatory Meditations before my Approach to the Lord's Supper* (1682; 1693–1725), eschewing that path, ironically makes instead all the real world symbolic of scriptural theme and doctrine, and composes thereby one of the most useful compendia of American biblical typology from the period.

The 18th century, with its tendency towards rationalism in both theology and poetry, is not rich in eucharistic themes in literature. As a fresh convert to Catholicism, Dryden in *The Hind and the Panther*

(1687) had expressed a weariness with eucharistic controversy now felt by many:

> Could he his god-head veil with flesh and bloud
> And not veil these again to be our food?
> His grace in both is equal in extent,
> The first affords us life, the second nourishment.
> And if he can, why all this frantick pain
> To construe what his clearest words contain,
> And make a riddle what he made so plain?
> To take up half on trust, and half to try,
> Name it not faith, but bungling biggottry. (1.134–42)

Poems and hymns by Isaac Watts ('When I Survey the Wondrous Cross') and Philip Doddridge ('My God, and Is Thy Table Spread') refer to the elements as 'sacred pledges' of the actual sacrifice on Calvary, a theme still found in Reformed hymnody in the 19th century, as in Horatio Bonar's 'For the bread and for the wine, / For the pledge that seals him mine' ('The Supper of Thanksgiving', 1870). Other hymns, expressions of the evangelical revival, hearken back to a Catholic formulation such as is found in the longer version of John Wesley's 'Author of Life Divine' (1745) and Charles Wesley's 'The Eucharistic Mystery' and 'Jesu, my Lord and God Bestow' (1745). The former of these hymns takes up the incomprehensibility of the eucharistic mystery in terms which recall Herbert; the latter specifically recollects a Catholic understanding of the sacrament:

> And make the real sign
> a sure and effectual means of grace...
> Only do thou my heart prepare
> To find thy real presence there,
> And all thy fullness gain.

It is in the Calvinist *Olney Hymns*, especially those of William Cowper (which draw their imagery largely from the Old Testament), that the most arresting depiction of the sacramental trope occurs:

> There is a fountain filled with blood
> Drawn from Emmanuel's veins;

And sinners, plunged beneath that flood,
Lose all their guilty stains. ('Praise for the Fountain
Opened', Zechariah 13:1; cf. 'Welcome to the Table')

In one of the many ironies of ecclesiastical history in the 18th century, this was to become a popular eucharistic hymn among those Reformed, Baptist, and Congregational churches and chapels most keen to disavow Catholic doctrine of the Real Presence because it was felt to provoke a ghoulish imagination. Yet the idea of the Eucharist as a sacrament of thanksgiving, re-emphasized in the 17th century by Richard Hooker (*Ecclesiastical Polity*) and Jeremy Taylor (*The Worthy Communicant*), survived intact in virtually all English Christian traditions, validating the succinct definition of Dr Johnson in his *Dictionary*: 'the sacramental act in which the death of our Redeemer is commemorated with a thankful remembrance; the sacrament of the Lord's Supper'.

The Eucharist has, of course, provided inspiration for great music of every era, from the Gregorian chant to the recent *Requiem* of Andrew Lloyd Webber. On the Continent, the 18th century was a particularly fruitful period for musical settings for the Mass, such as Bach's 'B-Minor Mass', his cantatas, and 'St Matthew's Passion', and shorter meditations on the sacrament such as Mozart's *Ave Verum Corpus*'. In Protestant England, however, all of Handel's oratorios are on Old Testament subjects; it was a thin period for church music on the grand scale, with only Samuel Wesley (1766–1837), the son of Charles Wesley, composing notable settings for the texts of Holy Communion.

In the early part of the 19th century, especially in American literature, the sacrament had a less than prominent literary history. In part this was due to the decreased importance it occupied in the worship life of Reformed, Congregational, and Baptist churches, which, following Zwingli and some of the early radical reformers among the Anabaptists, variously reduced observance of the Eucharist to four times a year (adopted by Reformed churches) or, at most, to one Sunday each month (among some of the Baptists). Further, formal religious consciousness was becoming more and more subtended by an empiricist and, in the modern linear sense of the word, 'historical' self-consciousness, even as popular spirituality was tending towards subjectivism. In poetry, the 'Communion Hymn' of William Cullen Bryant is characterized by misty, romantic sentiment:

> In tender memory of his grave
> The mystic bread we take,
> And muse upon the life he gave
> So freely for our sake.

The more profound communion in Bryant's verse, as in much poetry of the period, is with Nature (e.g., 'Thanatopsis'). Longfellow's 'Midnight Mass for the Dying Year' is charged with the 'real presence' of Nature rather than of God; his 'The Children of the Lord's Supper', presented as a translation from a Swedish tale by Bishop Tegner, concerns the sense of awe and reverie felt by children preparing for their first communion – here presented as a bit of anthropological exotica. Whittier's *Snow-Bound* takes a more macabre turn, with a ship's captain offering to feed his starving sailors on his own body; when at the last minute a school of porpoises arrive, '"Take, eat," he said, "and be content. / These fishes in my stead are sent..."' Such uneasiness with the sacrament could prompt a more openly hostile view such as D.H. Lawrence expresses in his essay on Melville in *Studies in Classic American Literature,* where he observes that there is an odd inconsistency in Melville's horror at the cannibalism of the Typees:

> He might have spared himself his shudder... If the savages
> like to partake of their sacrament... and to say, directly:
> 'This is thy body, which I take from thee and eat. This is
> thy blood, which I sip in annihilation of thee,' why surely
> their sacred ceremony was as awe inspiring as the one
> Jesus substituted.

In England during this period, the Oxford (or Tractarian) movement, under Keble, J.H. Newman, Froude, and others, concerned with 'national apostasy' (see Keble's 1833 sermon of that title), set out to reform prevalent Erastian and latitudinarian tendencies in the Church of England. They launched a series of *Tracts for the Times* which attracted the support of still others, including Edward B. Pusey, and urged a movement in liturgy, worship, and theology towards the

191

Roman rite. Pusey, after Newman's departure as the Tractarian leader, preached his famous sermon 'The Holy Eucharist, a Comfort to the Penitent' in 1843. It was quickly condemned by the Oxford Chancellor and six doctors of divinity for its advocacy of the doctrine of the Real Presence, but this merely had the effect of guaranteeing its publication and wide circulation. While only Newman among the most prominent members became a Catholic (later Cardinal), the movement did much to revive medieval views of the Church and its sacraments such as influenced Tennyson, William Morris, Christina Rossetti, and the Pre-Raphaelites, among others. It also prompted the translation for Anglican use of a number of medieval eucharistic hymns, including the 'Adoro Te', 'Pange Lingua Gloriosi', and 'Lauda Sion Salvatorem' of St Thomas Aquinas (trans. John Mason Neale). While Tennyson's Holy Grail, like much of the flowery romanticism of Morris and cloudy religiosity of the Pre-Raphaelites generally, applies eucharistic language to the creation of a symbolic mystical iconography, the poetry of Gerard Manley Hopkins makes sacramental language the font of all understanding which may be called 'poetic'. In 'The Bugler's First Communion', he deflects the Tennysonian theme in regarding the 'housel', as it was called in the Middle Ages, of 'an our day's God's own Galahad' from the priest's point of view. As a priest, he is attracted to the diversity and oddity of all those whose 'pure fasted faces draw unto this feast', whose bent and feeble knees 'God shall strengthen' ('Easter Communion'); the deep sense of communion within the multifaceted Body of Christ receiving the sacrament causes him to write:

> The dappled die-away
> Cheek and the wimpled lip,
> The gold wisp, the airy-grey
> Eye, all in fellowship –
> This, all this beauty blooming,
> This, all this freshness fuming,
> Give God while worth consuming.
> ('Morning, Midday, and Evening Sacrifice')

The impact of the Oxford Movement expresses itself in the 20th century in a variety of ways. One of these is the conversion to Anglo-

Catholic faith and practice of T.S. Eliot, whose historical understanding of the Eucharist lies behind the reverent irony of these lines from 'East Coker':

> The dripping blood our only drink,
> The bloody flesh our only food;
> In spite of which we like to think
> That we are sound, substantial flesh and blood.

Within the tradition of Hopkins as well as Eliot is David Jones, whose *Anathemata* is woven through with eucharistic motifs, especially those of anamnesis and the Real Presence (e.g., 8.227–29, 241, etc.). These themes are explored psychologically by Graham Greene in his novels *The Power and the Glory* (1940), *The Heart of the Matter* (1948), and *Brighton Rock* (1938). Greene's fiction is one of the prominent influences on Canadian Mennonite novelist Rudy Wiebe, whose *Blue Mountains of China* (1970) contains a chapter, 'Drink Ye All of It', in which David Epp, who led his own small community in a successful 'exodus' from Russia into China in the oppressions of 1927, then goes back, sacrificing himself, so that the authorities will not take vengeance upon those families who have chosen not to flee.

For J.R.R. Tolkien, the whole character of the happy ending in Western Christian narrative, especially of the type we call 'fairy story', is charged with a *consolatum* which evokes the symbolic significance of the Eucharist; hence he calls its special sense of joy and release to life a 'euchatastrophe', a 'far-off gleam or echo of *evangelium* in the real world' ('On Fairy Stories'). If Tolkien is right, the persistence of eucharistic imagery in literature may be due in some measure to its power as an integrator of biblical narrative and symbol, not only of the Last Supper and atonement directly but of all of the narrative and typology leading up to it. The sacrifice to which the believing person appeals invokes participation in the catastrophes of human experience which render it necessary: as Margaret Avison's 'For the Murderous: The Beginning of Time' suggests, it is also stories like that of the self-willed and failed sacrifice of Cain, with its aftermath in the spilling of Abel's innocent blood, which still speak (cf. Hebrews 11:4) in the Eucharist, leading as they do to a point where

> In time the paschal lamb
> before the slaying did
> what has made new the wine
> and broken bread. (sunblue, 49)

so that blood for blood no more need be required.

David L. Jeffrey
University of Ottawa
I. Howard Marshall
University of Aberdeen

Nativity of Christ

The nativity (birth) of Jesus Christ is chronicled in extensive narratives in the first and second chapters of both Matthew and Luke. Both versions emphasize the divine nature of Jesus' conception, his birth from a virgin, and his destiny as the Christ (Messiah) appointed to be the saviour of Israel and the world.

Matthew and Luke agree that at the time of Jesus' conception, his mother Mary and his guardian Joseph are engaged but have not yet had sexual relations (Matthew 1:18; Luke 1:27, 34). Thus Jesus is identified as being a descendant of David's line, the 'Son of David' through Joseph by adoption (Matthew 1:16, 20; Luke 1:27, 32; 2:4). In both gospels an angelic announcement heralds Jesus' birth (Matthew 1:20–23; Luke 1:30–35), identifying 'Jesus' as the child's name (Matthew 1:21; Luke 1:31) and proclaiming him as 'Saviour' (Matthew 1:21; Luke 1:31). Both accounts name Bethlehem as Jesus' birthplace (Matthew 2:23; Luke 2:39). The birth is chronologically situated during Herod the Great's reign (Matthew 2:1; Luke 1:5).

The accounts of Matthew and Luke, however, differ significantly in their inclusion of different events and personae as well as in their decisions to focus attention on the nativity from the perspectives of Joseph in Matthew and Mary in Luke.

Matthew begins with a genealogy of Jesus' Davidic descent through Joseph (1:17). In 1:18–25, Matthew reports on Joseph's reaction to the news that Mary has conceived a child 'of the Holy Spirit' (1:20). 'An angel of the Lord' (1:21) appears to Joseph in a

194

dream to convince him of the veracity of the divine nature of Jesus' conception and proclaim him as the long-awaited 'Emmanuel', the promised saviour of Israel (1:21, 23).

In Matthew 2 the actual birth is recorded (2:1). The universal significance of the nativity is communicated through the story of the Gentile Wise Men who travel in search of 'the King of the Jews' guided by a star (2:2). They pay him homage with symbolic gifts referring to his kingship, royal priesthood, and future passion and death: gold, frankincense, and myrrh (2:1). Herod's enmity towards the foretold Messiah and the consequent avoidance of him by the magi (2:12), as well as the flight of Mary, Joseph, and Jesus into Egypt (2:13) and Herod's slaughter of Bethlehem's male children (2:16) foreshadow the future conflict between Jesus and political authority. Divinely initiated dreams (1:20; 2:12, 13) and quotations from Old Testament prophecy (1:23; 2:6, 18) are important literary devices in Matthew.

Luke uses the narrative of John the Baptist's birth (1:5 – 2:25) to foreshadow Jesus' nativity. The focus is on Mary's reaction to the angelic pronouncement of Jesus' birth and her acceptance of her role in the divine plan (1:38). Luke contextualizes the nativity during the Roman census. Jesus' birth in lowly circumstances (the stable of an inn) contrasts with the accolades of the heavenly host (2:7, 14). Human recognition is afforded him by shepherds (2:15–17) and by the prophet Simeon and the prophetess Anna at the Temple (2:22–39). The Temple episode emphasizes Jesus' fulfilment of Jewish prophecy. Unique to Luke's account are the three canticles of praise recited by Mary (1:46–55), Zechariah (1:68–79), and Simeon (2:29–32).

Because the biblical nativity narratives are so rich in dramatic events, there are stong literary traditions associated with each element and possible topic, including the annunciation, the incarnation, the slaughter of the innocents, John the Baptist, Mary, Joseph, shepherds, magi, Herod, Simeon, and Anna. The birth of Jesus itself, however, is central to a host of literary adaptations, most of which illustrate the remarkable warmth with which the event is annually recollected in Christian tradition. As the history of Christmas celebration shows, however, the subject was far less popular among the Fathers of the Church and early medieval Christians (e.g., Tertullian, Origen, St

Jerome), largely because of their desire to avoid any association with celebrations of the natal feast of Roman emperors and pagan deities. Thus, while St Augustine was obliged to defend against gnostic and Manichean views of the incarnation – Faustus had characterized the event as 'the shameful birth of Jesus from a woman' (see *Contra Faustum,* 32.7; cf. 11.1) – and to stress the real humanity of Christ and the actuality of his physical birth, even he denied the Feast of the Nativity a place among signal celebrations of the Christian year. Although it gradually acquired such a place, exegetical commentary directed to the event itself is exceedingly spare until the late Middle Ages, and narrative or poetic adaptations even more rare. Two hymns by Prudentius in the 4th century, one the still popular *'Corde natus ex parentis'* ('Of the Father's Love Begotten'), emphasize not the event, but rather the significance of the incarnation theologically:

> He is Alpha and Omega,
> He the Source, the Ending he,
> Of the things that are, that have been,
> And that future years shall see...

Quem Quaeritis tropes in monastic liturgy of the 11th century emphasize the fact of the incarnation and the joy of the *pastores'* discovery; the great 12th-century hymn *'Veni Emmanuel'* ('O Come, O Come, Emmanuel') anticipates the Second Coming rather than focusing on the nativity. The subject goes virtually untreated in Old English poetry, even in the *Advent Lyrics of the Exeter Book,* again in deference to the controlling theological concept of the incarnation. Visual and plastic representation is correspondingly almost non-existent during this period; when the Christ child is depicted with Mary before the 13th century, he is shown as a *homunculus,* a miniature man, not as a realistic infant. This occurs not because medieval painters did not know how to paint real babies, but because their intent was to depict the idea of the incarnation iconographically; Mary is not seated beside a manger, but typically enthroned in a 'chair' which is at once a 'tower of David' and 'true Jerusalem' – a castle, or the walled city of St John's Revelation.

Nativity literature owes its sudden growth of popularity after the 13th century to the humanizing Christology and affective, emotional spirituality of the Franciscan revival. For St Francis, the heart of the message of the incarnation was that Christ from his splendour of divine majesty had condescended to identify with human nature – not with elevated rank or social position, but with the poorest and humblest of persons. Christ's birth in a crude cave-stable, his being laid in a manger and among the animals, and the revelation of the event first to poor people (Mary, Joseph, the shepherds) are all of crucial significance for Francis. Indeed, part of what requires radical identification with Christ in his singularly innocent suffering is that from the first he has radically identified with humanity in its universal condition of suffering in a sinful world. The first recorded nativity pageant is in 1223, when Francis obtained ecclesiastical permission to set up a crèche and pageant in an Italian church, complete with live animals, straw, and an actual baby. Looking at the completed scene, he is said to have been so overcome with emotion that he leaped into the set, snatching up the baby into his arms and breaking out in songs of praise to God. The subsequent influence of Franciscan spirituality on expansionary retellings of the biblical narratives (e.g., the widely popular *Meditationes Vitae Christi* and its translations, including Nicholas Love's *Mirrour of the Blessed Lyf of Jesu Christ*, 1400, upon the growth and development of nativity plays, lyrics, carols, and graphic representation), has been widely studied (see Van Marle; Fleming; Jeffrey). These incorporate many elements from early (2nd–5th century) apocryphal narratives such as the Protevangelium of James, the pseudo-gospels of Matthew and Thomas, the so-called History of Joseph the Carpenter, and Gospel of the Infancy.

Among the best nativity lyrics in English, none of which is earlier than the late 14th century, is John Grimestone's 'In bedlem is a child i-born' (ed. C. Brown, *Religious Lyrics of the XIVth Century*, no. 57). It encapsulates the entire narrative in eighty lines.

Grimestone, a Franciscan friar, wrote also 'A Lullaby to Christ in the Cradle', 'Christ weeps in the Cradle for the Sin of Mankind' (Brown, nos. 65, 59), and an effective imaginary dialogue between the newborn Jesus and his mother titled by its editor 'The Christ Child Shivering with Cold', in which the atonement is already anticipated as the reason for Christ's being born – hence the 'cradle' makes Mary think of a bier, and the cave a grave (no. 75).

The 15th and 16th centuries witnessed a popular diffusion of carols, dance songs adapted to Christian worship which were often (though not exclusively) associated with the nativity. Many of these celebrate not just the Bethlehem story but the entire plan of salvation. Exemplary is a 15th-century carol with the refrain 'Now may we syngyn as it is, / *Quod puer natus est nobis*' (ed. R. Greene, *The Early English Carols*, no. 19); the first stanza is indicative:

> This babe to vs that now is bore,
> Wyndyrful werkys he hath iwrowt;
> He wil not lese that was ilore,
> But baldly ayen it bowth.
> And thus it is,
> Forsothe, iwys,
> He askyth nouth but that is hys.

Others recapitulate the basic nativity narrative (e.g., Greene, no. 28), focus on one element (e.g., no. 32), or recount prophecies of the event (no. 68); still others are merely brief *lauda in exultatio*, like 'Honnd by honnd we schalle ous take' (no. 12), probably intended to be danced as well as sung, or praise of the 'gift' of the season itself such as the 16th-century carol 'Marke we mery in hall and bowr; / Thys tyme was born owr Savyowr' (no. 27):

> In this tyme God hath sent
> Hys own Son to be present,
> To dwell with us in verament.
> God, that ys owr Savyowr.

William Dunbar's 'Of the Nativitie of Christ' is an early 16th-century Scottish adaptation of the Latin hymn '*Hodie Puer Natus Est*'. The late medieval Corpus Christi plays, with their recapitulation in dramatic form of biblical salvation history, offered the best English opportunity for presentation of the nativity narrative, and rustic but effective re-enactments are to be found in all the major cycles (York, Chester, N-Town, Towneley). The Towneley Cycle's chief dramatist, the so-called Wakefield Master, produced two plays featuring the nativity, his 'First Shepherd's Play' and better-known comic 'Second Shepherd's Play'. While the latter closes with a vivid tableau (Joseph, Mary, the Child, and adoration of the shepherd), the first play is more fully responsive to the biblical narrative and presents a moving, even worshipful re-enactment. The closing scene of the 'Second Shepherd's Play' (746–49), however, poignantly captures the paradoxical double meaning of the moment – a joy already tinged with an incalculable sense of impending doom:

> 1 Pastor: Fare well, lady, so fare to beholde,
>   With thy childe on thi kne.
> 2 Pastor: Bot he lygys full cold!
>   Lord, well is me!

Reformation attitudes towards the celebration of Christmas were not always affirmative. Luther was one, however, whose celebration was vigorously and joyously medieval, and the carol he wrote on Luke 2:10 for his little son (1540) is of the angel's 'glad tidings'. 'To you this night is born a child,' it begins, then goes on to draw a lesson obverse to that heralded by the Franciscans – that the poverty into which Christ was born was God's way of declaring his scorn of 'this world's honour, wealth and might'. The carol then becomes a child's Christmas prayer:

> Ah, dearest Jesus, holy child,
> Make thee a bed, soft, undefiled,
> Within my heart, that it may be
> A quiet chamber kept for thee. (trans. C. Winkworth)

English poetry of the period holds many fine treatments of the subject, both Catholic and Protestant. Among Catholic poems Thomas Ford's 'A Heavenly Visitor' is a sober querying of Puritan disregard for the Feast of Christ's nativity, observing that though none would fail to do their utmost in regal preparation were Christ known to be coming to earth the next day, he is dishonoured by contemporary neglect of his first coming:

> We wallow in our sin
> Christ cannot find a chamber in the inn.
> We entertain him always like a stranger
> And as at first, still lodge him in a manger.

199

The 16th-century Jesuit poet Robert Southwell wrote several nativity poems, among them his visionary 'The Burning Babe' as well as an incarnation meditation, 'A Child my Choice' and the lovely carol, 'Behold a silly [simple] tender Babe'. Richard Crashaw (who converted to Catholicism after refusing to sign the Puritans' Covenant in 1644) wrote a complex antiphonal 'Hymn of the Nativity' composed from the shepherds' point of view. It concludes with the 'shepherds' singing in chorus:

> To thee, meek Majesty, soft King
> Of simple graces and sweet loves!
> Each of us his lamb will bring,
> Each his pair of silver doves!
> At last, in fire of thy fair eyes
> Ourselves become our own best sacrifice!

Francis Quarles' 'The Child Jesus' is complemented in its sense of paradox by Giles Fletcher's section on the nativity in his *Christs Victorie and Triumph in Heaven and Earth,* one stanza of which reads:

> A Child he was, and had not learn't to speake,
> That with his word the world before did make;
> His mother's armes him bore, he was so weake,
> That with one hand the vaults of Heau'n could shake;
> See how small roome my infant Lord doth take,
> Whom all the world is not enough to hold!
> Who of his yeares, or of his age hath told?
> Neuer such age so young, neuer a child so old.

The playwright Ben Jonson composed a poem emphasizing the motif of Christ in the manger as the glowing fire or light of the world: 'I sing the birth was born tonight, / The Author both of life and light.' As in late Renaissance paintings of the nativity scene, so in these two poems of Crashaw and Jonson the darkness of the stable is lit from within the manger by the Christ child himself.

In contrast, John Donne's 'Nativitie' ('Holy Sonnet 3'), an address to the Virgin, reads like a précis of the biblical infancy narrative, and has little of the dramatic power of much 16th-century nativity poetry. The first part of Henry Vaughan's 'Christ's Nativity', a two-part lyric in his *Silex Scintillans* (1650), is in the form of a classic aspiration:

> I would I had in my best part
> Fit Roomes for thee! Or that my heart
> Were so clean as
> Thy manger was!
> But I am filth, and obscene,
> Yet, if thou wilt, thou canst make clean. (19–24)

Mid-17th-century literary adaptations of the nativity story must have been severely restrained by rigid Puritan opposition to observance of the major Christian festivals. On 8 June 1647, the celebration of Christmas, Easter, Whitsun (Pentecost), and all saints' days 'heretofore superstitiously used and observed' was abolished by an Act of Parliament. It is thus somewhat ironic that Milton, with his thoroughgoing Puritan sympathies, should have written the most important nativity poem of the period, his ode 'On the Morning of Christ's Nativity' (1629). Its theme, however, is the early Christian one of the triumph of the infant Christ over the pagan gods. The poem begins by celebrating the Christmas season as replacement for the pagan *Natalis invicta:*

> This is the Month, and this the happy morn
> Wherein the Son of Heav'n's eternal King,
> Of wedded Maid, and Virgin Mother born,
> Our great redemption from above did bring…

Milton then moves on to characterize the birth as an act of battle with Satan as the adversary, concluding (after 244 lines) with an image of Mary, guarded by armoured angels, leaning over the manger:

> Her sleeping Lord with Handmaid Lamp attending:
> And all about the Courtly Stable,
> Bright-harness'd Angels sit in order serviceable.

Milton's poem was to exercise a powerful influence on subsequent treatments of the subject, including those by Edward Caswall and Elizabeth Barrett Browning.

Eighteenth-century nativity hymns by Isaac Watts ('Joy to the

World', 1719) and Charles Wesley ('Hark the Herald Angels Sing', 1739), both of whom had inherited a strong Puritan sensibility, are among the most noteworthy from that period. But it is Hannah More, the noted evangelical feminist, who best calls up the old Franciscan emphasis on the meaning of Christ's birth into poverty. In her 'Oh, how wondrous is the story,' she turns from the scene and its import of human salvation to her reading audience:

> Come, ye rich, survey the stable
> Where your infant Saviour lies;
> From your full, o'erflowing table
> Send the hungry good supplies.
>
> Boast not your ennobled stations;
> Boast not that you're highly fed;
> Jesus – hear it, all ye nations! –
> Had not where to lay his head.

But her insistence on the responsibility of the rich is then balanced by her assurance that there is something in Christ's poverty to encourage and comfort the poor:

> Come, ye poor, some comfort gather;
> Faint not in the race you run:
> Hard the lot your gracious Father
> Gave his dear, his only Son.

While none of this theme survives in E.B. Browning's 'The Virgin Mary to the Child Jesus', Mary's extended soliloquy in this poem as she watches her baby sleep constitutes possibly the richest English meditation in the affective tradition since the late medieval period. In the fifth of its thirteen stanzas Mary muses over the events of the day:

> We sate among the stalls at Bethlehem.
> The dumb kine from their fodder turning them,
> Softened their horned faces
> To almost human gazes
> Towards the newly Born.
> The simple shepherds from the star-lit brooks
> Brought visionary looks,

As yet in their astonished hearing rung
The strange, sweet angel-tongue.
The magi of the East, in sandals worn,
Knelt reverent, sweeping round,
With long pale beard their gifts upon the ground,
The incense, myrrh, and gold,
These baby hands were impotent to hold.
So, let all earthlies and celestials wait
Upon thy royal state!
Sleep, sleep, my kingly One!

Other 19th-century nativity meditations include Coleridge's 'The Shepherds', Christina Rossetti's lyric 'In the Bleak Midwinter', since set to music, Bliss Carman's 'Christmas Song', and Thomas Hardy's 'The Oxen'.

Modern plays and pageants have been written by the score since the 19th century; relatively few have literary significance. Exceptions include Longfellow's *The Golden Legend* (1851), a true nativity play, John Masefield's one-act *The Coming of Christ* (1928), Dorothy Sayers' *The Man Born to Be King* (1941–42), and a curious dramatic poem by Ezra Pound, *Christmas Prologue* (1910). In its Emmaus-like retrospect, one of the magi converses about the nativity with the shepherds. Of these Longfellow's play is the most erudite, drawing largely on pseudepigraphal and apocryphal texts – the Protevangelium, Arabic Gospel of the Infancy, Pseudo-Matthew, Gospel of Thomas, and the History of Joseph the Carpenter.

The turn of the century was notable for an outpouring of verse from Catholic poets, often relatively new converts: Francis Thompson's 'Little Jesus', Alice Meynell's 'Unto Us a Son is Given', and G.K. Chesterton's 'A Christmas Carol' are examples. A generation later, in the United States, different influences prevailed: Sara Teasdale's 'A Christmas Carol' is indebted to Christina Rossetti, and Edna St Vincent Millay's 'To Jesus on his Birthday' is more secular in its governing sensibility. William Faulkner's *A Fable* (1954) is a mythic invocation of biblical narrative in which the hero is born at Christmas in a Middle Eastern stable; his sister cannot remember whether they 'were driven from the inn itself or just turned away'. For most modern readers, however, it is probably T.S. Eliot's 'Journey of the Magi' (1927) which most traditionally declares the paradoxical nature of the birth of Jesus, the poverty which proves richer than wealth, weakness stronger than imperial might, a birth whose purpose is death, that death may be conquered. Here it is one of the Wise Men who looks back on the Bethlehem event, his lingering question an acknowledgment that, as Alice Meynell ('No Sudden Thing of Glory', 1896) and William Everson ('The Coming', 1962) also suggest, simple adoration was not enough:

> this Birth was
> Hard and bitter agony for us, like Death, our death.
> We returned to our places, these Kingdoms,
> But no longer at ease here, in the old dispensation,
> With an alien people clutching their gods.
> I should be glad of another death.

David L. Jeffrey
University of Ottawa
Lenore Gussin
New York, New York

Passion of Christ

Passion, an anglicized form of the late Latin *passio*, is used by ecclesiastical writers to refer to the suffering and death of Jesus on the cross and to the narratives of these events in the gospels (Matthew 26–27; Mark 14–16; Luke 22–23; John 18–19). The Latin term and its cognates translate the New Testament Greek word group 'suffer' (*pascho, pathos, pathema*), and in all but one instance (Hebrews 2:9) the New Testament employs the plural of the noun (*pathemata*) of the sufferings of Jesus (2 Corinthians 1:5–6; Philippians 3:10; Hebrews 2:10; 1 Peter 4:13).

In English literature one of the most imaginative and reverent passages relating to the passion of Christ is provided by Langland's *Piers Plowman*. The poet sees in his dream the Tree of Charity with its roots of Mercy and trunk of Pity (B.16.3–5); on Easter morning the poet calls his wife and daughter to honour God's resurrection: they are to creep on their knees to the cross and kiss it, a reference to the adoration of the cross (18.428); the poet dreams that he sees Piers all stained with blood and bearing a cross, and Conscience explains that the figure is Christ (19.6–8); and finally, the dreamer sees Grace give Piers the cross with which to make Holy Church (19.321–22). For Langland the cross is also a talisman for warding off spiritual danger or evil. This persists as a perennial image in gothic and horror fiction.

There are numerous, generally less emotional, references to the passion and cross in Chaucer: in his ABC addressed to the Virgin (60, 82, 162); at the conclusion of *Troilus and Criseyde* (5.1842–46); in *The Man of Law's Tale*, the prayer of Custance addressed to the cross (*Canterbury Tales*, 2.449–62); in *The Clerk's Tale*, Griselda's prayer (4.556, 558); and in *The Parson's Tale* (10.258, 271, 667, 819).

The dramatic enactment of the crucifixion forms the central aspect of all four English Mystery cycles. In the York 'Mortificacio Christi' Jesus' address from the cross is especially effective with its line, 'On roode am I ragged and rente', twice repeated (36.120, 253, 304; cf. plays no. 34 and 35, as well as those in the Towneley, Coventry, and Chester cycles).

After the Reformation there is little innovation in the tradition of the passion and crucifixion. References occur throughout English literature, but most are conventional reflections, among the best known of which involves the characterization and narration of the pilgrimage of Spenser's Redcrosse Knight, champion of Christian holiness (*Faerie Queene*, 1.1.2). St Thomas More's poem 'Consider Well' is a traditional Catholic invitation to meditation on the passion even in the midst of 'our disport, our revel, and our play'.

In Shakespeare, references occur chiefly in the history plays, as in *1 Henry IV* (1.1.20.27) where Henry refers both to the blessed cross and the bitter cross (cf. *Richard II*, 4.1.94, 241; *3 Henry VI*, 4.4.21). Seventeenth-century poetry continues the tradition of meditation on the cross, as in John Davies' long poem *The Holy Roode or Christs Crosse*. Richard Crashaw maintains the traditions of Franciscan (Capuchin) meditation on the passion in numerous vivid poems, including 'O these wakeful wonds of Thine! / Are they mouths? or are they eyes?' ('On the Wounds of our Crucified Lord') and his highly charged poem 'On the Bleeding Wounds of our Crucified Lord':

Jesu, no more, it is full tide;
From thy head and from thy feet,
From thy hands and from thy side,
All thy purple rivers meet.

Crashaw's baroque litany of poems in his 'The Office of the Holy Cross', with its sequence of poetic versicle, responsor, hymn, antiphon, versicle, responsor, and prayer for each of the eight canonical *horae,* constitutes perhaps the richest of 17th-century English meditations on the passion; it draws consciously on the 13th-century 'Hours of the Passion' of William Shoreham.

John Donne's poetry combines most of the earlier traditions with ingenuity and strong personal feeling. Most remarkable is his 64-line poem entitled 'The Crosse', in which he refers to the cross as an altar, speaks of stretching his arms to form his own cross, contrasts material and spiritual crosses, and ends with the 'Crosse of Christ'. Other meditations on the passion include his 'The Progresse of the Soul', 'Hymn to God, my God, in my sicknesse', the sonnet 'Crucifying', 'Satyre 4', and 'Goodfriday, 1613. Riding Westward'. Herbert also represents a high point in 17th-century meditative poetry on the passion. His 'Sacrifice', a 252-line poem, belongs to the *O vos omnes* tradition of Christ's appeal from the cross (cf. John Grimestone's 14th-century '*O Vos Omnes*', ed. C. Brown, *Religious Lyrics of the XIVth Century*, no. 74). Related poems include 'Easter', 'Affliction', 'Conscience', 'The Crosse', 'The Church Militant', and 'L'Envoy'.

Sir Thomas Browne's *The Garden of Cyrus* includes numerous expressions of admiration for landscape design inviting meditation because it incorporates the 'metaphysical cross'; in his *Religio Medici*, though eschewing Capuchin-styled adoration of the cross, he confesses to its importance in his spiritual reflection: 'At the sight of a Crosse or Crucifix I can dispence with my hat, but scarce with the thought and memory of my Saviour; I cannot laugh at but rather pity the fruitlesse journeys of Pilgrims, or contemne the miserable condition of Friers; for though misplaced in circumstance, there is something in it of devotion...' (1.3). Milton's 'The Passion' is an early, unfinished poem; two other references to the cross in Milton's poetry prophesy its place in the scheme of salvation: in 'Hymn on the Morning of Christ's Nativity', 'The Babe lies yet in smiling Infancy / That on the bitter Cross / Must redeem our loss' (151–53), and in *Paradise Lost* Michael tells Adam that in future ages God's Son will be 'nailed to the Cross' (12.413–17). In Bunyan's *Pilgrim's Progress* a vision of the cross causes Christian's burden to fall at last from his shoulders.

Despite the influence of the Wesleys and the Great Revival of the 18th century, relatively few important cross poems were written and the passion in general was eschewed as a subject for 'polite' literature. William Cowper provides a notable exception, though his treatment tends to be abstract by comparison with his 17th-century forebears, as, for example, in the closing lines of his 'The Progress of Error', in which 'the Cross, once seen is death to ev'ry vice: / Else he that hung there suffer'd all his pain, / Bled, groan'd, and agoniz'd, and died, in vain.' On the other hand, like some of the Puritan and Reformed hymn writers before him, he uses the blood of Christ metonymically for the passion and the cross in a fashion almost as vivid as the French Capuchins, the painter Matthias Grünewald, or Richard Crashaw. One of the most popular of his *Olney Hymns* (no. 15) begins:

> There is a fountain fill'd with blood
> Drawn from Emmanuel's veins;
> And sinners, plung'd beneath that flood,
> Lose all their guilty stains

and includes lines reminiscent of St Bonaventure or Jacopone:

> E'er since, by faith, I saw the stream
> Thy flowing wounds supply;
> Redeeming love has been my theme,
> And shall be till I die.

Among the Romantic poets, the most important in relation to this subject is Blake, who alludes to the cross in *The Four Zoas*, Night the Eighth (ed. Keynes, 325, 331, 338, 593–95); *Milton* (5.3; 22.58); and *Jerusalem* (652, 688, 695). Especially interesting is Blake's continuation of the tradition of the vision of the cross at the Last

Judgment (444; cf. *The Everlasting Gospel*, 749, 751, 759). In Wordsworth references to the cross are conventional: *The Prelude*, 6.484; *The White Doe of Rylstone* (124, 356, 663); *The Excursion*, 5.907; *Ecclesiastical Sonnets*, 3.40.9. In Coleridge, *Christabel* (389) and *The Rime of the Ancient Mariner* (141–42) are noteworthy. Shelley's references reflect his opposition to established Christianity: for example, *Queen Mab* (7.138, 174, 219, 229) and *Hellas* (224, 501, 603, 638, 1018). In *Don Juan* Byron ironically echoes Colossians 1:20: 'the crimson cross... red with no redeeming gore' (8.972–74).

Among 19th-century novelists Scott refers to relics of the cross in novels set in the Middle Ages: *Ivanhoe*, chapter 5; *Quentin Durward*, chapter 33; *The Talisman*, chapter 4. A more imaginative use of this tradition appears at the end of Melville's *Billy Budd*. In later 19th-century poetry, Longfellow's sonnet 'The Cross of Snow' and Sidney Lanier's 'A Ballad of the Trees and the Master' are remarkably original and moving. The poetry of Tennyson contains a number of references to the cross: 'Sea Dreams' (186); 'Vastness' (15); 'Happy' (3, 6, 12); and in *The Idylls of the King*, 'The Coming of Arthur' (271–74), 'Balin and Balan' (108, 451–53), and 'The Last Tournament' (493). Christina Rossetti recollects the passion in 'What Is It Jesus Saith', 'Tuesday Holy Week', 'Good Friday Morning', and 'General Assembly'; cf. E.A. Robinson's sonnet, 'Calvary'. In the poetry of Hopkins the image of Christ and his cross figures in 'Rosa Mystica', *The Wreck of the Deutschland*, especially stanza 24, and 'Pilate'.

Yeats deals with the crucifixion in three verse dramas: *Land of the Heart's Desire*, *Calvary*, and *Resurrection*. Lawrence's poems, including 'Reminder', 'Meeting among the Mountains', and 'The Cross', reveal his interest in the cross as an instrument of suffering and as a recurring form of life, as also does his 'The Man who Died'. Robert Frost in 'The Peaceful Shepherd' projects an ironic view of 'the Cross of Faith' in league with 'the Crown of Rule', 'the Scales of Trade', and 'the Sword', and a cross substitute becomes a symbol of human suffering in Hemingway's *The Old Man and the Sea*. The most memorable reference to the cross in Joyce is the sermon in *A Portrait of the Artist as a Young Man*, chapter 3; it is the subject of frequent wordplay in *Finnegans Wake*.

In 20th-century fiction, sermons on the cross appear not only in Joyce's *Portrait* but also in the conclusion of Faulkner's *The Sound and the Fury* and in Flannery O'Connor's *The Violent Bear It Away*, chapter 5. *Helena*, by Evelyn Waugh, is a fictional retelling of the story of the finding of the True Cross. Various modern 'fifth gospels' offer revisionist versions of the passion in which the hero suffers violent death at the hands of his adversaries (see T. Ziolkowski, *Fictional Transfigurations of Jesus*, 1972, 290).

Twentieth-century poems on the passion and cross include several by Joyce Kilmer, A.E. Housman's 'Easter Hymn', Ezra Pound's 'Ballad of the Goodly Fere', and Edith Sitwell's 'Still Falls the Rain'. Perhaps the best of the longer 20th-century cross poems are David Jones' *Anathemata* and 'Tribune's Visitation', while Geoffrey Hill's 'Canticle for Good Friday' and '*Lachrimae*' present more typical modern views.

Esther C. Quinn
New York, New York
John R. Donahue, SJ
University of Notre Dame

Pharisees

Pharisees were religious observants (Hebrew *perushim*, 'set apart'; Greek *pharisaioi*), members of a Jewish religious and political party active during the period of the Second Temple, and the one most frequently mentioned in the New Testament. They were an elite and scholarly brotherhood, many of them members of the school of Hillel (and later Gamaliel). The (probably false) derivation of their name from Hebrew *pesher*, 'interpretation', may be due to their subtle and argumentative exegesis. Unlike the scribes, who were formally trained in rabbinic law, most Pharisees were laymen. Their concern was oral law, or *Halakah*, which they taught as a 'tradition (*paradosis*) of the elders' (cf. Mark 7:1–13; Matthew 15:1–9) handed down from Moses and of equal authority with the Torah. By elaboration and observance of oral law they strove to create a community committed to a 'walk' (*halak; halakah*) of purity, fasting, prayer, tithing, and separation from the wider society of the 'unclean', and in this way to fulfil the injunction of Leviticus 11:44 and Exodus 19:6. Commentary on

Leviticus 11:44 reflects the Pharisees' sense of calling: 'Be holy ones (*qadoshim*) for I am holy (*qadosh*), that is: "As I am holy so you should be holy ones (*qadoshim*); as I am a separated one (*parush*) so should you be separated ones (*perushim*)"' (Sipra 39a; cf. Mekilta Exodus 19:6). As distinct from the Sadducees, who were more strictly biblicist, the Pharisees admitted a process of development in their magisterial legal tradition, which eventually contained several hundred extracanonical prohibitions and commandments. The view of Josephus (*Vita* 2.10–12; *Jewish War* 2.8.14; *Antiquities* 18.1.3, etc.) is that they were the most powerful political force in Jewish society of the first century. In contrast to the Sadducees they were eschatologically oriented, believing not only in life after death and the resurrection of the body, but in the advent of the Messiah and the Day of Judgment. As a powerful and elitist party, the Pharisees attracted the criticism of other sects (including the community at Qumran), and indeed of their own rabbinic successors.

Though numerous early Christian converts were Pharisees (notably St Paul and Nicodemus), the associations which continue from the New Testament, especially because of the words of Jesus recorded in the gospels, are extremely negative. Pharisees are typically condemned for exalting the 'letter of the law' while remaining obtuse to its 'spirit' or intention (Matthew 3:7; 23:13–35; Luke 18:9–14). Jesus' characterization of them as 'whited sepulchres' and a 'generation of vipers' was influential enough that 'Pharisee' has become in Western literature substantially synonymous with 'self-righteous', 'charlatan', 'fundamentalist', 'bigot', and 'hypocrite'.

Hypocrisy is the focus of many of Jesus' own comments. The parable of the Pharisee recorded in Luke 18:9–14, for example, contrasts the religious disposition of two characters – a Pharisee and a publican. The Pharisee is confident that as a result of his good works he enjoys God's favour and can pray with special assurance of receiving divine blessing. The publican or tax collector, an outcast in Jewish society because of a deserved reputation for dishonesty and ungodliness, has no confidence in himself and, acknowledging his sin, merely casts himself on the mercy of God. Jesus' observation that 'this man went down to his house justified rather than the other' was doubtless intended to shock his audience, although it reiterated a familiar biblical principle that self-exaltation (especially as indicated in contempt for others) leads to humiliation, and humility to exaltation.

The politics of religion have frequently occasioned literary reference to the Pharisees as exemplars of hypocrisy or false piety. Intersectarian quarrels in the Middle Ages, especially as reflected in the antifraternal and antimendicant satire of William of St Amour, Jean de Meun's *Roman de la Rose*, Langland's *Piers Plowman* (B.15.100–112, in which Pharisees are called 'a dunghill full of snakes'), and Chaucer's *Friar's Tale* and *Summoner's Tale*, frequently allude to Jesus' condemnations of the Pharisees. The widow-persecuting summoner of *The Friar's Tale* answers nicely to Bunyan's context in *The Pilgrim's Progress*, where in response to religious trick questions concerning true piety by Mr Hold-the-World, Christian answers: 'The Hypocritical Pharisees were also of this Religion, long prayers were their pretence, but to get widows houses was their intent, and greater damnation from God was their Judgment, Luke 20.46, 47.'

'Pharisaism' has, unsurprisingly, been a charge levelled by all manner of religious groups against perceived adversaries from the 14th century well into the modern period. The Wycliffite *Leaven of the Pharisees* is directed against friars; Tyndale's 'Pharisees' of a century later are 'papists' of any vocation; and those which appear in Dryden's *The Hind and the Panther* are illegitimate progeny of the Reformation. Concern for the 'spirit' as distinct from the external 'letter' of religion is evident in Donne's 'Pharisaicall Dissemblers' who 'feigne devotion' ('Holy Sonnet 8'), and for Herbert 'things inwardly good to have an eye to the world may be pharisaicall' ('Reasons for Arthur Woodnoth's living…'). Carlyle, in his *Characteristics*, argues that 'as soon as Prophecy among the Hebrews had ceased, then did the reign of Argumentation begin; and the ancient Theocracy, in its Sadduceeisms and Phariseeisms, and vain jangling of sects and doctors, give token that the soul of [religion] had fled.' Melville in *Billy Budd* says of Claggart's hidden evil nature: 'The Pharisee is the Guy Fawkes prowling in the hid chambers underlying some natures like Claggart's.'

Among the best known of modern novelists to draw on these allusions is François Mauriac, whose *Le noeud de vipeurs* and *La*

Pharisienne are studies in contemporary perversion of the spirit of faith by 'religious' manipulation and hypocrisy.

David L. Jeffrey
University of Ottawa
I. Howard Marshall
University of Aberdeen

Temptation of Christ

Matthew (4:1–11) and Luke (4:1–13) offer the fullest accounts of the temptation of Jesus during his fast in the desert. After a period of forty days without food, Satan came to him and tempted him in three ways. In the first instance, he taunted, 'If thou be the Son of God, command this stone that it be made bread.' Jesus answered him, saying, 'It is written, That man shall not live by bread alone, but by every word of God.' Next, according to Luke's account, the devil took Jesus up into a high mountain, showing him 'all the kingdoms of the world in a moment of time' and proposing, 'All this power will I give thee, and the glory of them: for that is delivered unto me; and to whomsoever I will I give it. If thou therefore wilt worship me, all shall be thine.' Jesus, unmoved, rebuked him for his blasphemous presumption: 'Get thee behind me, Satan: for it is written, Thou shalt worship the Lord thy God, and him only shalt thou serve.' Satan then brought Jesus to a pinnacle of the Temple in Jerusalem and challenged him to cast himself down: if he were really the Son of God, he would surely be protected from harm by angels, Satan argued, citing Psalm 91:11–12. Jesus replied simply, 'Thou shalt not tempt the Lord thy God,' and the devil departed, at which point 'angels came and ministered unto him'. In the Matthean account the order of the last two temptations is inverted.

The forty days' fast of Jesus is seen by commentators from St Augustine (e.g., *De consensu Evangelistarum*, 4.9) to Matthew Henry (*Commentary* 5.31) as paralleling those of Moses (Exodus 34:28) and Elijah (1 Kings 19:8); Henry imagines further that the temptation of Jesus accordingly occurred 'probably in the great wilderness of Sinai'.

Augustine, who established the main lines of medieval exegesis on the passage, describes the three temptations as 'by food, that is, by

the lust of the flesh... by vain boasting... and... by curiosity'
(*Enarrationes in Psalmos* 9.13). Later commentators tended to view the
three temptations as paralleling those by which Adam fell, described
as gluttony, vainglory, and avarice. St Gregory the Great, who follows
this schema in one of his homilies, is quoted by Peter Lombard in his
influential *Sententiae* (2.21.5):

> The Ancient Enemy raised himself in three temptations,
> against our first parents, for then he tempted them with
> gluttony, vainglory and avarice. And in tempting he was
> triumphant, for he made them subject to him through their
> consent. Indeed, he tempted them with gluttony, when he
> showed them the food of the forbidden tree and persuaded
> them to eat. He tempted them with vainglory when he said,
> 'you shall be as Gods' [Genesis 3:5]. And having made
> progress to this point he tempted them through avarice
> when he spoke of 'knowing good and evil'. For avarice has
> as its object not only money, but loftiness of estate. The
> desire which seeks elation is rightly called avarice in this
> sense.

Lombard then draws the parallel:

> But in the same way that he [Satan] overcame the first man,
> he lay subdued before the Second. He tempted him also
> with gluttony when he said, 'Command that these stones be
> made bread' [Matthew 4:3]. He tempted him with vainglory
> when he said, 'If thou be the Son of God cast thyself down.'
> And with avarice for loftiness and power, he tempted him
> when he showed him all the world, saying, 'All these things
> will I give thee if falling down thou wilt adore me.'

The commentary of the Venerable Bede on Matthew's version of the
temptation narrative (*Patrologia Latina*, 92.19–20) offers an early
English example of the established typology; in his comments on
Luke's version Bede adds other biblical parallels, including the three
excuses in the parable of the wedding feast (Luke 14:16ff.) and the
temptation described in John's First Epistle as 'the lust of the flesh,
and the lust of the eyes, and the pride of life' (1 John 2:16). Later

commentators elaborate the motif of the triple temptation with reference to the 'three foes of man', the World, the Flesh, and the Devil.

The earliest English literary adaptation of the narrative of the temptation of Christ is in the Old English *Christ and Satan* (665–710), in which the age-old struggle between Christ and Satan for the souls of men is summed up with an exemplary model for resistance to diabolic temptation. The 13th-century *Cursor Mundi* and 14th-century *Stanzaic Life of Christ* both treat the text in light of the parallels suggested in the commentaries. The temptation provides an important subject for the Corpus Christi drama, notably N-Town (22), York (22), and Chester (12), the latter of which pairs it with the narrative of the woman taken in adultery. In York the devil confides in the audience that he will 'assaye' Christ with gluttony, vainglory, and 'couetise'.

With the Reformation came a shift in typology and a replacement of medieval paradigms of moral theology with an emphasis on justifying faith. Calvin sees a typological parallel not with Eden but with Sinai: the fasting of Christ in preparation for his ministry is likened to Moses' being taken apart by God to receive the Law (*Harmony of the Gospels*, 1.134). Calvin rejects the medieval identification of the first temptation with gluttony, saying that 'it is ridiculous to speak of the immoderate display of gluttony in the case of a hungry man seeking food to satisfy his nature... What kind of high living is there in bread?... So we gather that Satan had made a direct attack on Christ's faith, that by overcoming it he might drive Christ into illicit and corrupt ways of finding food' (1.137). The Son of God was tempted for the sake of mankind, says Calvin, 'that by his victory he might win us the triumph' (1.135). It was also significant for our example: 'The first thing worth noting is that Christ uses scripture as a shield against [Satan], and this is the true way of fighting, if we wish to win a sure victory' (1.135).

John Bale's *A brief comedy or interlude concernynge the temptacyon of Our Lorde and Sauer Jesus Christ by Sathan in the desart* (1537) is a dramatic representation along largely medieval lines, despite its Reformation polemic, and adds as part of the temptation to kingdoms of this world an offer of 'fayre women, of countenaunce ameable, /

With all kyndes of meates, to the body delectable.' In Giles Fletcher's *Christ's Victorie, and Triumph* (1610) Satan disguises himself as 'A good old Hermit... / That for devotion had the world forsaken' (2.16, 20) – a stratagem which the author may have derived from the popular 'Temptations of St Anthony' (cf. Spenser, *Faerie Queene*, 1.1.29–35). Joseph Beaumont's *Psyche: Or Loves Mysterie in XX Cantos, Displaying the Intercourse betwixt Christ and the Soule* (1648) presents Satan as a wealthy monarch with a long train of servants offering food and aid to the hungry Christ if he will only consent to prove his divine entitlement by performing a miracle. When Christ rejects the offer, the entire pageant vanishes into thin air, leaving only 'Ashes, which so strongly smelt / That other Stincks compar'd with this, might seem / Perfumes' (9.241).

Protestant writers frequently parallel the temptation of Christ to Satan's 'tempting' of Job. Henry Oxenden's *Jobus Triumphans* (1656) concludes with such a comparison, and allusions to Job flavour Beaumont's *Psyche*. These texts, along with numerous other Protestant 'Christiads' identify Rome (and by implication the Roman Church) as the principal kingdom offered to Christ.

The best-known English poem on the subject is Milton's *Paradise Regained* (1671), which he based on the Luke version because it suited his 'grand design' to place the 'temptation of the tower' last. Milton combines the older medieval motif – showing Christ's heroic resistance to Satan as redressing Adam's disobedience (2.129–39) – with Calvin's emphasis, that Satan, often abusing scripture for his own purposes, can best be answered from out of a firm command of scripture. Milton's Satan discovers that while 'persuasive rhetoric' had been powerful enough to defeat Eve (4.1–9), the 'It is written' of scripture is more powerful still. Christ refutes Satan not with rational argument but with revelation (4.285ff.).

Carlyle's *Sartor Resartus* has Professor Teufelsdröckh exclaiming (at the beginning of 'The Everlasting Yea'): 'Temptations in the Wilderness! Have we not all to be tried with such?' In his contemporary reading 'Our wilderness is the wide World in an Atheistic century; our Forty Days are long years of suffering and fasting: nevertheless, to these also comes an end.' In Somerset Maugham's *Of Human Bondage* Philip, looking down from a hill in

Heidelberg, 'thought how the tempter had stood with Jesus on a high mountain and shown him the kingdoms of the earth. To Philip... it seemed that it was the whole world that was spread before him, and he was eager to step down and enjoy it. He was far from degrading fears and free from prejudice... He was his own master at last. From old habit, unconsciously he thanked God that he no longer believed in him.' A more traditional response is represented by T.S. Eliot in *Murder in the Cathedral*. Thomas is approached by a series of tempters whose seductions parallel those faced by Christ in the wilderness: the first tempts him to gratify bodily appetite; the second to seize power over 'all the kingdoms of the earth'; and the third to misappropriate spiritual power. A final, unanticipated tempter ('I expected three visitors, not four,' says Thomas, 476–77) tries to lure him into the sin of spiritual pride.

David L. Jeffrey
University of Ottawa

THE GREAT SAYINGS OF JESUS

Part Two: The Sermon On The Mount

Part Three: Proverbs and Shorter Sayings

Part Four: The Major Parables

Part Five: Jesus Disputes With The Scribes And Pharisees

Epilogue: From the Transfiguration to the Resurrection

From the Nativity to the Death of John the Baptist

THE ANNUNCIATION
Luke 1:26–35, 38, 46–55

And in the sixth month the angel Gabriel was sent from God unto a city of Galilee, named Nazareth, To a virgin espoused to a man whose name was Joseph, of the house of David; and the virgin's name was Mary. And the angel came in unto her, and said, Hail, thou that art highly favoured, the Lord is with thee: blessed art thou among women. And when she saw him, she was troubled at his saying, and cast in her mind what manner of salutation this should be.

And the angel said unto her, Fear not, Mary: for thou hast found favour with God. And, behold, thou shalt conceive in thy womb, and bring forth a son, and shalt call his name JESUS. He shall be great, and shall be called the Son of the Highest: and the Lord God shall give unto him the throne of his father David: And he shall reign over the house of Jacob for ever; and of his kingdom there shall be no end.

Then said Mary unto the angel, How shall this be, seeing I know not a man?

And the angel answered and said unto her, The Holy Ghost shall come upon thee, and the power of the Highest shall overshadow thee: therefore also that holy thing which shall be born of thee shall be called the Son of God...

And Mary said, Behold the handmaid of the Lord; be it unto me according to thy word. And the angel departed from her...

And Mary said, My soul doth magnify the Lord, And my spirit hath rejoiced in God my Saviour. For he hath regarded the low estate of his handmaiden: for, behold, from henceforth all generations shall call me blessed. For he that is mighty hath done to me great things;

and holy is his name. And his mercy is on them that fear him from generation to generation.

He hath shewed strength with his arm; he hath scattered the proud in the imagination of their hearts. He hath put down the mighty from their seats, and exalted them of low degree. He hath filled the hungry with good things; and the rich he hath sent empty away. He hath holpen his servant Israel, in remembrance of his mercy; As he spake to our fathers, to Abraham, and to his seed for ever.

THE NATIVITY
Luke 2:1–20; Matthew 2:1–12

And it came to pass in those days, that there went out a decree from Caesar Augustus, that all the world should be taxed. (And this taxing was first made when Cyrenius was governor of Syria.) And all went to be taxed, every one into his own city.

And Joseph also went up from Galilee, out of the city of Nazareth, into Judaea, unto the city of David, which is called Bethlehem; (because he was of the house and lineage of David:) To be taxed with Mary his espoused wife, being great with child.

And so it was, that, while they were there, the days were accomplished that she should be delivered. And she brought forth her firstborn son, and wrapped him in swaddling clothes, and laid him in a manger; because there was no room for them in the inn.

And there were in the same country shepherds abiding in the field, keeping watch over their flock by night. And, lo, the angel of the Lord came upon them, and the glory of the Lord shone round about them: and they were sore afraid.

And the angel said unto them, Fear not: for, behold, I bring you good tidings of great joy, which shall be to all people. For unto you is born this day in the city of David a Saviour, which is Christ the Lord. And this shall be a sign unto you; Ye shall find the babe wrapped in swaddling clothes, lying in a manger.

And suddenly there was with the angel a multitude of the heavenly host praising God, and saying, Glory to God in the highest, and on earth peace, good will toward men.

And it came to pass, as the angels were gone away from them into heaven, the shepherds said one to another, Let us now go even unto Bethlehem, and see this thing which is come to pass, which the Lord hath made known unto us.

And they came with haste, and found Mary, and Joseph, and the babe lying in a manger. And when they had seen it, they made known abroad the saying which was told them concerning this child. And all they that heard it wondered at those things which were told them by the shepherds. But Mary kept all these things, and pondered them in her heart. And the shepherds returned, glorifying and praising God for all the things that they had heard and seen, as it was told unto them...

Now when Jesus was born in Bethlehem of Judaea in the days of Herod the king, behold, there came wise men from the east to Jerusalem, Saying, Where is he that is born King of the Jews? for we have seen his star in the east, and are come to worship him.

When Herod the king had heard these things, he was troubled, and all Jerusalem with him. And when he had gathered all the chief priests and scribes of the people together, he demanded of them where Christ should be born.

And they said unto him, In Bethlehem of Judaea: for thus it is written by the prophet, And thou Bethlehem, in the land of Juda, art not the least among the princes of Juda: for out of thee shall come a Governor, that shall rule my people Israel.

Then Herod, when he had privily called the wise men, enquired of them diligently what time the star appeared. And he sent them to Bethlehem, and said, Go and search diligently for the young child; and when ye have found him, bring me word again, that I may come and worship him also.

When they had heard the king, they departed; and, lo, the star, which they saw in the east, went before them, till it came and stood over where the young child was. When they saw the star, they rejoiced with exceeding great joy. And when they were come into the house, they saw the young child with Mary his mother, and fell down, and worshipped him: and when they had opened their treasures, they presented unto him gifts; gold, and frankincense, and myrrh.

And being warned of God in a dream that they should not return to Herod, they departed into their own country another way.

THE FLIGHT INTO EGYPT
Matthew 2:13–23

And when they were departed, behold, the angel of the Lord appeareth to Joseph in a dream, saying, Arise, and take the young child and his mother, and flee into Egypt, and be thou there until I bring thee word: for Herod will seek the young child to destroy him.

When he arose, he took the young child and his mother by night, and departed into Egypt: And was there until the death of Herod: that it might be fulfilled which was spoken of the Lord by the prophet, saying, Out of Egypt have I called my son.

Then Herod, when he saw that he was mocked of the wise men, was exceeding wroth, and sent forth, and slew all the children that were in Bethlehem, and in all the coasts thereof, from two years old and under, according to the time which he had diligently enquired of the wise men.

Then was fulfilled that which was spoken by Jeremy the prophet, saying, In Rama was there a voice heard, lamentation, and weeping, and great mourning, Rachel weeping for her children, and would not be comforted, because they are not.

But when Herod was dead, behold, an angel of the Lord appeareth in a dream to Joseph in Egypt, Saying, Arise, and take the young child and his mother, and go into the land of Israel: for they are dead which sought the young child's life.

And he arose, and took the young child and his mother, and came into the land of Israel. But when he heard that Archelaus did reign in Judaea in the room of his father Herod, he was afraid to go thither: notwithstanding, being warned of God in a dream, he turned aside into the parts of Galilee: And he came and dwelt in a city called Nazareth.

THE BOY JESUS IN THE TEMPLE
Luke 2:42–52

And when he was twelve years old, they went up to Jerusalem after the custom of the feast. And when they had fulfilled the days, as they returned, the child Jesus tarried behind in Jerusalem; and Joseph and his mother knew not of it.

But they, supposing him to have been in the company, went a day's journey; and they sought him among their kinsfolk and acquaintance. And when they found him not, they turned back again to Jerusalem, seeking him.

And it came to pass, that after three days they found him in the temple, sitting in the midst of the doctors, both hearing them, and asking them questions. And all that heard him were astonished at his understanding and answers. And when they saw him, they were amazed: and his mother said unto him, Son, why hast thou thus dealt with us? behold, thy father and I have sought thee sorrowing.

And he said unto them, How is it that ye sought me? wist ye not that I must be about my Father's business? And they understood not the saying which he spake unto them.

And he went down with them, and came to Nazareth, and was subject unto them: but his mother kept all these sayings in her heart. And Jesus increased in wisdom and stature, and in favour with God and man.

JESUS IS BAPTIZED BY JOHN
Luke 3:1–6, 15–22

Now in the fifteenth year of the reign of Tiberius Caesar, Pontius Pilate being governor of Judaea, and Herod being tetrarch of Galilee, and his brother Philip tetrarch of Ituraea and of the region of Trachonitis, and Lysanias the tetrarch of Abilene, Annas and Caiaphas being the high priests, the word of God came unto John the son of Zacharias in the wilderness. And he came into all the country about Jordan, preaching the baptism of repentance for the remission of sins; As it is written in the book of the words of Esaias the prophet, saying, The voice of one crying in the wilderness, Prepare ye the way of the Lord, make his paths straight. Every valley shall be filled, and every mountain and hill shall be brought low; and the crooked shall be made straight, and the rough ways shall be made smooth; And all flesh shall see the salvation of God...

And as the people were in expectation, and all men mused in

their hearts of John, whether he were the Christ, or not; John answered, saying unto them all, I indeed baptize you with water; but one mightier than I cometh, the latchet of whose shoes I am not worthy to unloose: he shall baptize you with the Holy Ghost and with fire: Whose fan is in his hand, and he will throughly purge his floor, and will gather the wheat into his garner; but the chaff he will burn with fire unquenchable. And many other things in his exhortation preached he unto the people.

But Herod the tetrarch, being reproved by him for Herodias his brother Philip's wife, and for all the evils which Herod had done, Added yet this above all, that he shut up John in prison.

Now when all the people were baptized, it came to pass, that Jesus also being baptized, and praying, the heaven was opened, And the Holy Ghost descended in a bodily shape like a dove upon him, and a voice came from heaven, which said, Thou art my beloved Son; in thee I am well pleased.

THE TEMPTATION
Luke 4:1–13

And Jesus being full of the Holy Ghost returned from Jordan, and was led by the Spirit into the wilderness, Being forty days tempted of the devil. And in those days he did eat nothing: and when they were ended, he afterward hungered.

And the devil said unto him, If thou be the Son of God, command this stone that it be made bread. And Jesus answered him, saying, It is written, That man shall not live by bread alone, but by every word of God.

And the devil, taking him up into an high mountain, shewed unto him all the kingdoms of the world in a moment of time. And the devil said unto him, All this power will I give thee, and the glory of them: for that is delivered unto me; and to whomsoever I will I give it. If thou therefore wilt worship me, all shall be thine. And Jesus answered and said unto him, Get thee behind me, Satan: for it is written, Thou shalt worship the Lord thy God, and him only shalt thou serve.

And he brought him to Jerusalem, and set him on a pinnacle of the temple, and said unto him, If thou be the Son of God, cast thyself down from hence: For it is written, He shall give his angels charge over thee, to keep thee: And in their hands they shall bear thee up, lest at any time thou dash thy foot against a stone. And Jesus answering said unto him, It is said, Thou shalt not tempt the Lord thy God. And when the devil had ended all the temptation, he departed from him for a season.

THE STILLING OF THE STORM
Luke 8:22–25

Now it came to pass on a certain day, that he went into a ship with his disciples: and he said unto them, Let us go over unto the other side of the lake. And they launched forth. But as they sailed he fell asleep: and there came down a storm of wind on the lake; and they were filled with water, and were in jeopardy.

And they came to him, and awoke him, saying, Master, master, we perish. Then he arose, and rebuked the wind and the raging of the water: and they ceased, and there was a calm.

And he said unto them, Where is your faith? And they being afraid wondered, saying one to another, What manner of man is this! for he commandeth even the winds and water, and they obey him.

THE GADARENE SWINE
Mark 5:1–19

And they came over unto the other side of the sea, into the country of the Gadarenes.

And when he was come out of the ship, immediately there met him out of the tombs a man with an unclean spirit, Who had his dwelling among the tombs; and no man could bind him, no, not with chains: Because that he had been often bound with fetters and chains, and the chains had been plucked asunder by him, and the fetters broken in pieces: neither could any man tame him. And always, night and day, he was in the mountains, and in the tombs, crying, and cutting himself with stones.

But when he saw Jesus afar off, he ran and worshipped him, And cried with a loud voice, and said, What have I to do with thee, Jesus, thou Son of the most high God? I adjure thee by God, that thou torment me not. For he said unto him, Come out of the man, thou unclean spirit. And he asked him, What is thy name? And he answered, saying, My name is Legion: for we are many. And he besought him much that he would not send them away out of the country.

Now there was there nigh unto the mountains a great herd of swine feeding. And all the devils besought him, saying, Send us into the swine, that we may enter into them.

And forthwith Jesus gave them leave. And the unclean spirits went out, and entered into the swine: and the herd ran violently down a steep place into the sea, (they were about two thousand;) and were choked in the sea.

And they that fed the swine fled, and told it in the city, and in the country. And they went out to see what it was that was done. And they come to Jesus, and see him that was possessed with the devil, and had the legion, sitting, and clothed, and in his right mind: and they were afraid.

And they that saw it told them how it befell to him that was possessed with the devil, and also concerning the swine. And they began to pray him to depart out of their coasts.

And when he was come into the ship, he that had been possessed with the devil prayed him that he might be with him. Howbeit Jesus suffered him not, but saith unto him, Go home to thy friends, and tell them how great things the Lord hath done for thee, and hath had compassion on thee.

JAIRUS' DAUGHTER AND THE WOMAN WITH AN ISSUE OF BLOOD
Mark 5:21–43

And when Jesus was passed over again by ship unto the other side, much people gathered unto him: and he was nigh unto the sea.

And, behold, there cometh one of the rulers of the synagogue, Jairus by name; and when he saw him, he fell at his feet, And besought him greatly, saying, My little daughter lieth at the point of death: I pray thee, come and lay thy hands on her, that she may be healed; and she shall live.

And Jesus went with him; and much people followed him, and thronged him. And a certain woman, which had an issue of blood twelve years, And had suffered many things of many physicians, and had spent all that she had, and was nothing bettered, but rather grew worse, When she had heard of Jesus, came in the press behind, and touched his garment.

For she said, If I may touch but his clothes, I shall be whole. And straightway the fountain of her blood was dried up; and she felt in her body that she was healed of that plague.

And Jesus, immediately knowing in himself that virtue had gone out of him, turned him about in the press, and said, Who touched my clothes?

And his disciples said unto him, Thou seest the multitude thronging thee, and sayest thou, Who touched me? And he looked round about to see her that had done this thing.

But the woman fearing and trembling, knowing what was done in her, came and fell down before him, and told him all the truth.

And he said unto her, Daughter, thy faith hath made thee whole; go in peace, and be whole of thy plague.

While he yet spake, there came from the ruler of the synagogue's house certain which said, Thy daughter is dead: why troublest thou the Master any further?

As soon as Jesus heard the word that was spoken, he saith unto the ruler of the synagogue, Be not afraid, only believe. And he suffered no man to follow him, save Peter, and James, and John the brother of James.

And he cometh to the house of the ruler of the synagogue, and seeth the tumult, and them that wept and wailed greatly. And when he was come in, he saith unto them, Why make ye this ado, and weep? the damsel is not dead, but sleepeth.

And they laughed him to scorn. But when he had put them all out, he taketh the father and the mother of the damsel, and them that

THE GREAT SAYINGS OF JESUS

were with him, and entereth in where the damsel was lying. And he took the damsel by the hand, and said unto her, Talitha cumi; which is, being interpreted, Damsel, I say unto thee, arise. And straightway the damsel arose, and walked; for she was of the age of twelve years. And they were astonished with a great astonishment.

And he charged them straitly that no man should know it; and commanded that something should be given her to eat.

THE FEEDING OF THE FIVE THOUSAND
Mark 6:31–44

And he said unto them, Come ye yourselves apart into a desert place, and rest a while: for there were many coming and going, and they had no leisure so much as to eat. And they departed into a desert place by ship privately.

And the people saw them departing, and many knew him, and ran afoot thither out of all cities, and outwent them, and came together unto him.

And Jesus, when he came out, saw much people, and was moved with compassion toward them, because they were as sheep not having a shepherd: and he began to teach them many things.

And when the day was now far spent, his disciples came unto him, and said, This is a desert place, and now the time is far passed: Send them away, that they may go into the country round about, and into the villages, and buy themselves bread: for they have nothing to eat.

He answered and said unto them, Give ye them to eat. And they say unto him, Shall we go and buy two hundred pennyworth of bread, and give them to eat?

He saith unto them, How many loaves have ye? go and see. And when they knew, they say, Five, and two fishes.

And he commanded them to make all sit down by companies upon the green grass. And they sat down in ranks, by hundreds, and by fifties. And when he had taken the five loaves and the two fishes, he looked up to heaven, and blessed, and brake the loaves, and gave them to his disciples to set before them; and the two fishes divided he among them all. And they did all eat, and were filled.

And they took up twelve baskets full of the fragments, and of the fishes. And they that did eat of the loaves were about five thousand men.

JESUS WALKS ON THE WATER
Matthew 14:22–33

And straightway Jesus constrained his disciples to get into a ship, and to go before him unto the other side, while he sent the multitudes away. And when he had sent the multitudes away, he went up into a mountain apart to pray: and when the evening was come, he was there alone. But the ship was now in the midst of the sea, tossed with waves: for the wind was contrary. And in the fourth watch of the night Jesus went unto them, walking on the sea.

And when the disciples saw him walking on the sea, they were troubled, saying, It is a spirit; and they cried out for fear. But straightway Jesus spake unto them, saying, Be of good cheer; it is I; be not afraid.

And Peter answered him and said, Lord, if it be thou, bid me come unto thee on the water. And he said, Come. And when Peter was come down out of the ship, he walked on the water, to go to Jesus. But when he saw the wind boisterous, he was afraid; and beginning to sink, he cried, saying, Lord, save me.

And immediately Jesus stretched forth his hand, and caught him, and said unto him, O thou of little faith, wherefore didst thou doubt?

And when they were come into the ship, the wind ceased. Then they that were in the ship came and worshipped him, saying, Of a truth thou art the Son of God.

THE DEATH OF JOHN THE BAPTIST
Matthew 14:1–12

At that time Herod the tetrarch heard of the fame of Jesus, And said unto his servants, This is John the Baptist; he is risen from the dead;

233

and therefore mighty works do shew forth themselves in him. For Herod had laid hold on John, and bound him, and put him in prison for Herodias' sake, his brother Philip's wife. For John said unto him, It is not lawful for thee to have her. And when he would have put him to death, he feared the multitude, because they counted him as a prophet.

But when Herod's birthday was kept, the daughter of Herodias danced before them, and pleased Herod. Whereupon he promised with an oath to give her whatsoever she would ask. And she, being before instructed of her mother, said, Give me here John Baptist's head in a charger.

And the king was sorry: nevertheless for the oath's sake, and them which sat with him at meat, he commanded it to be given her. And he sent, and beheaded John in the prison. And his head was brought in a charger, and given to the damsel: and she brought it to her mother. And his disciples came, and took up the body, and buried it, and went and told Jesus.

Part One
Jesus Teaches His Disciples

THE CALL OF THE DISCIPLES
Mark 1:16–20

Now as he walked by the sea of Galilee, he saw Simon and Andrew his brother casting a net into the sea: for they were fishers. And Jesus said unto them, Come ye after me, and I will make you to become fishers of men. And straightway they forsook their nets, and followed him. And when he had gone a little further thence, he saw James the son of Zebedee, and John his brother, who also were in the ship mending their nets. And straightway he called them: and they left their father Zebedee in the ship with the hired servants, and went after him...

JESUS COMMISSIONS THE TWELVE
Matthew 10

And when he had called unto him his twelve disciples, he gave them power against unclean spirits, to cast them out, and to heal all manner of sickness and all manner of disease.

Now the names of the twelve apostles are these; The first, Simon, who is called Peter, and Andrew his brother; James the son of Zebedee, and John his brother; Philip, and Bartholomew; Thomas, and Matthew the publican; James the son of Alphaeus, and Lebbaeus, whose surname was Thaddaeus; Simon the Canaanite, and Judas Iscariot, who also betrayed him.

These twelve Jesus sent forth, and commanded them, saying, Go not into the way of the Gentiles, and into any city of the Samaritans enter ye not: But go rather to the lost sheep of the house of Israel. And as ye go, preach, saying, The kingdom of heaven is at hand. Heal the sick, cleanse the lepers, raise the dead, cast out devils: freely ye have received, freely give. Provide neither gold, nor silver, nor brass in your purses, Nor scrip for your journey, neither two coats, neither shoes, nor yet staves: for the workman is worthy of his meat.

And into whatsoever city or town ye shall enter, enquire who in it is worthy; and there abide till ye go thence. And when ye come into an house, salute it. And if the house be worthy, let your peace come upon it: but if it be not worthy, let your peace return to you. And whosoever shall not receive you, nor hear your words, when ye depart out of that house or city, shake off the dust of your feet. Verily I say unto you, It shall be more tolerable for the land of Sodom and Gomorrha in the day of judgment, than for that city.

Behold, I send you forth as sheep in the midst of wolves: be ye therefore wise as serpents, and harmless as doves. But beware of men: for they will deliver you up to the councils, and they will scourge you in their synagogues; And ye shall be brought before governors and kings for my sake, for a testimony against them and the Gentiles. But when they deliver you up, take no thought how or what ye shall speak: for it shall be given you in that same hour what ye shall speak. For it is not ye that speak, but the Spirit of your Father which speaketh in you.

And the brother shall deliver up the brother to death, and the father the child: and the children shall rise up against their parents, and cause them to be put to death. And ye shall be hated of all men for my name's sake: but he that endureth to the end shall be saved. But when they persecute you in this city, flee ye into another: for verily I say unto you, Ye shall not have gone over the cities of Israel, till the Son of man be come.

The disciple is not above his master, nor the servant above his lord. It is enough for the disciple that he be as his master, and the servant as his lord. If they have called the master of the house Beelzebub, how much more shall they call them of his household? Fear them not therefore: for there is nothing covered, that shall not be revealed; and hid, that shall not be known. What I tell you in darkness, that speak ye in light: and what ye hear in the ear, that preach ye upon the housetops. And fear not them which kill the body, but are not able to kill the soul: but rather fear him which is able to destroy both soul and body in hell.

Are not two sparrows sold for a farthing? and one of them shall not fall on the ground without your Father. But the very hairs of your head are all numbered. Fear ye not therefore, ye are of more value than many sparrows. Whosoever therefore shall confess me before men, him will I confess also before my Father which is in heaven. But whosoever shall deny me before men, him will I also deny before my Father which is in heaven.

Think not that I am come to send peace on earth: I came not to send peace, but a sword. For I am come to set a man at variance against his father, and the daughter against her mother, and the daughter in law against her mother in law. And a man's foes shall be they of his own household. He that loveth father or mother more than me is not worthy of me: and he that loveth son or daughter more than me is not worthy of me. And he that taketh not his cross, and followeth after me, is not worthy of me.

He that findeth his life shall lose it: and he that loseth his life for my sake shall find it. He that receiveth you receiveth me, and he that receiveth me receiveth him that sent me. He that receiveth a prophet in the name of a prophet shall receive a prophet's reward; and he that receiveth a righteous man in the name of a righteous man shall receive a righteous man's reward. And whosoever shall give to drink unto one of these little ones a cup of cold water only in the name of a disciple, verily I say unto you, he shall in no wise lose his reward.

THE KEYS OF THE KINGDOM
Matthew 16:13–23

When Jesus came into the coasts of Caesarea Philippi, he asked his disciples, saying, Whom do men say that I the Son of man am?

And they said, Some say that thou art John the Baptist: some, Elias; and others, Jeremias, or one of the prophets.

He saith unto them, But whom say ye that I am?

And Simon Peter answered and said, Thou art the Christ, the Son of the living God.

And Jesus answered and said unto him, Blessed art thou, Simon Bar-jona: for flesh and blood hath not revealed it unto thee, but my

Father which is in heaven. And I say also unto thee, That thou art Peter, and upon this rock I will build my church; and the gates of hell shall not prevail against it. And I will give unto thee the keys of the kingdom of heaven: and whatsoever thou shalt bind on earth shall be bound in heaven: and whatsoever thou shalt loose on earth shall be loosed in heaven. Then charged he his disciples that they should tell no man that he was Jesus the Christ.

From that time forth began Jesus to shew unto his disciples, how that he must go unto Jerusalem, and suffer many things of the elders and chief priests and scribes, and be killed, and be raised again the third day.

Then Peter took him, and began to rebuke him, saying, Be it far from thee, Lord: this shall not be unto thee. But he turned, and said unto Peter, Get thee behind me, Satan: thou art an offence unto me: for thou savourest not the things that be of God, but those that be of men.

WHOSOEVER WILL SAVE HIS LIFE
SHALL LOSE IT
Matthew 16:24–27

Then said Jesus unto his disciples, If any man will come after me, let him deny himself, and take up his cross, and follow me. For whosoever will save his life shall lose it: and whosoever will lose his life for my sake shall find it. For what is a man profited, if he shall gain the whole world, and lose his own soul? or what shall a man give in exchange for his soul?

For the Son of man shall come in the glory of his Father with his angels; and then he shall reward every man according to his works.

SUFFER THE LITTLE CHILDREN
TO COME UNTO ME
Mark 10:13–16

And they brought young children to him, that he should touch them: and his disciples rebuked those that brought them.

But when Jesus saw it, he was much displeased, and said unto them, Suffer the little children to come unto me, and forbid them not: for of such is the kingdom of God. Verily I say unto you, Whosoever shall not receive the kingdom of God as a little child, he shall not enter therein.

And he took them up in his arms, put his hands upon them, and blessed them.

EXCEPT YE BECOME AS LITTLE CHILDREN
Matthew 18:1–7, 10

At the same time came the disciples unto Jesus, saying, Who is the greatest in the kingdom of heaven?

And Jesus called a little child unto him, and set him in the midst of them, And said, Verily I say unto you, Except ye be converted, and become as little children, ye shall not enter into the kingdom of heaven. Whosoever therefore shall humble himself as this little child, the same is greatest in the kingdom of heaven. And whoso shall receive one such little child in my name receiveth me. But whoso shall offend one of these little ones which believe in me, it were better for him that a millstone were hanged about his neck, and that he were drowned in the depth of the sea.

Woe unto the world because of offences! for it must needs be that offences come; but woe to that man by whom the offence cometh!

...Take heed that ye despise not one of these little ones; for I say unto you, That in heaven their angels do always behold the face of my Father which is in heaven.

WHERE TWO OR THREE ARE GATHERED
Matthew 18:15–22

Moreover if thy brother shall trespass against thee, go and tell him his fault between thee and him alone: if he shall hear thee, thou hast gained thy brother. But if he will not hear thee, then take with thee one or two more, that in the mouth of two or three witnesses every word may be established. And if he shall neglect to hear them, tell it unto the church: but if he neglect to hear the church, let him be unto thee as an heathen man and a publican.

Verily I say unto you, Whatsoever ye shall bind on earth shall be bound in heaven: and whatsoever ye shall loose on earth shall be loosed in heaven. Again I say unto you, That if two of you shall agree on earth as touching any thing that they shall ask, it shall be done for them of my Father which is in heaven. For where two or three are gathered together in my name, there am I in the midst of them.

Then came Peter to him, and said, Lord, how oft shall my brother sin against me, and I forgive him? till seven times?

Jesus saith unto him, I say not unto thee, Until seven times: but, Until seventy times seven.

EUNUCHS FOR THE KINGDOM OF HEAVEN
Matthew 19:9–12

And I say unto you, Whosoever shall put away his wife, except it be for fornication, and shall marry another, committeth adultery: and whoso marrieth her which is put away doth commit adultery.

His disciples say unto him, If the case of the man be so with his wife, it is not good to marry. But he said unto them, All men cannot receive this saying, save they to whom it is given. For there are some eunuchs, which were so born from their mother's womb: and there are some eunuchs, which were made eunuchs of men: and there be eunuchs, which have made themselves eunuchs for the kingdom of heaven's sake. He that is able to receive it, let him receive it.

A CAMEL THROUGH THE EYE OF A NEEDLE
Mark 10:17–27

And when he was gone forth into the way, there came one running, and kneeled to him, and asked him, Good Master, what shall I do that I may inherit eternal life?

And Jesus said unto him, Why callest thou me good? there is none good but one, that is, God. Thou knowest the commandments, Do not commit adultery, Do not kill, Do not steal, Do not bear false witness, Defraud not, Honour thy father and mother.

And he answered and said unto him, Master, all these have I observed from my youth.

Then Jesus beholding him loved him, and said unto him, One thing thou lackest: go thy way, sell whatsoever thou hast, and give to the poor, and thou shalt have treasure in heaven: and come, take up the cross, and follow me.

And he was sad at that saying, and went away grieved: for he had great possessions.

And Jesus looked round about, and saith unto his disciples, How hardly shall they that have riches enter into the kingdom of God!

And the disciples were astonished at his words. But Jesus answereth again, and saith unto them, Children, how hard is it for them that trust in riches to enter into the kingdom of God! It is easier for a camel to go through the eye of a needle, than for a rich man to enter into the kingdom of God.

And they were astonished out of measure, saying among themselves, Who then can be saved?

And Jesus looking upon them saith, With men it is impossible, but not with God: for with God all things are possible.

THE LAST SHALL BE FIRST
Mark 10:28–31

Then Peter began to say unto him, Lo, we have left all, and have followed thee.

And Jesus answered and said, Verily I say unto you, There is no man that hath left house, or brethren, or sisters, or father, or mother, or wife, or children, or lands, for my sake, and the gospel's, But he shall receive an hundredfold now in this time, houses, and brethren, and sisters, and mothers, and children, and lands, with persecutions; and in the world to come eternal life. But many that are first shall be last; and the last first.

WHOSOEVER WILL BE GREAT AMONG YOU
Mark 10:35–45

And James and John, the sons of Zebedee, come unto him, saying, Master, we would that thou shouldest do for us whatsoever we shall desire. And he said unto them, What would ye that I should do for you?

They said unto him, Grant unto us that we may sit, one on thy right hand, and the other on thy left hand, in thy glory. But Jesus said unto them, Ye know not what ye ask: can ye drink of the cup that I drink of? and be baptized with the baptism that I am baptized with?

And they said unto him, We can. And Jesus said unto them, Ye shall indeed drink of the cup that I drink of; and with the baptism that I am baptized withal shall ye be baptized: But to sit on my right hand and on my left hand is not mine to give; but it shall be given to them for whom it is prepared.

And when the ten heard it, they began to be much displeased with James and John.

But Jesus called them to him, and saith unto them, Ye know that they which are accounted to rule over the Gentiles exercise lordship over them; and their great ones exercise authority upon them. But so shall it not be among you: but whosoever will be great among you, shall be your minister: And whosoever of you will be the chiefest, shall be servant of all. For even the Son of man came not to be ministered unto, but to minister, and to give his life a ransom for many.

HAVE FAITH IN GOD
Mark 11:12–14, 19–24

And on the morrow, when they were come from Bethany, he was hungry: And seeing a fig tree afar off having leaves, he came, if haply he might find any thing thereon: and when he came to it, he found nothing but leaves; for the time of figs was not yet.

And Jesus answered and said unto it, No man eat fruit of thee hereafter for ever. And his disciples heard it...

And when even was come, he went out of the city. And in the morning, as they passed by, they saw the fig tree dried up from the roots. And Peter calling to remembrance saith unto him, Master, behold, the fig tree which thou cursedst is withered away.

And Jesus answering saith unto them, Have faith in God. For verily I say unto you, That whosoever shall say unto this mountain, Be thou removed, and be thou cast into the sea; and shall not doubt in his heart, but shall believe that those things which he saith shall come to pass; he shall have whatsoever he saith. Therefore I say unto you, What things soever ye desire, when ye pray, believe that ye receive them, and ye shall have them.

HE THAT IS NOT AGAINST US
Luke 9:49–50

And John answered and said, Master, we saw one casting out devils in thy name; and we forbad him, because he followeth not with us.

And Jesus said unto him, Forbid him not: for he that is not against us is for us.

NOT TO DESTROY, BUT TO SAVE
Luke 9:51–56

And it came to pass, when the time was come that he should be received up, he stedfastly set his face to go to Jerusalem, And sent messengers before his face: and they went, and entered into a village of the Samaritans, to make ready for him.

And they did not receive him, because his face was as though he would go to Jerusalem.

And when his disciples James and John saw this, they said, Lord, wilt thou that we command fire to come down from heaven, and consume them, even as Elias did?

But he turned, and rebuked them, and said, Ye know not what manner of spirit ye are of. For the Son of man is not come to destroy men's lives, but to save them. And they went to another village.

243

LET THE DEAD BURY THEIR DEAD
Luke: 9:57–62

And it came to pass, that, as they went in the way, a certain man said unto him, Lord, I will follow thee whithersoever thou goest. And Jesus said unto him, Foxes have holes, and birds of the air have nests; but the Son of man hath not where to lay his head.

And he said unto another, Follow me. But he said, Lord, suffer me first to go and bury my father. Jesus said unto him, Let the dead bury their dead: but go thou and preach the kingdom of God.

And another also said, Lord, I will follow thee; but let me first go bid them farewell, which are at home at my house. And Jesus said unto him, No man, having put his hand to the plough, and looking back, is fit for the kingdom of God.

SATAN'S FALL
Luke 10:1, 17–20

After these things the Lord appointed other seventy also, and sent them two and two before his face into every city and place, whither he himself would come...

And the seventy returned again with joy, saying, Lord, even the devils are subject unto us through thy name. And he said unto them, I beheld Satan as lightning fall from heaven. Behold, I give unto you power to tread on serpents and scorpions, and over all the power of the enemy: and nothing shall by any means hurt you. Notwithstanding in this rejoice not, that the spirits are subject unto you; but rather rejoice, because your names are written in heaven.

NO MAN KNOWETH WHOM THE SON IS
Luke 10:21–24

In that hour Jesus rejoiced in spirit, and said, I thank thee, O Father, Lord of heaven and earth, that thou hast hid these things from the wise and prudent, and hast revealed them unto babes: even so, Father; for so it seemed good in thy sight. All things are delivered to me of my Father: and no man knoweth who the Son is, but the Father; and who the Father is, but the Son, and he to whom the Son will reveal him.

And he turned him unto his disciples, and said privately, Blessed are the eyes which see the things that ye see: For I tell you, that many prophets and kings have desired to see those things which ye see, and have not seen them; and to hear those things which ye hear, and have not heard them.

ONE THING IS NEEDFUL
Luke 10:38–42

Now it came to pass, as they went, that he entered into a certain village: and a certain woman named Martha received him into her house. And she had a sister called Mary, which also sat at Jesus' feet, and heard his word. But Martha was cumbered about much serving, and came to him, and said, Lord, dost thou not care that my sister hath left me to serve alone? bid her therefore that she help me.

And Jesus answered and said unto her, Martha, Martha, thou art careful and troubled about many things: But one thing is needful: and Mary hath chosen that good part, which shall not be taken away from her.

THE TEST OF DISCIPLESHIP
Luke 14:28–33

For which of you, intending to build a tower, sitteth not down first, and counteth the cost, whether he have sufficient to finish it? Lest haply, after he hath laid the foundation, and is not able to finish it, all that behold it begin to mock him, Saying, This man began to build, and was not able to finish. Or what king, going to make war against another king, sitteth not down first, and consulteth whether he be able with ten thousand to meet him that cometh against him with twenty thousand? Or else, while the other is yet a great way off, he sendeth an ambassage, and desireth conditions of peace.

So likewise, whosoever he be of you that forsaketh not all that he hath, he cannot be my disciple.

REMEMBER LOT'S WIFE
Luke 17:22–37

And he said unto the disciples, The days will come, when ye shall desire to see one of the days of the Son of man, and ye shall not see it. And they shall say to you, See here; or, see there: go not after them, nor follow them. For as the lightning, that lighteneth out of the one part under heaven, shineth unto the other part under heaven; so shall also the Son of man be in his day. But first must he suffer many things, and be rejected of this generation. And as it was in the days of Noe, so shall it be also in the days of the Son of man. They did eat, they drank, they married wives, they were given in marriage, until the day that Noe entered into the ark, and the flood came, and destroyed them all.

Likewise also as it was in the days of Lot; they did eat, they drank, they bought, they sold, they planted, they builded; But the same day that Lot went out of Sodom it rained fire and brimstone from heaven, and destroyed them all. Even thus shall it be in the day when the Son of man is revealed.

In that day, he which shall be upon the housetop, and his stuff in the house, let him not come down to take it away: and he that is in the field, let him likewise not return back. Remember Lot's wife.

Whosoever shall seek to save his life shall lose it; and whosoever shall lose his life shall preserve it. I tell you, in that night there shall be two men in one bed; the one shall be taken, and the other shall be left. Two women shall be grinding together; the one shall be taken, and the other left. Two men shall be in the field; the one shall be taken, and the other left.

And they answered and said unto him, Where, Lord? And he said unto them, Wheresoever the body is, thither will the eagles be gathered together.

THE WIDOW'S MITE
Mark 12:41–44

And Jesus sat over against the treasury, and beheld how the people cast money into the treasury: and many that were rich cast in much.

And there came a certain poor widow, and she threw in two mites, which make a farthing.

And he called unto him his disciples, and saith unto them, Verily I say unto you, That this poor widow hath cast more in, than all they which have cast into the treasury: For all they did cast in of their abundance; but she of her want did cast in all that she had, even all her living.

THE MOUNT OLIVET PROPHECY
Mark 13

And as he went out of the temple, one of his disciples saith unto him, Master, see what manner of stones and what buildings are here!

And Jesus answering said unto him, Seest thou these great buildings? there shall not be left one stone upon another, that shall not be thrown down.

And as he sat upon the mount of Olives over against the temple, Peter and James and John and Andrew asked him privately, Tell us, when shall these things be? and what shall be the sign when all these things shall be fulfilled?

And Jesus answering them began to say, Take heed lest any man deceive you: For many shall come in my name, saying, I am Christ; and shall deceive many. And when ye shall hear of wars and rumours of wars, be ye not troubled: for such things must needs be; but the end shall not be yet. For nation shall rise against nation, and kingdom against kingdom: and there shall be earthquakes in divers places, and there shall be famines and troubles: these are the beginnings of sorrows.

But take heed to yourselves: for they shall deliver you up to councils; and in the synagogues ye shall be beaten: and ye shall be brought before rulers and kings for my sake, for a testimony against them. And the gospel must first be published among all nations. But when they shall lead you, and deliver you up, take no thought beforehand what ye shall speak, neither do ye premeditate: but whatsoever shall be given you in that hour, that speak ye: for it is not ye that speak, but the Holy Ghost.

Now the brother shall betray the brother to death, and the father the son; and children shall rise up against their parents, and shall cause them to be put to death. And ye shall be hated of all men for my name's sake: but he that shall endure unto the end, the same shall be saved.

But when ye shall see the abomination of desolation, spoken of by Daniel the prophet, standing where it ought not, (let him that readeth understand,) then let them that be in Judaea flee to the mountains: And let him that is on the housetop not go down into the house, neither enter therein, to take any thing out of his house: And let him that is in the field not turn back again for to take up his garment. But woe to them that are with child, and to them that give suck in those days! And pray ye that your flight be not in the winter.

For in those days shall be affliction, such as was not from the beginning of the creation which God created unto this time, neither shall be. And except that the Lord had shortened those days, no flesh should be saved: but for the elect's sake, whom he hath chosen, he hath shortened the days.

And then if any man shall say to you, Lo, here is Christ; or, lo, he is there; believe him not: For false Christs and false prophets shall rise, and shall shew signs and wonders, to seduce, if it were possible, even the elect. But take ye heed: behold, I have foretold you all things.

But in those days, after that tribulation, the sun shall be darkened, and the moon shall not give her light, And the stars of heaven shall fall, and the powers that are in heaven shall be shaken. And then shall they see the Son of man coming in the clouds with great power and glory. And then shall he send his angels, and shall gather together his elect from the four winds, from the uttermost part of the earth to the uttermost part of heaven.

Now learn a parable of the fig tree; When her branch is yet tender, and putteth forth leaves, ye know that summer is near: So ye in like manner, when ye shall see these things come to pass, know that it is nigh, even at the doors.

Verily I say unto you, that this generation shall not pass, till all these things be done. Heaven and earth shall pass away: but my words shall not pass away. But of that day and that hour knoweth no man, no, not the angels which are in heaven, neither the Son, but the Father. Take ye heed, watch and pray: for ye know not when the time is. For the Son of man is as a man taking a far journey, who left his house, and gave authority to his servants, and to every man his work, and commanded the porter to watch.

Watch ye therefore: for ye know not when the master of the house cometh, at even, or at midnight, or at the cockcrowing, or in the morning: Lest coming suddenly he find you sleeping. And what I say unto you I say unto all, Watch.

Part Two

The Sermon
on the Mount

PROLOGUE
Matthew 5:1–2

And seeing the multitudes, he went up into a mountain:
and when he was set, his disciples came unto him:
And he opened his mouth, and taught them...

THE BEATITUDES
Matthew 5:3–12

Blessed are the poor in spirit: for theirs is the kingdom of heaven.

Blessed are they that mourn: for they shall be comforted.

Blessed are the meek: for they shall inherit the earth.

Blessed are they which do hunger and thirst after righteousness: for they shall be filled.

Blessed are the merciful: for they shall obtain mercy.

Blessed are the pure in heart: for they shall see God.

Blessed are the peacemakers: for they shall be called the children of God.

Blessed are they which are persecuted for righteousness' sake: for theirs is the kingdom of heaven.

Blessed are ye, when men shall revile you, and persecute you, and shall say all manner of evil against you falsely, for my sake.

Rejoice, and be exceeding glad: for great is your reward in heaven: for so persecuted they the prophets which were before you.

THE SALT OF THE EARTH
Matthew 5:13

Ye are the salt of the earth: but if the salt have lost his savour, wherewith shall it be salted? it is thenceforth good for nothing, but to be cast out, and to be trodden under foot of men.

THE LIGHT OF THE WORLD
Matthew 5:14–16

Ye are the light of the world. A city that is set on an hill cannot be hid. Neither do men light a candle, and put it under a bushel, but on a candlestick; and it giveth light unto all that are in the house. Let your light so shine before men, that they may see your good works, and glorify your Father which is in heaven.

THE FULFILMENT OF THE LAW
Matthew 5:17–20

Think not that I am come to destroy the law, or the prophets: I am not come to destroy, but to fulfil. For verily I say unto you, Till heaven and earth pass, one jot or one tittle shall in no wise pass from the law, till all be fulfilled.

Whosoever therefore shall break one of these least commandments, and shall teach men so, he shall be called the least in the kingdom of heaven: but whosoever shall do and teach them, the same shall be called great in the kingdom of heaven. For I say unto you, That except your righteousness shall exceed the righteousness of the scribes and Pharisees, ye shall in no case enter into the kingdom of heaven.

MURDER AND ANGER
Matthew 5:21–26

Ye have heard that it was said by them of old time, Thou shalt not kill; and whosoever shall kill shall be in danger of the judgment: But I say unto you, That whosoever is angry with his brother without a cause shall be in danger of the judgment: and whosoever shall say to his brother, Raca, shall be in danger of the council: but whosoever shall say, Thou fool, shall be in danger of hell fire.

Therefore if thou bring thy gift to the altar, and there rememberest that thy brother hath ought against thee; Leave there thy gift before the altar, and go thy way; first be reconciled to thy brother, and then come and offer thy gift.

Agree with thine adversary quickly, whiles thou art in the way with him; lest at any time the adversary deliver thee to the judge, and the judge deliver thee to the officer, and thou be cast into prison. Verily I say unto thee, Thou shalt by no means come out thence, till thou hast paid the uttermost farthing.

ADULTERY AND LUST
Matthew 5:27–30

Ye have heard that it was said by them of old time, Thou shalt not commit adultery: But I say unto you, That whosoever looketh on a woman to lust after her hath committed adultery with her already in his heart.

And if thy right eye offend thee, pluck it out, and cast it from thee: for it is profitable for thee that one of thy members should perish, and not that thy whole body should be cast into hell.

And if thy right hand offend thee, cut it off, and cast it from thee: for it is profitable for thee that one of thy members should perish, and not that thy whole body should be cast into hell.

DIVORCE
Matthew 5:31–32

It hath been said, Whosoever shall put away his wife, let him give her a writing of divorcement: But I say unto you, That whosoever shall put away his wife, saving for the cause of fornication, causeth her to commit adultery: and whosoever shall marry her that is divorced committeth adultery.

SWEAR NOT AT ALL
Matthew 5:33–37

Again, ye have heard that it hath been said by them of old time, Thou shalt not forswear thyself, but shalt perform unto the Lord thine oaths: But I say unto you, Swear not at all; neither by heaven; for it is God's throne: Nor by the earth; for it is his footstool: neither by Jerusalem; for it is the city of the great King. Neither shalt thou swear by thy head, because thou canst not make one hair white or black. But let your communication be, Yea, yea; Nay, nay: for whatsoever is more than these cometh of evil.

TURN THE OTHER CHEEK
Matthew 5:38–42

Ye have heard that it hath been said, An eye for an eye, and a tooth for a tooth: But I say unto you, That ye resist not evil: but whosoever shall smite thee on thy right cheek, turn to him the other also.

And if any man will sue thee at the law, and take away thy coat, let him have thy cloke also. And whosoever shall compel thee to go a mile, go with him twain. Give to him that asketh thee, and from him that would borrow of thee turn not thou away.

LOVE YOUR ENEMIES
Matthew 5:43–48

Ye have heard that it hath been said, Thou shalt love thy neighbour, and hate thine enemy. But I say unto you, Love your enemies, bless them that curse you, do good to them that hate you, and pray for them which despitefully use you, and persecute you; That ye may be the children of your Father which is in heaven: for he maketh his sun to rise on the evil and on the good, and sendeth rain on the just and on the unjust.

For if ye love them which love you, what reward have ye? do not even the publicans the same? And if ye salute your brethren only, what do ye more than others? do not even the publicans so? Be ye therefore perfect, even as your Father which is in heaven is perfect.

ALMSGIVING
Matthew 6:1–4

Take heed that ye do not your alms before men, to be seen of them:
otherwise ye have no reward of your Father which is in heaven.

Therefore when thou doest thine alms, do not sound a trumpet
before thee, as the hypocrites do in the synagogues and in the streets,
that they may have glory of men. Verily I say unto you, They have their
reward. But when thou doest alms, let not thy left hand know what
thy right hand doeth: That thine alms may be in secret: and thy Father
which seeth in secret himself shall reward thee openly.

PRAYER
Matthew 6:5–8

And when thou prayest, thou shalt not be as the hypocrites are: for
they love to pray standing in the synagogues and in the corners of the
streets, that they may be seen of men. Verily I say unto you, They have
their reward. But thou, when thou prayest, enter into thy closet, and
when thou hast shut thy door, pray to thy Father which is in secret;
and thy Father which seeth in secret shall reward thee openly.

But when ye pray, use not vain repetitions, as the heathen do:
for they think that they shall be heard for their much speaking. Be not
ye therefore like unto them: for your Father knoweth what things ye
have need of, before ye ask him.

THE LORD'S PRAYER
Matthew 6:9–13

After this manner therefore pray ye: Our Father which art in heaven,
Hallowed be thy name. Thy kingdom come. Thy will be done in earth,
as it is in heaven.

Give us this day our daily bread. And forgive us our debts, as
we forgive our debtors.

And lead us not into temptation, but deliver us from evil: For
thine is the kingdom, and the power, and the glory, for ever. Amen.

FORGIVENESS
Matthew 6:14–15

For if ye forgive men their trespasses, your heavenly Father will also forgive you: But if ye forgive not men their trespasses, neither will your Father forgive your trespasses.

FASTING
Matthew 6:16–18

Moreover when ye fast, be not, as the hypocrites, of a sad countenance: for they disfigure their faces, that they may appear unto men to fast. Verily I say unto you, They have their reward.

But thou, when thou fastest, anoint thine head, and wash thy face; That thou appear not unto men to fast, but unto thy Father which is in secret: and thy Father, which seeth in secret, shall reward thee openly.

TREASURE UPON EARTH
Matthew 6:19–21

Lay not up for yourselves treasures upon earth, where moth and rust doth corrupt, and where thieves break through and steal: But lay up for yourselves treasures in heaven, where neither moth nor rust doth corrupt, and where thieves do not break through nor steal: For where your treasure is, there will your heart be also.

THE LIGHT OF THE BODY
Matthew 6:22–23

The light of the body is the eye: if therefore thine eye be single, thy whole body shall be full of light. But if thine eye be evil, thy whole body shall be full of darkness. If therefore the light that is in thee be darkness, how great is that darkness!

NO MAN CAN SERVE TWO MASTERS
Matthew 6:24

No man can serve two masters: for either he will hate the one, and love the other; or else he will hold to the one, and despise the other. Ye cannot serve God and mammon.

SEEK YE FIRST THE KINGDOM OF GOD
Matthew 6:25–34

Therefore I say unto you, Take no thought for your life, what ye shall eat, or what ye shall drink; nor yet for your body, what ye shall put on. Is not the life more than meat, and the body than raiment? Behold the fowls of the air: for they sow not, neither do they reap, nor gather into barns; yet your heavenly Father feedeth them. Are ye not much better than they?

Which of you by taking thought can add one cubit unto his stature? And why take ye thought for raiment? Consider the lilies of the field, how they grow; they toil not, neither do they spin: And yet I say unto you, That even Solomon in all his glory was not arrayed like one of these. Wherefore, if God so clothe the grass of the field, which to day is, and to morrow is cast into the oven, shall he not much more clothe you, O ye of little faith?

Therefore take no thought, saying, What shall we eat? or, What shall we drink? or, Wherewithal shall we be clothed? (For after all these things do the Gentiles seek:) for your heavenly Father knoweth that ye have need of all these things. But seek ye first the kingdom of God, and his righteousness; and all these things shall be added unto you. Take therefore no thought for the morrow: for the morrow shall take thought for the things of itself. Sufficient unto the day is the evil thereof.

JUDGE NOT
Matthew 7:1–5

Judge not, that ye be not judged. For with what judgment ye judge, ye shall be judged: and with what measure ye mete, it shall be measured to you again. And why beholdest thou the mote that is in thy brother's eye, but considerest not the beam that is in thine own eye?

Or how wilt thou say to thy brother, Let me pull out the mote out of thine eye; and, behold, a beam is in thine own eye? Thou hypocrite, first cast out the beam out of thine own eye; and then shalt thou see clearly to cast out the mote out of thy brother's eye.

PEARLS BEFORE SWINE
Matthew 7:6

Give not that which is holy unto the dogs, neither cast ye your pearls before swine, lest they trample them under their feet, and turn again and rend you.

SEEK AND YE SHALL FIND
Matthew 7:7–11

Ask, and it shall be given you; seek, and ye shall find; knock, and it shall be opened unto you: For every one that asketh receiveth; and he that seeketh findeth; and to him that knocketh it shall be opened.

Or what man is there of you, whom if his son ask bread, will he give him a stone? Or if he ask a fish, will he give him a serpent? If ye then, being evil, know how to give good gifts unto your children, how much more shall your Father which is in heaven give good things to them that ask him?

THE GOLDEN RULE
Matthew 7:12

Therefore all things whatsoever ye would that men should do to you, do ye even so to them: for this is the law and the prophets.

STRAIT AND NARROW
Matthew 7:13–14

Enter ye in at the strait gate: for wide is the gate, and broad is the way, that leadeth to destruction, and many there be which go in thereat: Because strait is the gate, and narrow is the way, which leadeth unto life, and few there be that find it.

WOLVES IN SHEEP'S CLOTHING
Matthew 7:15

Beware of false prophets, which come to you in sheep's clothing, but inwardly they are ravening wolves.

BY THEIR FRUITS YE SHALL KNOW THEM
Matthew 7:16–20

Ye shall know them by their fruits. Do men gather grapes of thorns, or figs of thistles? Even so every good tree bringeth forth good fruit; but a corrupt tree bringeth forth evil fruit.

A good tree cannot bring forth evil fruit, neither can a corrupt tree bring forth good fruit. Every tree that bringeth not forth good fruit is hewn down, and cast into the fire. Wherefore by their fruits ye shall know them.

I NEVER KNEW YOU
Matthew 7:21–23

Not every one that saith unto me, Lord, Lord, shall enter into the kingdom of heaven; but he that doeth the will of my Father which is in heaven.

Many will say to me in that day, Lord, Lord, have we not prophesied in thy name? and in thy name have cast out devils? and in thy name done many wonderful works? And then will I profess unto them, I never knew you: depart from me, ye that work iniquity.

WISE AND FOOLISH BUILDERS
Matthew 7:24–27

Therefore whosoever heareth these sayings of mine, and doeth them, I will liken him unto a wise man, which built his house upon a rock: And the rain descended, and the floods came, and the winds blew, and beat upon that house; and it fell not: for it was founded upon a rock.

And every one that heareth these sayings of mine, and doeth them not, shall be likened unto a foolish man, which built his house upon the sand: And the rain descended, and the floods came, and the winds blew, and beat upon that house; and it fell: and great was the fall of it.

EPILOGUE
Matthew 7:28–29

And it came to pass, when Jesus had ended these sayings, the people were astonished at his doctrine: For he taught them as one having authority, and not as the scribes.

Part Three

Proverbs and Shorter Sayings

REPENT AND BELIEVE
Mark 1:15

The time is fulfilled, and the kingdom of God is at hand: repent ye, and believe the gospel.

LIGHT UNDER A BUSHEL
Mark 4:21–22

Is a candle brought to be put under a bushel, or under a bed? and not to be set on a candlestick? For there is nothing hid, which shall not be manifested; neither was any thing kept secret, but that it should come abroad.

THE SEED OF THE KINGDOM
Mark 4:26–29

So is the kingdom of God, as if a man should cast seed into the ground; And should sleep, and rise night and day, and the seed should spring and grow up, he knoweth not how.

For the earth bringeth forth fruit of herself; first the blade, then the ear, after that the full corn in the ear. But when the fruit is brought forth, immediately he putteth in the sickle, because the harvest is come.

THE MUSTARD SEED
Mark 4:30–32

Whereunto shall we liken the kingdom of God? or with what comparison shall we compare it? It is like a grain of mustard seed, which, when it is sown in the earth, is less than all the seeds that be in the earth: But when it is sown, it groweth up, and becometh greater than all herbs, and shooteth out great branches; so that the fowls of the air may lodge under the shadow of it.

A PROPHET IS NOT WITHOUT HONOUR
Mark 6:4

A prophet is not without honour, but in his own country, and among his own kin, and in his own house.

THE SALT OF THE GOSPEL
Mark 9:50

Salt is good: but if the salt have lost his saltness, wherewith will ye season it? Have salt in yourselves, and have peace one with another.

TRUE FORGIVENESS
Mark 11:25–26

And when ye stand praying, forgive, if ye have ought against any: that your Father also which is in heaven may forgive you your trespasses. But if ye do not forgive, neither will your Father which is in heaven forgive your trespasses.

THE POOR WITH YOU ALWAYS
Mark 14:7

For ye have the poor with you always, and whensoever ye will ye may do them good: but me ye have not always.

MY YOKE IS EASY
Matthew 11:28–30

Come unto me, all ye that labour and are heavy laden, and I will give you rest. Take my yoke upon you, and learn of me; for I am meek and lowly in heart: and ye shall find rest unto your souls. For my yoke is easy, and my burden is light.

THE LEAVEN
Matthew 13:33

The kingdom of heaven is like unto leaven, which a woman took, and hid in three measures of meal, till the whole was leavened.

THE HIDDEN TREASURE
Matthew 13:44

Again, the kingdom of heaven is like unto treasure hid in a field; the which when a man hath found, he hideth, and for joy thereof goeth and selleth all that he hath, and buyeth that field.

THE PEARL OF GREAT PRICE
Matthew 13:45–46

Again, the kingdom of heaven is like unto a merchant man, seeking goodly pearls: Who, when he had found one pearl of great price, went and sold all that he had, and bought it.

THE DRAGNET
Matthew 13:47–50

Again, the kingdom of heaven is like unto a net, that was cast into the sea, and gathered of every kind: Which, when it was full, they drew to shore, and sat down, and gathered the good into vessels, but cast the bad away.

So shall it be at the end of the world: the angels shall come forth, and sever the wicked from among the just, And shall cast them into the furnace of fire: there shall be wailing and gnashing of teeth.

TREASURE NEW AND OLD
Matthew 13:52

Every scribe which is instructed unto the kingdom of heaven is like unto a man that is an householder, which bringeth forth out of his treasure things new and old.

FOUR WOES
Luke 6:24–26

Woe unto you that are rich! for ye have received your consolation.
Woe unto you that are full! for ye shall hunger.
Woe unto you that laugh now! for ye shall mourn and weep.
Woe unto you, when all men shall speak well of you! for so did their fathers to the false prophets.

MEASURE FOR MEASURE
Luke 6:37–38

Judge not, and ye shall not be judged: condemn not, and ye shall not be condemned: forgive, and ye shall be forgiven: Give, and it shall be given unto you; good measure, pressed down, and shaken together, and running over, shall men give into your bosom. For with the same measure that ye mete withal it shall be measured to you again.

THE BLIND LEAD THE BLIND
Luke 6:39

Can the blind lead the blind? shall they not both fall into the ditch?

THE DISCIPLE AND MASTER
Luke 6:40

The disciple is not above his master: but every one that is perfect shall be as his master.

TRUE FAMILY
Luke 8:19–21

Then came to him his mother and his brethren, and could not come at him for the press.

And it was told him by certain which said, Thy mother and thy brethren stand without, desiring to see thee. And he answered and said unto them, My mother and my brethren are these which hear the word of God, and do it.

TRUE BLESSING
Luke 11:27–28

And it came to pass, as he spake these things, a certain woman of the company lifted up her voice, and said unto him, Blessed is the womb that bare thee, and the paps which thou hast sucked.

But he said, Yea rather, blessed are they that hear the word of God, and keep it.

BEWARE OF COVETOUSNESS
Luke 12:13–15

And one of the company said unto him, Master, speak to my brother, that he divide the inheritance with me.

And he said unto him, Man, who made me a judge or a divider over you? And he said unto them, Take heed, and beware of covetousness: for a man's life consisteth not in the abundance of the things which he possesseth.

EXCEPT YE REPENT
Luke 13:1–5

There were present at that season some that told him of the Galilaeans, whose blood Pilate had mingled with their sacrifices. And Jesus answering said unto them, Suppose ye that these Galilaeans were sinners above all the Galilaeans, because they suffered such things? I tell you, Nay: but, except ye repent, ye shall all likewise perish. Or those eighteen, upon whom the tower in Siloam fell, and slew them, think ye that they were sinners above all men that dwelt in Jerusalem? I tell you, Nay: but, except ye repent, ye shall all likewise perish.

FRIEND, GO UP HIGHER
Luke 14:8–11

When thou art bidden of any man to a wedding, sit not down in the highest room; lest a more honourable man than thou be bidden of him; And he that bade thee and him come and say to thee, Give this man place; and thou begin with shame to take the lowest room. But when thou art bidden, go and sit down in the lowest room; that when he that bade thee cometh, he may say unto thee, Friend, go up higher: then shalt thou have worship in the presence of them that sit at meat with thee. For whosoever exalteth himself shall be abased; and he that humbleth himself shall be exalted.

TRUE GENEROSITY
Luke 14:12–14

Then said he also to him that bade him, When thou makest a dinner or a supper, call not thy friends, nor thy brethren, neither thy kinsmen, nor thy rich neighbours; lest they also bid thee again, and a recompence be made thee. But when thou makest a feast, call the poor, the maimed, the lame, the blind: And thou shalt be blessed; for they cannot recompense thee: for thou shalt be recompensed at the resurrection of the just.

TRUE FAITHFULNESS
Luke 16:10–12

He that is faithful in that which is least is faithful also in much: and he that is unjust in the least is unjust also in much. If therefore ye have not been faithful in the unrighteous mammon, who will commit to your trust the true riches? And if ye have not been faithful in that which is another man's, who shall give you that which is your own?

A SERVANT'S DUTY
Luke 17:7–10

But which of you, having a servant plowing or feeding cattle, will say unto him by and by, when he is come from the field, Go and sit down to meat? And will not rather say unto him, Make ready wherewith I may sup, and gird thyself, and serve me, till I have eaten and drunken; and afterward thou shalt eat and drink? Doth he thank that servant because he did the things that were commanded him? I trow not.

So likewise ye, when ye shall have done all those things which are commanded you, say, We are unprofitable servants: we have done that which was our duty to do.

THE KINGDOM WITHIN
Luke 17:20–21

The kingdom of God cometh not with observation: Neither shall they say, Lo here! or, lo there! for, behold, the kingdom of God is within you.

Part Four

The Major Parables

THE SOWER
Mark 4:1–20

And he began again to teach by the sea side: and there was gathered
unto him a great multitude, so that he entered into a ship, and sat in
the sea; and the whole multitude was by the sea on the land.

And he taught them many things by parables, and said unto
them in his doctrine, Hearken; Behold, there went out a sower to sow:
And it came to pass, as he sowed, some fell by the way side, and the
fowls of the air came and devoured it up. And some fell on stony
ground, where it had not much earth; and immediately it sprang up,
because it had no depth of earth: But when the sun was up, it was
scorched; and because it had no root, it withered away. And some fell
among thorns, and the thorns grew up, and choked it, and it yielded
no fruit. And other fell on good ground, and did yield fruit that sprang
up and increased; and brought forth, some thirty, and some sixty, and
some an hundred. And he said unto them, He that hath ears to hear,
let him hear.

And when he was alone, they that were about him with the
twelve asked of him the parable. And he said unto them, Unto you it
is given to know the mystery of the kingdom of God: but unto them
that are without, all these things are done in parables: That seeing
they may see, and not perceive; and hearing they may hear, and not
understand; lest at any time they should be converted, and their sins
should be forgiven them. And he said unto them, Know ye not this
parable? and how then will ye know all parables?

The sower soweth the word. And these are they by the way side,
where the word is sown; but when they have heard, Satan cometh
immediately, and taketh away the word that was sown in their hearts.
And these are they likewise which are sown on stony ground; who,

when they have heard the word, immediately receive it with gladness; And have no root in themselves, and so endure but for a time: afterward, when affliction or persecution ariseth for the word's sake, immediately they are offended. And these are they which are sown among thorns; such as hear the word, And the cares of this world, and the deceitfulness of riches, and the lusts of other things entering in, choke the word, and it becometh unfruitful. And these are they which are sown on good ground; such as hear the word, and receive it, and bring forth fruit, some thirtyfold, some sixty, and some an hundred.

THE WHEAT AND THE TARES
Matthew 13:24–30, 36–43

Another parable put he forth unto them, saying, The kingdom of heaven is likened unto a man which sowed good seed in his field: But while men slept, his enemy came and sowed tares among the wheat, and went his way. But when the blade was sprung up, and brought forth fruit, then appeared the tares also.

So the servants of the householder came and said unto him, Sir, didst not thou sow good seed in thy field? from whence then hath it tares?

He said unto them, An enemy hath done this. The servants said unto him, Wilt thou then that we go and gather them up?

But he said, Nay; lest while ye gather up the tares, ye root up also the wheat with them. Let both grow together until the harvest: and in the time of harvest I will say to the reapers, Gather ye together first the tares, and bind them in bundles to burn them: but gather the wheat into my barn...

Then Jesus sent the multitude away, and went into the house: and his disciples came unto him, saying, Declare unto us the parable of the tares of the field.

He answered and said unto them, He that soweth the good seed is the Son of man; The field is the world; the good seed are the children of the kingdom; but the tares are the children of the wicked one; The enemy that sowed them is the devil; the harvest is the end of the world; and the reapers are the angels. As therefore the tares are gathered and burned in the fire; so shall it be in the end of this world.

The Son of man shall send forth his angels, and they shall gather out of his kingdom all things that offend, and them which do iniquity; And shall cast them into a furnace of fire: there shall be wailing and gnashing of teeth. Then shall the righteous shine forth as the sun in the kingdom of their Father. Who hath ears to hear, let him hear.

THE UNFORGIVING SERVANT
Matthew 18:23–35

Therefore is the kingdom of heaven likened unto a certain king, which would take account of his servants. And when he had begun to reckon, one was brought unto him, which owed him ten thousand talents. But forasmuch as he had not to pay, his lord commanded him to be sold, and his wife, and children, and all that he had, and payment to be made. The servant therefore fell down, and worshipped him, saying, Lord, have patience with me, and I will pay thee all. Then the lord of that servant was moved with compassion, and loosed him, and forgave him the debt.

But the same servant went out, and found one of his fellowservants, which owed him an hundred pence: and he laid hands on him, and took him by the throat, saying, Pay me that thou owest. And his fellowservant fell down at his feet, and besought him, saying, Have patience with me, and I will pay thee all. And he would not: but went and cast him into prison, till he should pay the debt.

So when his fellowservants saw what was done, they were very sorry, and came and told unto their lord all that was done. Then his lord, after that he had called him, said unto him, O thou wicked servant, I forgave thee all that debt, because thou desiredst me: Shouldest not thou also have had compassion on thy fellowservant, even as I had pity on thee? And his lord was wroth, and delivered him to the tormentors, till he should pay all that was due unto him.

So likewise shall my heavenly Father do also unto you, if ye from your hearts forgive not every one his brother their trespasses.

THE LABOURERS IN THE VINEYARD
Matthew 20:1–16

For the kingdom of heaven is like unto a man that is an householder, which went out early in the morning to hire labourers into his vineyard. And when he had agreed with the labourers for a penny a day, he sent them into his vineyard.

And he went out about the third hour, and saw others standing idle in the marketplace, And said unto them: Go ye also into the vineyard, and whatsoever is right I will give you. And they went their way. Again he went out about the sixth and ninth hour, and did likewise. And about the eleventh hour he went out, and found others standing idle, and saith unto them, Why stand ye here all the day idle? They say unto him, Because no man hath hired us. He saith unto them, Go ye also into the vineyard; and whatsoever is right, that shall ye receive.

So when even was come, the lord of the vineyard saith unto his steward, Call the labourers, and give them their hire, beginning from the last unto the first. And when they came that were hired about the eleventh hour, they received every man a penny. But when the first came, they supposed that they should have received more; and they likewise received every man a penny. And when they had received it, they murmured against the goodman of the house, Saying, These last have wrought but one hour, and thou hast made them equal unto us, which have borne the burden and heat of the day. But he answered one of them, and said, Friend, I do thee no wrong: didst not thou agree with me for a penny? Take that thine is, and go thy way: I will give unto this last, even as unto thee. Is it not lawful for me to do what I will with mine own? Is thine eye evil, because I am good? So the last shall be first, and the first last: for many be called, but few chosen.

THE WICKED HUSBANDMEN
Matthew 21:33–46

Hear another parable: There was a certain householder, which planted a vineyard, and hedged it round about, and digged a winepress in it, and built a tower, and let it out to husbandmen, and went into a far country: And when the time of the fruit drew near, he sent his servants to the husbandmen, that they might receive the fruits of it. And the husbandmen took his servants, and beat one, and killed another, and stoned another. Again, he sent other servants more than the first: and they did unto them likewise. But last of all he sent unto them his son, saying, They will reverence my son.

But when the husbandmen saw the son, they said among themselves, This is the heir; come, let us kill him, and let us seize on his inheritance. And they caught him, and cast him out of the vineyard, and slew him.

When the lord therefore of the vineyard cometh, what will he do unto those husbandmen?

They say unto him, He will miserably destroy those wicked men, and will let out his vineyard unto other husbandmen, which shall render him the fruits in their seasons.

Jesus saith unto them, Did ye never read in the scriptures, The stone which the builders rejected, the same is become the head of the corner: this is the Lord's doing, and it is marvellous in our eyes? Therefore say I unto you, The kingdom of God shall be taken from you, and given to a nation bringing forth the fruits thereof. And whosoever shall fall on this stone shall be broken: but on whomsoever it shall fall, it will grind him to powder.

And when the chief priests and Pharisees had heard his parables, they perceived that he spake of them. But when they sought to lay hands on him, they feared the multitude, because they took him for a prophet.

THE WISE AND FOOLISH VIRGINS
Matthew 25:1–13

Then shall the kingdom of heaven be likened unto ten virgins, which took their lamps, and went forth to meet the bridegroom.

And five of them were wise, and five were foolish. They that were foolish took their lamps, and took no oil with them: But the wise took oil in their vessels with their lamps. While the bridegroom tarried, they all slumbered and slept.

And at midnight there was a cry made, Behold, the bridegroom cometh; go ye out to meet him. Then all those virgins arose, and trimmed their lamps. And the foolish said unto the wise, Give us of your oil; for our lamps are gone out. But the wise answered, saying, Not so; lest there be not enough for us and you: but go ye rather to them that sell, and buy for yourselves.

And while they went to buy, the bridegroom came; and they that were ready went in with him to the marriage: and the door was shut.

Afterward came also the other virgins, saying, Lord, Lord, open to us. But he answered and said, Verily I say unto you, I know you not.

Watch therefore, for ye know neither the day nor the hour wherein the Son of man cometh.

THE UNPROFITABLE SERVANT
Matthew 25:14–30

For the kingdom of heaven is as a man travelling into a far country, who called his own servants, and delivered unto them his goods. And unto one he gave five talents, to another two, and to another one; to every man according to his several ability; and straightway took his journey.

Then he that had received the five talents went and traded with the same, and made them other five talents. And likewise he that had received two, he also gained other two. But he that had received one went and digged in the earth, and hid his lord's money.

After a long time the lord of those servants cometh, and reckoneth with them. And so he that had received five talents came and brought other five talents, saying, Lord, thou deliveredst unto me five talents: behold, I have gained beside them five talents more. His lord said unto him, Well done, thou good and faithful servant: thou hast been faithful over a few things, I will make thee ruler over many things: enter thou into the joy of thy lord.

He also that had received two talents came and said, Lord, thou deliveredst unto me two talents: behold, I have gained two other talents beside them. His lord said unto him, Well done, good and faithful servant; thou hast been faithful over a few things, I will make thee ruler over many things: enter thou into the joy of thy lord.

Then he which had received the one talent came and said, Lord, I knew thee that thou art an hard man, reaping where thou hast not sown, and gathering where thou hast not strawed: And I was afraid, and went and hid thy talent in the earth: lo, there thou hast that is thine.

His lord answered and said unto him, Thou wicked and slothful servant, thou knewest that I reap where I sowed not, and gather where I have not strawed: Thou oughtest therefore to have put my money to the exchangers, and then at my coming I should have received mine own with usury. Take therefore the talent from him, and give it unto him which hath ten talents. For unto every one that hath shall be given, and he shall have abundance: but from him that hath not shall be taken away even that which he hath. And cast ye the unprofitable servant into outer darkness: there shall be weeping and gnashing of teeth.

THE SHEEP AND THE GOATS
Matthew 25:31–46

When the Son of man shall come in his glory, and all the holy angels with him, then shall he sit upon the throne of his glory: And before him shall be gathered all nations: and he shall separate them one from another, as a shepherd divideth his sheep from the goats: And he shall set the sheep on his right hand, but the goats on the left.

Then shall the King say unto them on his right hand, Come, ye blessed of my Father, inherit the kingdom prepared for you from the foundation of the world: For I was an hungred, and ye gave me meat: I was thirsty, and ye gave me drink: I was a stranger, and ye took me in: Naked, and ye clothed me: I was sick, and ye visited me: I was in prison, and ye came unto me.

Then shall the righteous answer him, saying, Lord, when saw we thee an hungred, and fed thee? or thirsty, and gave thee drink? When saw we thee a stranger, and took thee in? or naked, and clothed thee? Or when saw we thee sick, or in prison, and came unto thee?

And the King shall answer and say unto them, Verily I say unto you, Inasmuch as ye have done it unto one of the least of these my brethren, ye have done it unto me. Then shall he say also unto them on the left hand, Depart from me, ye cursed, into everlasting fire, prepared for the devil and his angels: For I was an hungred, and ye gave me no meat: I was thirsty, and ye gave me no drink: I was a stranger, and ye took me not in: naked, and ye clothed me not: sick, and in prison, and ye visited me not.

Then shall they also answer him, saying, Lord, when saw we thee an hungred, or athirst, or a stranger, or naked, or sick, or in prison, and did not minister unto thee?

Then shall he answer them, saying, Verily I say unto you, Inasmuch as ye did it not to one of the least of these, ye did it not to me. And these shall go away into everlasting punishment: but the righteous into life eternal.

THE GOOD SAMARITAN
Luke 10:25–37

And, behold, a certain lawyer stood up, and tempted him, saying, Master, what shall I do to inherit eternal life?

He said unto him, What is written in the law? how readest thou? And he answering said, Thou shalt love the Lord thy God with all thy heart, and with all thy soul, and with all thy strength, and with all thy mind; and thy neighbour as thyself.

And he said unto him, Thou hast answered right: this do, and thou shalt live. But he, willing to justify himself, said unto Jesus, And who is my neighbour?

And Jesus answering said, A certain man went down from Jerusalem to Jericho, and fell among thieves, which stripped him of his raiment, and wounded him, and departed, leaving him half dead. And by chance there came down a certain priest that way: and when he saw him, he passed by on the other side. And likewise a Levite, when he was at the place, came and looked on him, and passed by on the other side. But a certain Samaritan, as he journeyed, came where he was: and when he saw him, he had compassion on him, And went to him, and bound up his wounds, pouring in oil and wine, and set him on his own beast, and brought him to an inn, and took care of him. And on the morrow when he departed, he took out two pence, and gave them to the host, and said unto him, Take care of him; and whatsoever thou spendest more, when I come again, I will repay thee.

Which now of these three, thinkest thou, was neighbour unto him that fell among the thieves?

And he said, He that shewed mercy on him. Then said Jesus unto him, Go, and do thou likewise.

THE RICH FOOL
Luke 12:16–21

And he spake a parable unto them, saying, The ground of a certain rich man brought forth plentifully: And he thought within himself, saying, What shall I do, because I have no room where to bestow my fruits? And he said, This will I do: I will pull down my barns, and build greater; and there will I bestow all my fruits and my goods. And I will say to my soul, Soul, thou hast much goods laid up for many years; take thine ease, eat, drink, and be merry.

But God said unto him, Thou fool, this night thy soul shall be required of thee: then whose shall those things be, which thou hast provided?

So is he that layeth up treasure for himself, and is not rich toward God.

THE FAITHFUL STEWARD
Luke 12:42–48

And the Lord said, Who then is that faithful and wise steward, whom his lord shall make ruler over his household, to give them their portion of meat in due season? Blessed is that servant, whom his lord when he cometh shall find so doing. Of a truth I say unto you, that he will make him ruler over all that he hath.

But and if that servant say in his heart, My lord delayeth his coming; and shall begin to beat the menservants and maidens, and to eat and drink, and to be drunken; The lord of that servant will come in a day when he looketh not for him, and at an hour when he is not aware, and will cut him in sunder, and will appoint him his portion with the unbelievers. And that servant, which knew his lord's will, and prepared not himself, neither did according to his will, shall be beaten with many stripes.

But he that knew not, and did commit things worthy of stripes, shall be beaten with few stripes. For unto whomsoever much is given, of him shall be much required: and to whom men have committed much, of him they will ask the more.

THE GREAT SUPPER
Luke 14:15–24

And when one of them that sat at meat with him heard these things, he said unto him, Blessed is he that shall eat bread in the kingdom of God.

Then said he unto him, A certain man made a great supper, and bade many: And sent his servant at supper time to say to them that were bidden, Come; for all things are now ready.

And they all with one consent began to make excuse. The first said unto him, I have bought a piece of ground, and I must needs go and see it: I pray thee have me excused. And another said, I have bought five yoke of oxen, and I go to prove them: I pray thee have me excused. And another said, I have married a wife, and therefore I cannot come.

So that servant came, and shewed his lord these things. Then the master of the house being angry said to his servant, Go out quickly into the streets and lanes of the city, and bring in hither the poor, and the maimed, and the halt, and the blind. And the servant said, Lord, it is done as thou hast commanded, and yet there is room.

And the lord said unto the servant, Go out into the highways and hedges, and compel them to come in, that my house may be filled. For I say unto you, That none of those men which were bidden shall taste of my supper.

THE MARRIAGE FEAST
Matthew 22:1–14

And Jesus answered and spake unto them again by parables, and said, The kingdom of heaven is like unto a certain king, which made a marriage for his son, And sent forth his servants to call them that were bidden to the wedding: and they would not come.

Again, he sent forth other servants, saying, Tell them which are bidden, Behold, I have prepared my dinner: my oxen and my fatlings are killed, and all things are ready: come unto the marriage. But they made light of it, and went their ways, one to his farm, another to his merchandise: And the remnant took his servants, and entreated them spitefully, and slew them. But when the king heard thereof, he was wroth: and he sent forth his armies, and destroyed those murderers, and burned up their city.

Then saith he to his servants, The wedding is ready, but they which were bidden were not worthy. Go ye therefore into the highways, and as many as ye shall find, bid to the marriage.

So those servants went out into the highways, and gathered together all as many as they found, both bad and good: and the wedding was furnished with guests. And when the king came in to see the guests, he saw there a man which had not on a wedding garment: And he saith unto him, Friend, how camest thou in hither not having a wedding garment? And he was speechless.

Then said the king to the servants, Bind him hand and foot, and take him away, and cast him into outer darkness; there shall be weeping and gnashing of teeth. For many are called, but few are chosen.

THE LOST SHEEP
Luke 15:4–7

What man of you, having an hundred sheep, if he lose one of them, doth not leave the ninety and nine in the wilderness, and go after that which is lost, until he find it? And when he hath found it, he layeth it on his shoulders, rejoicing. And when he cometh home, he calleth together his friends and neighbours, saying unto them, Rejoice with me; for I have found my sheep which was lost.

I say unto you, that likewise joy shall be in heaven over one sinner that repenteth, more than over ninety and nine just persons, which need no repentance.

THE LOST COIN
Luke 15:8–10

Either what woman having ten pieces of silver, if she lose one piece, doth not light a candle, and sweep the house, and seek diligently till she find it? And when she hath found it, she calleth her friends and her neighbours together, saying, Rejoice with me; for I have found the piece which I had lost.

Likewise, I say unto you, there is joy in the presence of the angels of God over one sinner that repenteth.

THE PRODIGAL SON
Luke 15:11–32

And he said, A certain man had two sons: And the younger of them said to his father, Father, give me the portion of goods that falleth to me. And he divided unto them his living. And not many days after the younger son gathered all together, and took his journey into a far country, and there wasted his substance with riotous living. And when he had spent all, there arose a mighty famine in that land; and he began to be in want. And he went and joined himself to a citizen of that country; and he sent him into his fields to feed swine. And he would fain have filled his belly with the husks that the swine did eat: and no man gave unto him.

And when he came to himself, he said, How many hired servants of my father's have bread enough and to spare, and I perish with hunger! I will arise and go to my father, and will say unto him, Father, I have sinned against heaven, and before thee, And am no more worthy to be called thy son: make me as one of thy hired servants.

And he arose, and came to his father. But when he was yet a great way off, his father saw him, and had compassion, and ran, and fell on his neck, and kissed him. And the son said unto him, Father, I have sinned against heaven, and in thy sight, and am no more worthy to be called thy son.

But the father said to his servants, Bring forth the best robe, and put it on him; and put a ring on his hand, and shoes on his feet: And bring hither the fatted calf, and kill it; and let us eat, and be merry: For this my son was dead, and is alive again; he was lost, and is found. And they began to be merry.

Now his elder son was in the field: and as he came and drew nigh to the house, he heard musick and dancing. And he called one of the servants, and asked what these things meant.

And he said unto him, Thy brother is come; and thy father hath killed the fatted calf, because he hath received him safe and sound. And he was angry, and would not go in: therefore came his father out, and intreated him. And he answering said to his father, Lo, these many years do I serve thee, neither transgressed I at any time thy commandment: and yet thou never gavest me a kid, that I might make merry with my friends: But as soon as this thy son was come, which hath devoured thy living with harlots, thou hast killed for him the fatted calf.

And he said unto him, Son, thou art ever with me, and all that I have is thine. It was meet that we should make merry, and be glad: for this thy brother was dead, and is alive again; and was lost, and is found.

THE UNJUST STEWARD
Luke 16:1–9

And he said also unto his disciples, There was a certain rich man, which had a steward; and the same was accused unto him that he had wasted his goods. And he called him, and said unto him, How is it that I hear this of thee? give an account of thy stewardship; for thou mayest be no longer steward.

Then the steward said within himself, What shall I do? for my lord taketh away from me the stewardship: I cannot dig; to beg I am ashamed. I am resolved what to do, that, when I am put out of the stewardship, they may receive me into their houses. So he called every one of his lord's debtors unto him, and said unto the first, How much owest thou unto my lord?

And he said, An hundred measures of oil. And he said unto him, Take thy bill, and sit down quickly, and write fifty. Then said he to another, And how much owest thou? And he said, An hundred measures of wheat. And he said unto him, Take thy bill, and write fourscore. And the lord commended the unjust steward, because he had done wisely: for the children of this world are in their generation wiser than the children of light.

And I say unto you, Make to yourselves friends of the mammon of unrighteousness; that, when ye fail, they may receive you into everlasting habitations.

DIVES AND LAZARUS
Luke 16:19–31

There was a certain rich man, which was clothed in purple and fine linen, and fared sumptuously every day: And there was a certain beggar named Lazarus, which was laid at his gate, full of sores, And desiring to be fed with the crumbs which fell from the rich man's table: moreover the dogs came and licked his sores.

And it came to pass, that the beggar died, and was carried by the angels into Abraham's bosom: the rich man also died, and was buried; And in hell he lift up his eyes, being in torments, and seeth Abraham afar off, and Lazarus in his bosom.

And he cried and said, Father Abraham, have mercy on me, and send Lazarus, that he may dip the tip of his finger in water, and cool my tongue; for I am tormented in this flame.

But Abraham said, Son, remember that thou in thy lifetime receivedst thy good things, and likewise Lazarus evil things: but now he is comforted, and thou art tormented. And beside all this, between us and you there is a great gulf fixed: so that they which would pass from hence to you cannot; neither can they pass to us, that would come from thence.

Then he said, I pray thee therefore, father, that thou wouldest send him to my father's house: For I have five brethren; that he may testify unto them, lest they also come into this place of torment.

Abraham saith unto him, They have Moses and the prophets; let them hear them.

And he said, Nay, father Abraham: but if one went unto them from the dead, they will repent.

And he said unto him, If they hear not Moses and the prophets, neither will they be persuaded, though one rose from the dead.

THE IMPORTUNATE WIDOW
Luke 18:1–8

And he spake a parable unto them to this end, that men ought always to pray, and not to faint; Saying, There was in a city a judge, which feared not God, neither regarded man: And there was a widow in that city; and she came unto him, saying, Avenge me of mine adversary.

And he would not for a while: but afterward he said within himself, Though I fear not God, nor regard man; Yet because this widow troubleth me, I will avenge her, lest by her continual coming she weary me.

And the Lord said, Hear what the unjust judge saith. And shall not God avenge his own elect, which cry day and night unto him, though he bear long with them? I tell you that he will avenge them speedily. Nevertheless when the Son of man cometh, shall he find faith on the earth?

THE PHARISEE AND THE PUBLICAN
Luke 18:9–14

And he spake this parable unto certain which trusted in themselves that they were righteous, and despised others: Two men went up into the temple to pray; the one a Pharisee, and the other a publican. The Pharisee stood and prayed thus with himself, God, I thank thee, that I am not as other men are, extortioners, unjust, adulterers, or even as this publican. I fast twice in the week, I give tithes of all that I possess. And the publican, standing afar off, would not lift up so much as his eyes unto heaven, but smote upon his breast, saying, God be merciful to me a sinner.

I tell you, this man went down to his house justified rather than the other: for every one that exalteth himself shall be abased; and he that humbleth himself shall be exalted.

Part Five

Jesus Disputes with the Scribes and Pharisees

THEY THAT ARE WHOLE NEED NOT A PHYSICIAN
Luke 5:27–32

And after these things he went forth, and saw a publican, named Levi, sitting at the receipt of custom: and he said unto him, Follow me. And he left all, rose up, and followed him.

And Levi made him a great feast in his own house: and there was a great company of publicans and of others that sat down with them. But their scribes and Pharisees murmured against his disciples, saying, Why do ye eat and drink with publicans and sinners? And Jesus answering said unto them, They that are whole need not a physician; but they that are sick. I came not to call the righteous, but sinners to repentance.

NEW WINE IN NEW BOTTLES
Luke 5:33–39

And they said unto him, Why do the disciples of John fast often, and make prayers, and likewise the disciples of the Pharisees; but thine eat and drink?

And he said unto them, Can ye make the children of the bridechamber fast, while the bridegroom is with them? But the days will come, when the bridegroom shall be taken away from them, and then shall they fast in those days.

And he spake also a parable unto them; No man putteth a piece of a new garment upon an old; if otherwise, then both the new maketh a rent, and the piece that was taken out of the new agreeth not with the old. And no man putteth new wine into old bottles; else the new wine will burst the bottles, and be spilled, and the bottles shall perish. But new wine must be put into new bottles; and both are preserved. No man also having drunk old wine straightway desireth new: for he saith, The old is better.

WISDOM IS JUSTIFIED OF ALL HER CHILDREN
Luke 7:29–35

And all the people that heard him, and the publicans, justified God, being baptized with the baptism of John. But the Pharisees and lawyers rejected the counsel of God against themselves, being not baptized of him.

And the Lord said, Whereunto then shall I liken the men of this generation? and to what are they like? They are like unto children sitting in the marketplace, and calling one to another, and saying, We have piped unto you, and ye have not danced; we have mourned to you, and ye have not wept. For John the Baptist came neither eating bread nor drinking wine; and ye say, He hath a devil. The Son of man is come eating and drinking; and ye say, Behold a gluttonous man, and a winebibber, a friend of publicans and sinners! But wisdom is justified of all her children.

HER SINS, WHICH ARE MANY, ARE FORGIVEN
Luke 7:36–50

And one of the Pharisees desired him that he would eat with him. And he went into the Pharisee's house, and sat down to meat.

And, behold, a woman in the city, which was a sinner, when she knew that Jesus sat at meat in the Pharisee's house, brought an alabaster box of ointment, And stood at his feet behind him weeping, and began to wash his feet with tears, and did wipe them with the hairs of her head, and kissed his feet, and anointed them with the ointment.

Now when the Pharisee which had bidden him saw it, he spake

within himself, saying, This man, if he were a prophet, would have known who and what manner of woman this is that toucheth him: for she is a sinner.

And Jesus answering said unto him, Simon, I have somewhat to say unto thee. And he saith, Master, say on.

There was a certain creditor which had two debtors: the one owed five hundred pence, and the other fifty. And when they had nothing to pay, he frankly forgave them both. Tell me therefore, which of them will love him most?

Simon answered and said, I suppose that he, to whom he forgave most. And he said unto him, Thou hast rightly judged.

And he turned to the woman, and said unto Simon, Seest thou this woman? I entered into thine house, thou gavest me no water for my feet: but she hath washed my feet with tears, and wiped them with the hairs of her head. Thou gavest me no kiss: but this woman since the time I came in hath not ceased to kiss my feet. My head with oil thou didst not anoint: but this woman hath anointed my feet with ointment. Wherefore I say unto thee, Her sins, which are many, are forgiven; for she loved much: but to whom little is forgiven, the same loveth little.

And he said unto her, Thy sins are forgiven. And they that sat at meat with him began to say within themselves, Who is this that forgiveth sins also? And he said to the woman, Thy faith hath saved thee; go in peace.

THE SABBATH WAS MADE FOR MAN
Mark 2:23 – 3:6

And it came to pass, that he went through the corn fields on the sabbath day; and his disciples began, as they went, to pluck the ears of corn. And the Pharisees said unto him, Behold, why do they on the sabbath day that which is not lawful?

And he said unto them, Have ye never read what David did, when he had need, and was an hungred, he, and they that were with him? How he went into the house of God in the days of Abiathar the high priest, and did eat the shewbread, which is not lawful to eat but

287

for the priests, and gave also to them which were with him? And he said unto them, The sabbath was made for man, and not man for the sabbath: Therefore the Son of man is Lord also of the sabbath.

And he entered again into the synagogue; and there was a man there which had a withered hand. And they watched him, whether he would heal him on the sabbath day; that they might accuse him.

And he saith unto the man which had the withered hand, Stand forth. And he saith unto them, Is it lawful to do good on the sabbath days, or to do evil? to save life, or to kill? But they held their peace.

And when he had looked round about on them with anger, being grieved for the hardness of their hearts, he saith unto the man, Stretch forth thine hand. And he stretched it out: and his hand was restored whole as the other.

And the Pharisees went forth, and straightway took counsel with the Herodians against him, how they might destroy him.

THE TRADITION OF MEN
Mark 7:1–23

Then came together unto him the Pharisees, and certain of the scribes, which came from Jerusalem. And when they saw some of his disciples eat bread with defiled, that is to say, with unwashen, hands, they found fault. For the Pharisees, and all the Jews, except they wash their hands oft, eat not, holding the tradition of the elders. And when they come from the market, except they wash, they eat not. And many other things there be, which they have received to hold, as the washing of cups, and pots, brasen vessels, and of tables.

Then the Pharisees and scribes asked him, Why walk not thy disciples according to the tradition of the elders, but eat bread with unwashen hands?

He answered and said unto them, Well hath Esaias prophesied of you hypocrites, as it is written, This people honoureth me with their lips, but their heart is far from me. Howbeit in vain do they worship me, teaching for doctrines the commandments of men. For laying aside the commandment of God, ye hold the tradition of men, as the washing of pots and cups: and many other such like things ye do.

And he said unto them, Full well ye reject the commandment of God, that ye may keep your own tradition. For Moses said, Honour thy father and thy mother; and, Whoso curseth father or mother, let him die the death: But ye say, If a man shall say to his father or mother, It is Corban, that is to say, a gift, by whatsoever thou mightest be profited by me; he shall be free. And ye suffer him no more to do ought for his father or his mother; Making the word of God of none effect through your tradition, which ye have delivered: and many such like things do ye.

And when he had called all the people unto him, he said unto them, Hearken unto me every one of you, and understand: There is nothing from without a man, that entering into him can defile him: but the things which come out of him, those are they that defile the man. If any man have ears to hear, let him hear.

And when he was entered into the house from the people, his disciples asked him concerning the parable. And he saith unto them, Are ye so without understanding also? Do ye not perceive, that whatsoever thing from without entereth into the man, it cannot defile him; Because it entereth not into his heart, but into the belly, and goeth out into the draught, purging all meats?

And he said, That which cometh out of the man, that defileth the man. For from within, out of the heart of men, proceed evil thoughts, adulteries, fornications, murders, thefts, covetousness, wickedness, deceit, lasciviousness, an evil eye, blasphemy, pride, foolishness: All these evil things come from within, and defile the man.

WHAT GOD HATH JOINED TOGETHER, LET NOT MAN PUT ASUNDER
Mark 10:2–11

And the Pharisees came to him, and asked him, Is it lawful for a man to put away his wife? tempting him. And he answered and said unto them, What did Moses command you? And they said, Moses suffered to write a bill of divorcement, and to put her away.

And Jesus answered and said unto them, For the hardness of your heart he wrote you this precept. But from the beginning of the creation

God made them male and female. For this cause shall a man leave his father and mother, and cleave to his wife; And they twain shall be one flesh: so then they are no more twain, but one flesh. What therefore God hath joined together, let not man put asunder.

And in the house his disciples asked him again of the same matter. And he saith unto them, Whosoever shall put away his wife, and marry another, committeth adultery against her.

A HOUSE DIVIDED AGAINST ITSELF
Matthew 12:22–29

Then was brought unto him one possessed with a devil, blind, and dumb: and he healed him, insomuch that the blind and dumb both spake and saw. And all the people were amazed, and said, Is not this the son of David?

But when the Pharisees heard it, they said, This fellow doth not cast out devils, but by Beelzebub the prince of the devils. And Jesus knew their thoughts, and said unto them, Every kingdom divided against itself is brought to desolation; and every city or house divided against itself shall not stand: And if Satan cast out Satan, he is divided against himself; how shall then his kingdom stand? And if I by Beelzebub cast out devils, by whom do your children cast them out? therefore they shall be your judges. But if I cast out devils by the Spirit of God, then the kingdom of God is come unto you. Or else how can one enter into a strong man's house, and spoil his goods, except he first bind the strong man? and then he will spoil his house.

THE UNPARDONABLE SIN
Matthew 12:30–32

He that is not with me is against me; and he that gathereth not with me scattereth abroad. Wherefore I say unto you, All manner of sin and blasphemy shall be forgiven unto men: but the blasphemy against the Holy Ghost shall not be forgiven unto men. And whosoever speaketh a word against the Son of man, it shall be forgiven him: but whosoever speaketh against the Holy Ghost, it shall not be forgiven him, neither in this world, neither in the world to come.

EVERY IDLE WORD
Matthew 12:34–37

O generation of vipers, how can ye, being evil, speak good things? for out of the abundance of the heart the mouth speaketh. A good man out of the good treasure of the heart bringeth forth good things: and an evil man out of the evil treasure bringeth forth evil things. But I say unto you, That every idle word that men shall speak, they shall give account thereof in the day of judgment. For by thy words thou shalt be justified, and by thy words thou shalt be condemned.

AN EVIL GENERATION
Matthew 12:38–45

Then certain of the scribes and of the Pharisees answered, saying, Master, we would see a sign from thee.

But he answered and said unto them, An evil and adulterous generation seeketh after a sign; and there shall no sign be given to it, but the sign of the prophet Jonas: For as Jonas was three days and three nights in the whale's belly; so shall the Son of man be three days and three nights in the heart of the earth. The men of Nineveh shall rise in judgment with this generation, and shall condemn it: because they repented at the preaching of Jonas; and, behold, a greater than Jonas is here.

The queen of the south shall rise up in the judgment with this generation, and shall condemn it: for she came from the uttermost parts of the earth to hear the wisdom of Solomon; and, behold, a greater than Solomon is here.

When the unclean spirit is gone out of a man, he walketh through dry places, seeking rest, and findeth none. Then he saith, I will return into my house from whence I came out; and when he is come, he findeth it empty, swept, and garnished. Then goeth he, and taketh with himself seven other spirits more wicked than himself, and they enter in and dwell there: and the last state of that man is worse than the first. Even so shall it be also unto this wicked generation.

YE CANNOT SERVE GOD AND MAMMON
Luke 16:13–15

No servant can serve two masters: for either he will hate the one, and love the other; or else he will hold to the one, and despise the other. Ye cannot serve God and mammon.

And the Pharisees also, who were covetous, heard all these things: and they derided him.

And he said unto them, Ye are they which justify yourselves before men; but God knoweth your hearts: for that which is highly esteemed among men is abomination in the sight of God.

SIGNS OF THE TIMES
Matthew 16:1–3

The Pharisees also with the Sadducees came, and tempting desired him that he would shew them a sign from heaven.

He answered and said unto them, When it is evening, ye say, It will be fair weather: for the sky is red. And in the morning, It will be foul weather to day: for the sky is red and lowring. O ye hypocrites, ye can discern the face of the sky; but can ye not discern the signs of the times?

BY WHAT AUTHORITY?
Matthew 21:23–27

And when he was come into the temple, the chief priests and the elders of the people came unto him as he was teaching, and said, By what authority doest thou these things? and who gave thee this authority?

And Jesus answered and said unto them, I also will ask you one thing, which if ye tell me, I in like wise will tell you by what authority I do these things. The baptism of John, whence was it? from heaven, or of men?

And they reasoned with themselves, saying, If we shall say, From heaven; he will say unto us, Why did ye not then believe him? But if we shall say, Of men; we fear the people; for all hold John as a prophet.

And they answered Jesus, and said, We cannot tell. And he said unto them, Neither tell I you by what authority I do these things.

THE TWO SONS
Matthew 21:28–32

But what think ye? A certain man had two sons; and he came to the first, and said, Son, go work to day in my vineyard. He answered and said, I will not: but afterward he repented, and went. And he came to the second, and said likewise. And he answered and said, I go, sir: and went not. Whether of them twain did the will of his father? They say unto him, The first. Jesus saith unto them, Verily I say unto you, That the publicans and the harlots go into the kingdom of God before you. For John came unto you in the way of righteousness, and ye believed him not: but the publicans and the harlots believed him: and ye, when ye had seen it, repented not afterward, that ye might believe him.

RENDER TO CAESAR THE THINGS THAT ARE CAESAR'S
Mark 12:13–17

And they send unto him certain of the Pharisees and of the Herodians, to catch him in his words.

And when they were come, they say unto him, Master, we know that thou art true, and carest for no man: for thou regardest not the person of men, but teachest the way of God in truth: Is it lawful to give tribute to Caesar, or not? Shall we give, or shall we not give?

But he, knowing their hypocrisy, said unto them, Why tempt ye me? bring me a penny, that I may see it. And they brought it. And he saith unto them, Whose is this image and superscription? And they said unto him, Caesar's.

And Jesus answering said unto them, Render to Caesar the things that are Caesar's, and to God the things that are God's. And they marvelled at him.

NOT THE GOD OF THE DEAD, BUT OF THE LIVING
Mark 12:18–27

Then come unto him the Sadducees, which say there is no resurrection; and they asked him, saying, Master, Moses wrote unto us, If a man's brother die, and leave his wife behind him, and leave no children, that his brother should take his wife, and raise up seed unto his brother. Now there were seven brethren: and the first took a wife, and dying left no seed. And the second took her, and died, neither left he any seed: and the third likewise. And the seven had her, and left no seed: last of all the woman died also. In the resurrection therefore, when they shall rise, whose wife shall she be of them? for the seven had her to wife.

And Jesus answering said unto them, Do ye not therefore err, because ye know not the scriptures, neither the power of God? For when they shall rise from the dead, they neither marry, nor are given in marriage; but are as the angels which are in heaven. And as touching the dead, that they rise: have ye not read in the book of Moses, how in the bush God spake unto him, saying, I am the God of Abraham, and the God of Isaac, and the God of Jacob? He is not the God of the dead, but the God of the living: ye therefore do greatly err.

THE TWO GREAT COMMANDMENTS
Mark 12:28–34

And one of the scribes came, and having heard them reasoning together, and perceiving that he had answered them well, asked him, Which is the first commandment of all?

And Jesus answered him, The first of all the commandments is, Hear, O Israel; The Lord our God is one Lord: And thou shalt love the Lord thy God with all thy heart, and with all thy soul, and with all thy mind, and with all thy strength: this is the first commandment. And the second is like, namely this, Thou shalt love thy neighbour as thyself. There is none other commandment greater than these.

And the scribe said unto him, Well, Master, thou hast said the truth: for there is one God; and there is none other but he: And to love him with all the heart, and with all the understanding, and with all the soul, and with all the strength, and to love his neighbour as himself, is more than all whole burnt offerings and sacrifices.

And when Jesus saw that he answered discreetly, he said unto him, Thou art not far from the kingdom of God. And no man after that durst ask him any question.

DAVID'S LORD
Mark 12:35–37

And Jesus answered and said, while he taught in the temple, How say the scribes that Christ is the Son of David? For David himself said by the Holy Ghost, The Lord said to my Lord, Sit thou on my right hand, till I make thine enemies thy footstool. David therefore himself calleth him Lord; and whence is he then his son? And the common people heard him gladly.

WOE UNTO YOU, SCRIBES AND PHARISEES!
Matthew 23

Then spake Jesus to the multitude, and to his disciples, Saying, The scribes and the Pharisees sit in Moses' seat: All therefore whatsoever they bid you observe, that observe and do; but do not ye after their works: for they say, and do not. For they bind heavy burdens and grievous to be borne, and lay them on men's shoulders; but they themselves will not move them with one of their fingers.

But all their works they do for to be seen of men: they make broad their phylacteries, and enlarge the borders of their garments, And love the uppermost rooms at feasts, and the chief seats in the synagogues, And greetings in the markets, and to be called of men, Rabbi, Rabbi. But be not ye called Rabbi: for one is your Master, even Christ; and all ye are brethren. And call no man your father upon the earth: for one is your Father, which is in heaven. Neither be ye called masters: for one is your Master, even Christ. But he that is greatest among you shall be your servant. And whosoever shall exalt himself shall be abased; and he that shall humble himself shall be exalted.

But woe unto you, scribes and Pharisees, hypocrites! for ye shut up the kingdom of heaven against men: for ye neither go in yourselves, neither suffer ye them that are entering to go in.

Woe unto you, scribes and Pharisees, hypocrites! for ye devour widows' houses, and for a pretence make long prayer: therefore ye shall receive the greater damnation.

Woe unto you, scribes and Pharisees, hypocrites! for ye compass sea and land to make one proselyte, and when he is made, ye make him twofold more the child of hell than yourselves.

Woe unto you, ye blind guides, which say, Whosoever shall swear by the temple, it is nothing; but whosoever shall swear by the gold of the temple, he is a debtor! Ye fools and blind: for whether is greater, the gold, or the temple that sanctifieth the gold? And, Whosoever shall swear by the altar, it is nothing; but whosoever sweareth by the gift that is upon it, he is guilty. Ye fools and blind: for whether is greater, the gift, or the altar that sanctifieth the gift? Whoso therefore shall swear by the altar, sweareth by it, and by all things thereon. And whoso shall swear by the temple, sweareth by it, and by him that dwelleth therein. And he that shall swear by heaven, sweareth by the throne of God, and by him that sitteth thereon.

Woe unto you, scribes and Pharisees, hypocrites! for ye pay tithe of mint and anise and cummin, and have omitted the weightier matters of the law, judgment, mercy, and faith: these ought ye to have done, and not to leave the other undone. Ye blind guides, which strain at a gnat, and swallow a camel.

Woe unto you, scribes and Pharisees, hypocrites! for ye make clean the outside of the cup and of the platter, but within they are full of extortion and excess. Thou blind Pharisee, cleanse first that which is within the cup and platter, that the outside of them may be clean also.

Woe unto you, scribes and Pharisees, hypocrites! for ye are like unto whited sepulchres, which indeed appear beautiful outward, but are within full of dead men's bones, and of all uncleanness. Even so ye also outwardly appear righteous unto men, but within ye are full of hypocrisy and iniquity.

Woe unto you, scribes and Pharisees, hypocrites! because ye build the tombs of the prophets, and garnish the sepulchres of the righteous, And say, If we had been in the days of our fathers, we would not have been partakers with them in the blood of the prophets. Wherefore ye be witnesses unto yourselves, that ye are the children of them which killed the prophets. Fill ye up then the measure of your fathers. Ye serpents, ye generation of vipers, how can ye escape the damnation of hell?

Wherefore, behold, I send unto you prophets, and wise men, and scribes: and some of them ye shall kill and crucify; and some of them shall ye scourge in your synagogues, and persecute them from city to city: That upon you may come all the righteous blood shed upon the earth, from the blood of righteous Abel unto the blood of Zacharias son of Barachias, whom ye slew between the temple and the altar. Verily I say unto you, All these things shall come upon this generation.

O Jerusalem, Jerusalem, thou that killest the prophets, and stonest them which are sent unto thee, how often would I have gathered thy children together, even as a hen gathereth her chickens under her wings, and ye would not! Behold, your house is left unto you desolate. For I say unto you, Ye shall not see me henceforth, till ye shall say, Blessed is he that cometh in the name of the Lord.

From the Transfiguration to the Resurrection

THE TRANSFIGURATION
Luke 9:28–36

And it came to pass about an eight days after these sayings, he took Peter and John and James, and went up into a mountain to pray. And as he prayed, the fashion of his countenance was altered, and his raiment was white and glistering.

And, behold, there talked with him two men, which were Moses and Elias: Who appeared in glory, and spake of his decease which he should accomplish at Jerusalem. But Peter and they that were with him were heavy with sleep: and when they were awake, they saw his glory, and the two men that stood with him. And it came to pass, as they departed from him, Peter said unto Jesus, Master, it is good for us to be here: and let us make three tabernacles; one for thee, and one for Moses, and one for Elias: not knowing what he said.

While he thus spake, there came a cloud, and overshadowed them: and they feared as they entered into the cloud. And there came a voice out of the cloud, saying, This is my beloved Son: hear him.

And when the voice was past, Jesus was found alone. And they kept it close, and told no man in those days any of those things which they had seen.

THE TRIUMPHAL ENTRY
Luke 19:28–44

And when he had thus spoken, he went before, ascending up to Jerusalem. And it came to pass, when he was come nigh to Bethphage and Bethany, at the mount called the mount of Olives, he sent two of his disciples, Saying, Go ye into the village over against you; in the which at your entering ye shall find a colt tied, whereon yet never man sat: loose him, and bring him hither. And if any man ask you, Why do ye loose him? thus shall ye say unto him, Because the Lord hath need of him.

And they that were sent went their way, and found even as he had said unto them. And as they were loosing the colt, the owners thereof said unto them, Why loose ye the colt? And they said, The Lord hath need of him.

And they brought him to Jesus: and they cast their garments upon the colt, and they set Jesus thereon. And as he went, they spread their clothes in the way.

And when he was come nigh, even now at the descent of the mount of Olives, the whole multitude of the disciples began to rejoice and praise God with a loud voice for all the mighty works that they had seen; Saying, Blessed be the King that cometh in the name of the Lord: peace in heaven, and glory in the highest. And some of the Pharisees from among the multitude said unto him, Master, rebuke thy disciples. And he answered and said unto them, I tell you that, if these should hold their peace, the stones would immediately cry out.

And when he was come near, he beheld the city, and wept over it, Saying, If thou hadst known, even thou, at least in this thy day, the things which belong unto thy peace! but now they are hid from thine eyes. For the days shall come upon thee, that thine enemies shall cast a trench about thee, and compass thee round, and keep thee in on every side, And shall lay thee even with the ground, and thy children within thee; and they shall not leave in thee one stone upon another; because thou knewest not the time of thy visitation.

THE CLEANSING OF THE TEMPLE
Matthew 21:10–17

And when he was come into Jerusalem, all the city was moved, saying, Who is this? And the multitude said, This is Jesus the prophet of Nazareth of Galilee. And Jesus went into the temple of God, and cast out all them that sold and bought in the temple, and overthrew the tables of the moneychangers, and the seats of them that sold doves, And said unto them, It is written, My house shall be called the house of prayer; but ye have made it a den of thieves.

And the blind and the lame came to him in the temple; and he healed them. And when the chief priests and scribes saw the wonderful things that he did, and the children crying in the temple, and saying, Hosanna to the Son of David; they were sore displeased, And said unto him, Hearest thou what these say? And Jesus saith unto them, Yea; have ye never read, Out of the mouth of babes and sucklings thou hast perfected praise? And he left them, and went out of the city into Bethany; and he lodged there.

THE LAST SUPPER
Matthew 26:17–35

Now the first day of the feast of unleavened bread the disciples came to Jesus, saying unto him, Where wilt thou that we prepare for thee to eat the passover? And he said, Go into the city to such a man, and say unto him, The Master saith, My time is at hand; I will keep the passover at thy house with my disciples. And the disciples did as Jesus had appointed them; and they made ready the passover.

Now when the even was come, he sat down with the twelve. And as they did eat, he said, Verily I say unto you, that one of you shall betray me. And they were exceeding sorrowful, and began every one of them to say unto him, Lord, is it I? And he answered and said, He that dippeth his hand with me in the dish, the same shall betray me. The Son of man goeth as it is written of him: but woe unto that man by whom the Son of man is betrayed! it had been good for that man if he had not been born.

Then Judas, which betrayed him, answered and said, Master, is it I? He said unto him, Thou hast said.

And as they were eating, Jesus took bread, and blessed it, and brake it, and gave it to the disciples, and said, Take, eat; this is my body. And he took the cup, and gave thanks, and gave it to them, saying, Drink ye all of it; For this is my blood of the new testament, which is shed for many for the remission of sins. But I say unto you,

I will not drink henceforth of this fruit of the vine, until that day when I drink it new with you in my Father's kingdom. And when they had sung an hymn, they went out into the mount of Olives.

Then saith Jesus unto them, All ye shall be offended because of me this night: for it is written, I will smite the shepherd, and the sheep of the flock shall be scattered abroad. But after I am risen again, I will go before you into Galilee.

Peter answered and said unto him, Though all men shall be offended because of thee, yet will I never be offended. Jesus said unto him, Verily I say unto thee, That this night, before the cock crow, thou shalt deny me thrice. Peter said unto him, Though I should die with thee, yet will I not deny thee. Likewise also said all the disciples.

THE AGONY IN THE GARDEN
Mark 14:32–42

And they came to a place which was named Gethsemane: and he saith to his disciples, Sit ye here, while I shall pray. And he taketh with him Peter and James and John, and began to be sore amazed, and to be very heavy; And saith unto them, My soul is exceeding sorrowful unto death: tarry ye here, and watch.

And he went forward a little, and fell on the ground, and prayed that, if it were possible, the hour might pass from him. And he said, Abba, Father, all things are possible unto thee; take away this cup from me: nevertheless not what I will, but what thou wilt.

And he cometh, and findeth them sleeping, and saith unto Peter, Simon, sleepest thou? couldest not thou watch one hour? Watch ye and pray, lest ye enter into temptation. The spirit truly is ready, but the flesh is weak.

And again he went away, and prayed, and spake the same words. And when he returned, he found them asleep again, (for their eyes were heavy,) neither wist they what to answer him.

And he cometh the third time, and saith unto them, Sleep on now, and take your rest: it is enough, the hour is come; behold, the Son of man is betrayed into the hands of sinners. Rise up, let us go; lo, he that betrayeth me is at hand.

THE BETRAYAL AND ARREST
Matthew 26:47–56

And while he yet spake, lo, Judas, one of the twelve, came, and with him a great multitude with swords and staves, from the chief priests and elders of the people. Now he that betrayed him gave them a sign, saying, Whomsoever I shall kiss, that same is he: hold him fast. And forthwith he came to Jesus, and said, Hail, master; and kissed him. And Jesus said unto him, Friend, wherefore art thou come? Then came they, and laid hands on Jesus, and took him.

And, behold, one of them which were with Jesus stretched out his hand, and drew his sword, and struck a servant of the high priest's, and smote off his ear. Then said Jesus unto him, Put up again thy sword into his place: for all they that take the sword shall perish with the sword. Thinkest thou that I cannot now pray to my Father, and he shall presently give me more than twelve legions of angels? But how then shall the scriptures be fulfilled, that thus it must be?

In that same hour said Jesus to the multitudes, Are ye come out as against a thief with swords and staves for to take me? I sat daily with you teaching in the temple, and ye laid no hold on me. But all this was done, that the scriptures of the prophets might be fulfilled. Then all the disciples forsook him, and fled.

PETER'S DENIAL
Luke 22:54–62

Then took they him, and led him, and brought him into the high priest's house. And Peter followed afar off. And when they had kindled a fire in the midst of the hall, and were set down together, Peter sat down among them.

But a certain maid beheld him as he sat by the fire, and earnestly looked upon him, and said, This man was also with him. And he denied him, saying, Woman, I know him not.

And after a little while another saw him, and said, Thou art also of them. And Peter said, Man, I am not. And about the space of one hour after another confidently affirmed, saying, Of a truth this fellow also was with him: for he is a Galilaean. And Peter said, Man, I know not what thou sayest.

And immediately, while he yet spake, the cock crew. And the Lord turned, and looked upon Peter. And Peter remembered the word of the Lord, how he had said unto him, Before the cock crow, thou shalt deny me thrice. And Peter went out, and wept bitterly.

THE TRIAL BEFORE THE HIGH PRIEST
Matthew 26:59–68

Now the chief priests, and elders, and all the council, sought false witness against Jesus, to put him to death; But found none: yea, though many false witnesses came, yet found they none. At the last came two false witnesses, And said, This fellow said, I am able to destroy the temple of God, and to build it in three days. And the high priest arose, and said unto him, Answerest thou nothing? what is it which these witness against thee?

But Jesus held his peace. And the high priest answered and said unto him, I adjure thee by the living God, that thou tell us whether thou be the Christ, the Son of God. Jesus saith unto him, Thou hast said: nevertheless I say unto you, Hereafter shall ye see the Son of man sitting on the right hand of power, and coming in the clouds of heaven.

Then the high priest rent his clothes, saying, He hath spoken blasphemy; what further need have we of witnesses? behold, now ye have heard his blasphemy. What think ye? They answered and said, He is guilty of death. Then did they spit in his face, and buffeted him; and others smote him with the palms of their hands, Saying, Prophesy unto us, thou Christ, Who is he that smote thee?

THE TRIAL BEFORE PILATE
Matthew 27:1–5, 11–31

When the morning was come, all the chief priests and elders of the people took counsel against Jesus to put him to death: And when they had bound him, they led him away, and delivered him to Pontius Pilate the governor.

Then Judas, which had betrayed him, when he saw that he was condemned, repented himself, and brought again the thirty pieces of silver to the chief priests and elders, Saying, I have sinned in that I have betrayed the innocent blood. And they said, What is that to us? see thou to that. And he cast down the pieces of silver in the temple, and departed, and went and hanged himself...

And Jesus stood before the governor: and the governor asked him, saying, Art thou the King of the Jews? And Jesus said unto him, Thou sayest. And when he was accused of the chief priests and elders, he answered nothing.

Then said Pilate unto him, Hearest thou not how many things they witness against thee? And he answered him to never a word; insomuch that the governor marvelled greatly.

Now at that feast the governor was wont to release unto the people a prisoner, whom they would. And they had then a notable prisoner, called Barabbas. Therefore when they were gathered together, Pilate said unto them, Whom will ye that I release unto you? Barabbas, or Jesus which is called Christ? For he knew that for envy they had delivered him.

When he was set down on the judgment seat, his wife sent unto him, saying, Have thou nothing to do with that just man: for I have suffered many things this day in a dream because of him. But the chief priests and elders persuaded the multitude that they should ask Barabbas, and destroy Jesus.

The governor answered and said unto them, Whether of the twain will ye that I release unto you? They said, Barabbas. Pilate saith unto them, What shall I do then with Jesus which is called Christ? They all say unto him, Let him be crucified. And the governor said, Why, what evil hath he done? But they cried out the more, saying, Let him be crucified.

When Pilate saw that he could prevail nothing, but that rather a tumult was made, he took water, and washed his hands before the multitude, saying, I am innocent of the blood of this just person: see ye to it. Then answered all the people, and said, His blood be on us, and on our children. Then released he Barabbas unto them: and when he had scourged Jesus, he delivered him to be crucified.

Then the soldiers of the governor took Jesus into the common hall, and gathered unto him the whole band of soldiers. And they stripped him, and put on him a scarlet robe. And when they had platted a crown of thorns, they put it upon his head, and a reed in his right hand: and they bowed the knee before him, and mocked him, saying, Hail, King of the Jews! And they spit upon him, and took the reed, and smote him on the head. And after that they had mocked him, they took the robe off from him, and put his own raiment on him, and led him away to crucify him.

THE CRUCIFIXION
Luke 23:26–56

And as they led him away, they laid hold upon one Simon, a Cyrenian, coming out of the country, and on him they laid the cross, that he might bear it after Jesus. And there followed him a great company of people, and of women, which also bewailed and lamented him.

But Jesus turning unto them said, Daughters of Jerusalem, weep not for me, but weep for yourselves, and for your children. For, behold, the days are coming, in the which they shall say, Blessed are the barren, and the wombs that never bare, and the paps which never gave suck. Then shall they begin to say to the mountains, Fall on us; and to the hills, Cover us. For if they do these things in a green tree, what shall be done in the dry?

And there were also two other, malefactors, led with him to be put to death. And when they were come to the place, which is called Calvary, there they crucified him, and the malefactors, one on the right hand, and the other on the left. Then said Jesus, Father, forgive them; for they know not what they do. And they parted his raiment, and cast lots.

And the people stood beholding. And the rulers also with them derided him, saying, He saved others; let him save himself, if he be Christ, the chosen of God. And the soldiers also mocked him, coming to him, and offering him vinegar, And saying, If thou be the king of the Jews, save thyself. And a superscription also was written over him in letters of Greek, and Latin, and Hebrew, THIS IS THE KING OF

THE JEWS. And one of the malefactors which were hanged railed on him, saying, If thou be Christ, save thyself and us. But the other answering rebuked him, saying, Dost not thou fear God, seeing thou art in the same condemnation? And we indeed justly; for we receive the due reward of our deeds: but this man hath done nothing amiss. And he said unto Jesus, Lord, remember me when thou comest into thy kingdom. And Jesus said unto him, Verily I say unto thee, To day shalt thou be with me in paradise.

And it was about the sixth hour, and there was a darkness over all the earth until the ninth hour. And the sun was darkened, and the veil of the temple was rent in the midst. And when Jesus had cried with a loud voice, he said, Father, into thy hands I commend my spirit: and having said thus, he gave up the ghost.

Now when the centurion saw what was done, he glorified God, saying, Certainly this was a righteous man. And all the people that came together to that sight, beholding the things which were done, smote their breasts, and returned. And all his acquaintance, and the women that followed him from Galilee, stood afar off, beholding these things.

And, behold, there was a man named Joseph, a counsellor; and he was a good man, and a just: (The same had not consented to the counsel and deed of them;) he was of Arimathaea, a city of the Jews: who also himself waited for the kingdom of God. This man went unto Pilate, and begged the body of Jesus. And he took it down, and wrapped it in linen, and laid it in a sepulchre that was hewn in stone, wherein never man before was laid.

And that day was the preparation, and the sabbath drew on. And the women also, which came with him from Galilee, followed after, and beheld the sepulchre, and how his body was laid. And they returned, and prepared spices and ointments; and rested the sabbath day according to the commandment.

THE RESURRECTION
Matthew 28:1–10

In the end of the sabbath, as it began to dawn toward the first day of the week, came Mary Magdalene and the other Mary to see the sepulchre. And, behold, there was a great earthquake: for the angel of the Lord descended from heaven, and came and rolled back the stone from the door, and sat upon it. His countenance was like lightning, and his raiment white as snow: And for fear of him the keepers did shake, and became as dead men. And the angel answered and said unto the women, Fear not ye: for I know that ye seek Jesus, which was crucified. He is not here: for he is risen, as he said. Come, see the place where the Lord lay. And go quickly, and tell his disciples that he is risen from the dead; and, behold, he goeth before you into Galilee; there shall ye see him: lo, I have told you.

And they departed quickly from the sepulchre with fear and great joy; and did run to bring his disciples word. And as they went to tell his disciples, behold, Jesus met them, saying, All hail. And they came and held him by the feet, and worshipped him. Then said Jesus unto them, Be not afraid: go tell my brethren that they go into Galilee, and there shall they see me.

THE ROAD TO EMMAUS
Luke 24:13–35

And, behold, two of them went that same day to a village called Emmaus, which was from Jerusalem about threescore furlongs. And they talked together of all these things which had happened.

And it came to pass, that, while they communed together and reasoned, Jesus himself drew near, and went with them. But their eyes were holden that they should not know him. And he said unto them, What manner of communications are these that ye have one to another, as ye walk, and are sad?

And the one of them, whose name was Cleopas, answering said unto him, Art thou only a stranger in Jerusalem, and hast not known the things which are come to pass there in these days? And he said unto them, What things? And they said unto him, Concerning Jesus of Nazareth, which was a prophet mighty in deed and word before God and all the people: And how the chief priests and our rulers delivered him to be condemned to death, and have crucified him. But we trusted that it had been he which should have redeemed Israel:

and beside all this, to day is the third day since these things were done. Yea, and certain women also of our company made us astonished, which were early at the sepulchre; And when they found not his body, they came, saying, that they had also seen a vision of angels, which said that he was alive. And certain of them which were with us went to the sepulchre, and found it even so as the women had said: but him they saw not.

Then he said unto them, O fools, and slow of heart to believe all that the prophets have spoken: Ought not Christ to have suffered these things, and to enter into his glory? And beginning at Moses and all the prophets, he expounded unto them in all the scriptures the things concerning himself.

And they drew nigh unto the village, whither they went: and he made as though he would have gone further. But they constrained him, saying, Abide with us: for it is toward evening, and the day is far spent. And he went in to tarry with them. And it came to pass, as he sat at meat with them, he took bread, and blessed it, and brake, and gave to them. And their eyes were opened, and they knew him; and he vanished out of their sight.

And they said one to another, Did not our heart burn within us, while he talked with us by the way, and while he opened to us the scriptures? And they rose up the same hour, and returned to Jerusalem, and found the eleven gathered together, and them that were with them, Saying, The Lord is risen indeed, and hath appeared to Simon. And they told what things were done in the way, and how he was known of them in breaking of bread.

THE GREAT COMMISSION
Matthew 28:16–20

Then the eleven disciples went away into Galilee, into a mountain where Jesus had appointed them. And when they saw him, they worshipped him: but some doubted.

And Jesus came and spake unto them, saying, All power is given unto me in heaven and in earth. Go ye therefore, and teach all nations, baptizing them in the name of the Father, and of the Son, and of the Holy Ghost: Teaching them to observe all things whatsoever I have commanded you: and, lo, I am with you alway, even unto the end of the world. Amen.

Index of Primary Sources